EAT

SLEEP

CYCLE

EAT, SLEEP, CYCLE

Summersdale Publishers Ltd
46 West Street
Chichester
West Sussex
PO19 1RP
UK

www.summersdale.com

Printed and bound by CPI Group (UK) Ltd, Croydon, CR0 4YY

ISBN: 978-1-84953-687-5

Substantial discounts on bulk quantities of Summersdale books are available to corporations, professional associations and other organisations. For details contact Nicky Douglas by telephone: +44 (0) 1243 756902, fax: +44 (0) 1243 786300 or email: nicky@summersdale.com.

EAT
SLEEP

CYCLE

A BIKE RIDE AROUND
THE COAST OF BRITAIN

ANNA HUGHES

summersdale

ABOUT THE AUTHOR

Anna works as a freelance cycling instructor and mechanic in London. Her cycle ride round the coast of Britain inspired her to sail around the same coastline a year later. She currently lives on a narrowboat in Hackney.

ACKNOWLEDGEMENTS

To all those who gave me a bed, shower, and food and to those who kept me company on the road.

To those who helped with early drafts of the book:

Adrian Scoffham, Steve Clough, Clare Dowling, Andy Adkin, David Showell and Becca Sayers. Special thanks to Richard Gibbens for your sustained and indispensable input, and to Sarah Frecknall, Mike Carter, David Charles and Clifton Hughes.

To Jennifer Barclay, my editor, and Chris Turton and Claire Plimmer at Summersdale, and to Ben Broomfield for the head shots.

CONTENTS

PART 1:

THE EAST COAST OF ENGLAND

Miles to go = 4,000
Days to go = 72

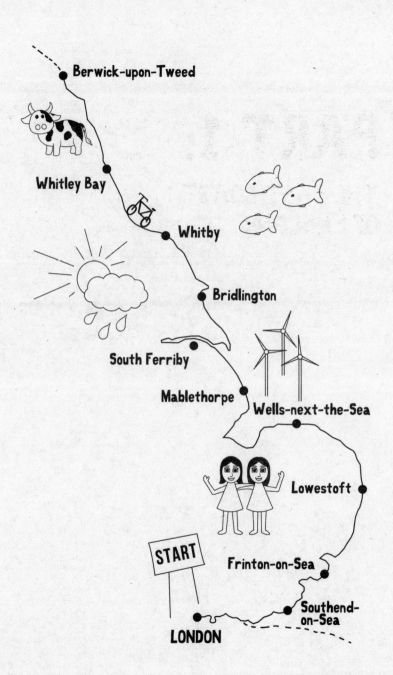

Berwick-upon-Tweed

Whitley Bay

Whitby

Bridlington

South Ferriby

Mablethorpe

Wells-next-the-Sea

Lowestoft

START

Frinton-on-Sea

Southend-on-Sea

LONDON

DAY 1:
LONDON TO SOUTHEND

56 miles

There is a cycle route across Rainham Marshes that winds its way through the RSPB nature reserve. It's easy to forget that it lies within the circle of the M25 as you ride along the smooth tarmac and wooden slats, your wheels kept well away from the soggy ground and tiny creeks that are so attractive to the birdlife that nests here. Coots glide along the still surface of the water, half-hidden behind bulrushes so high and plush that you soon feel lost in the maze.

Flocks of lapwings dart across tussocky grassland. Dragonflies dance between the reeds, and thrushes emerge from under bushes, startled by the whirr of bicycle wheels. If you're lucky you might spot an avocet or little egret feeding on the edge of the wetlands, and maybe even a peregrine falcon, hovering above the scattered scrub on the hunt for a snack.

The land is an oasis amid the industry of east London: puffing chimneys and pylons line each horizon. Away from the A13 the dull roar of the traffic recedes, replaced by birdsong and the rhythmic wash of the Thames. Barges lie half-submerged here, beached and abandoned on the muddy foreshore, constructed from concrete during World War Two when steel was in short supply. Now they are part of the birdlife habitat, guillemots nesting among their algae-covered hulls.

The path skirts the edge of a landfill site, crows and seagulls crowning piles of rubbish in great squawking clouds, scavenging for titbits among what we see fit to discard. Then the Queen Elizabeth II Bridge appears, carrying the M25 across the river to Dartford, the lorries that are caught in its endless circle mere toys at this distance. If the light is right, the concrete stays that hold the cables appear to glow bright white, shimmering above the water, the view causing your breath to catch for a moment as you stop at the side of the path, struck still by the perfect symmetry of the bridge. You are far enough from the city that the banks of the river retain something of what they might have looked like centuries ago, with water tickling the edge of marshland grasses, but close enough that, if you look the other way, the skyscrapers at Canary Wharf are still visible, the light on top of the pyramid at One Canada Square blinking with steady reliability.

This used to be MOD land, but the only traces of the firing ranges today are the odd pill box and the remains of shooting butts. Now it's part of Route 13 of the National Cycle Network, which makes its way towards this point from Tower Bridge, sometimes along the secluded Thames Path, sometimes adjacent to the busy A13. There, the path becomes engulfed in fumes from vehicles motoring towards Southend, or lies hidden behind steep banks strewn with plastic bags and litter. It's not always a pleasant ride. Even the quiet village of Rainham is indiscriminately swallowed by east London's sprawl.

But across the railway lies the haven of these wetlands, and a few miles downstream the mess of the suburbs is finally left behind and tiny Essex villages take their place. The cycle route becomes separated from the riverside by power stations, oil refineries and the unbridged Vange Creek, but rejoins the waterfront at Benfleet Yacht Club, where the boats that line the muddy waterways rest on bulbous hulls. A bumpy bridleway traces the river through Hadleigh Country Park, the deep ruts a challenge for all but the hardiest of bikes. The ruined tower of Hadleigh Castle overlooks the water from the hill, next to it the scars of the mountain bike track from the London Olympics. At low tide, the brave can ford the gap to Two Tree Island, splashing through the creek, before crossing the bridge to rejoin the cycle route.

The estuary suddenly opens up, and the settlements along its banks take on nautical names: Leigh-on-Sea, Westcliff-on-Sea, Southend-on-Sea. Here, the sea wall becomes crowded with boats, holidaymakers and oyster huts, the 'No cycling' signs directing you to the parallel road, where the gradient increases as the road traverses the cliffs. It's a crude reminder that Essex is not all flat.

Then, back down at sea level, it's once more traffic-free, the cycle path sandwiched between the promenade and rows of Victorian hotels. The 'caw-caw-caw' of seagulls becomes drowned by the screams from Adventure Island as you pass by Southend pier; at a mile long, it's the longest in the world, seeming almost to touch the other side. The estuary grows wider and wider as you travel past Thorpe Bay and Shoeburyness until, eventually, it melts into the North Sea.

This is what I'd been looking forward to when I set out to cycle around Britain. I'd ridden to Southend before, I'd spent the past two years working in Rainham and Benfleet and Basildon, and I couldn't wait for those ordinary places to become a part of my extraordinary journey, the culmination of months of planning and even longer spent dreaming.

For months I had been building up to this day, the day when I would finally head off into the unknown, exploring places so familiar yet so full of mystery. Like most people I'd always dreamt of adventure, but unlike most I'd reached the day when I'd run out of excuses and my dreams had turned into plans. It would have to be a cycling adventure; I'd always loved cycling for the joy and freedom it brings, for the beauty of travelling for miles and miles simply by keeping the pedals turning. And it would have to be the UK; as an environmentalist I wouldn't fly, and it felt wrong to explore another country when I knew so little about my own.

But by the time I had rounded Vange Creek on that first day, I was ready to give up. I'd been on the road for nearly seven hours and travelled less than 50 miles. Departing Tower Bridge in a flurry of flag waving and camera flashing seemed like a distant memory. I pulled into a pub car park and sank to the floor, my back to the wall, my head tilted backwards in exhaustion. I was desperately thirsty; my water bottles had long since been drained of their last drop, the August day hotter than I'd anticipated and the exertion of hauling 16 kg of luggage harder than I'd realised. The grime of the dry roads covered my bare skin, and angry splotches marked my shoulders from where I'd taken a tumble and landed in a pile of stinging nettles. It wasn't supposed to get hard yet – it was only day one, and this was the part I knew.

I had ridden long distances before: a few years back I'd cycled from Penzance to Brighton with a group of friends, and I'd always thought about going back and completing the journey, making my way slowly along the coastline, exploring some of the most beautiful and remote parts of Britain. Cycling in a big circle appealed to me. Earlier that year I had cycled the Capital Ring, a 78-mile route that winds its way round the periphery of London, through parks, along canals, down unassuming streets. I liked knowing that if I just kept following the signs, eventually I would get back to where I'd started. Cycling the coast would be the ultimate version of that trip, following the river from London until it became the sea, then following the sea for 4,000 miles until it reached the mouth of the Thames again, and finally back to London. I loved the simplicity of it. How hard could it be?

My friends were more cautious: 'Try a LEJOG first, Anna. Don't be too ambitious.' Riding from Land's End to John o'Groats (LEJOG, or in reverse JOGLE) was something I'd considered, but it's a ride that so many others have done, and I wanted to do something more unusual. I had made up my mind. I would ride the coast.

I'd sat looking at my UK wall chart often enough, visualising what it might be like. The Abbey at Whitby, the Fair at Scarborough, Land's End, the Humber Bridge, the Tower at Blackpool, St Michael's Mount in Penzance, the excitement, the discovery, the feeling of achievement when I made my triumphant return to Tower Bridge.

But less than a day into the adventure, here I was, sitting in a car park, exhausted and dispirited. It had looked so easy, but I'd left late, and I'd become lost, my determination to stay next to the water adding unnecessary miles and leading me again and again down a dead end. At one point, my cycle route had become little more than a concrete shelf balanced over the water, and I'd almost cried in frustration, fearful that my adventure would end before it had begun.

From Vange Creek, the cycle route would join the coastal bridleway through Hadleigh Country Park; this was a part to which I'd especially looked forward – a winding, creek-lined route I knew so well. But now, I was weary of riding. The bumpy track would add more time and distance, and wouldn't do my laden bike any favours – a convenient excuse. After having painstakingly hugged the shore of the Thames since central London, it was crushing to accept that the trip I had planned, and ridden so many times in my head, might not work out quite the way I had supposed it would. I couldn't believe that I was giving up on my resolve to follow every inch of the coast so soon after having set out. But my motivation had faded. I just wanted to reach my destination as quickly as possible. So I joined the traffic on the A13 as it crawled up Bread and Cheese Hill, wishing I had some bread and cheese to eat at the top as the old motor-car drivers would once have done while waiting for their engines to cool off.

My first glimpse of the water from the clifftop at Leigh-on-Sea made my surly mood evaporate.

'I can see the sea!'

That glimpse released a jumble of emotions: childish excitement, the thrill of discovery and nervousness for what I was about to undertake. I took a deep breath and freewheeled to the shore, hoping for the first of the daily swims I had promised myself. But at the promenade, all I could see was a mile of sludge and a distant blue stripe at its far end at the low tide. It didn't matter – there would be plenty more opportunities: I was cycling the coast, after all. I settled on the seafront, watching the sky turn to orange in the evening glow.

I had finished the first day's ride. It had been more challenging than I had imagined, but I had done it, and I was here, the first step taken, my adventure now set in motion. Across the Thames sat Kent, the lights on the shore starting to twinkle as the sunlight faded. All being well, I would be there in ten weeks' time, on my final day, cycling back to London. I had no idea what would happen between now and then, but I couldn't wait to find out.

DAY 2:
SOUTHEND TO FRINTON

60 miles

Some people say that the first day is the worst. You're not sure what you've let yourself in for, it's hard work and you're not used to riding a loaded bike. They're wrong – the second day is far harder. You still don't know what you've let yourself in for, it's still hard work and you're sore from the first day. My legs hurt, my knees hurt, my shoulders hurt. This was going to be a long trip.

I said as much to Graham as I limped down the stairs that morning; Graham was my colleague and friend who had given me a bed for the night and who would be riding with me that day. We had both worked as Bike It Officers for Sustrans, he in Southend and me in Basildon, our job to create a culture of cycling among school children. It was rewarding but exhausting work, and when my contract had come to an end I'd declined to have it renewed; this was a good opportunity to have my adventure.

'Is your saddle too low?' Graham asked as he dished out the eggs. I looked at him blankly. This was something I should probably know the answer to.

'Um, I haven't really thought about it.'

I was embarrassed to admit that, in the excitement of treating myself to a new touring bike, I'd not checked it was the right size for me. The rest of my planning had been meticulous. I already knew where I would be staying each night for the entire trip; I was a terrible camper, so had spent months contacting friends and strangers and distant relatives to ensure I had a bed to sleep in each night. But I'd paid less attention to my bike, the very thing that would make this venture a success or a failure.

'We'll have a look at it after breakfast,' Graham said, even though it was nearing the time we said we'd be leaving.

'But shouldn't we get going?'

'Anna! You can't ride a bike that's the wrong size for you for ten weeks straight. Come on, it won't take long. You'll thank me in the long run.'

With the rear wheel propped up in the training stand, I clambered on. Graham set to work, eyeing-up angles, measuring tubing, checking cables and bolts.

'That's odd,' he said, testing the saddle position by dangling a weighted line from one knee then the other.

'What?' I asked, suddenly concerned that my adventure was doomed.

'I think you have one leg shorter than the other!'

More fiddling and fettling followed as I stood anxiously by. My impatience at Graham's exactitude was a clear indication that I had much to learn. 'Uncle Graham' we used to call him at work, the youngsters among us bowing to his superior knowledge and experience as a life-long cyclist. I tried to do the same now, hoping my beautiful Ridgeback Voyage would pass the test.

'It's a good bike,' he concluded, after checking the wheels ran true.

'I greased the bearings in the hubs myself!'

I neglected to say that as I'd reassembled them I'd found one rolling around on the floor.

'Do you have a spare inner tube?' he asked.

'No...'

'Goodness me, you can't cycle four thousand miles without a spare tube. What if it bursts and you can't patch it? We'll call past the bike shop on our way.'

Once more I checked the time. 'But shouldn't we...'

Graham interrupted with a laugh. 'Stop clock-watching. This is more important.'

By the time I had a fresh inner tube added to my luggage I was itching to leave. Off we pedalled, past endless rows of front doors as we criss-crossed the grid of residential streets, eventually bridging the dual carriageway that kept Southend tucked neatly next to the sea. Beyond it lay the wide open countryside, where each road would become less wide and less busy than the last. I had finally shaken off the city and the suburbs, and here before me was nothing but space, a patchwork of fields disappearing over the edge of the vista, and the endless, endless sky.

Heat rose from the tarmac, our sun-cream-sticky arms covered in a light sweat as we rode side by side down hedge-lined roads, the trees heavy with summer foliage, pulling over to let the occasional vehicle pass. Villages came and went, all spacious detached houses and wooden fences, and expensive cars sitting on paved driveways.

'It's great coming down here when I'm not with the club,' Graham said. 'I must have ridden these roads hundreds of times, but usually I don't see anything except the tyre of the person in front.'

I smiled, but wished we would go faster. I tried unsuccessfully to hide my twitchiness.

'Anna, relax! There's no rush. Slow and steady wins the race. You remind me of some of the guys I ride with, zooming off ahead. They soon burn out. Anyway, what exactly are we rushing for? You have all the time in the world.'

I knew he was right but even so, I wanted to zoom ahead like those cycle club guys. I knew I could ride fast, much faster than this, and this was an opportunity to push myself while it was flat. I had a target, a destination, and I wanted to reach it.

Soon, the masts of boats became visible across the fields, our first glimpse of water that day at Maldon, 15 miles inland. I laughed wryly at the determination I'd had yesterday to hug the edge so strictly. There hadn't been a chance of doing that today, the unbridged rivers Roach, Crouch and Blackwater forcing us away from the coast, reaching deep into Essex like the capillaries of the sea. We rode through the outskirts of the town towards Marine Parade Park, where the waterfront was crowded with boats. Moored alongside the quay were old Thames barges that used to carry agricultural goods to London, their terracotta sails lashed tightly to wooden masts. Behind them sat rows of yachts in the marina, with yet more yachts tethered to the mooring buoys that dotted the water. Boats upon boats upon boats. I looked at them, feeling the lure of the sea, the history and folklore of our island so richly steeped in the water that holds us in its saline grip and hugs and releases, hugs and releases day after day.

The boats remained in sight long after we'd left Maldon, winding along the river valley towards Mersea Island, where the ferry to Point Clear would finally allow us to reach the coast. We rode carefully on to the causeway, the long straight tarmac flanked by huge wetlands; all of it, including the road, would be covered at high tide, giving the island a desolate feel, a sense of isolation that comes when, twice a day, a community is cut off from the mainland. Our road eventually ended in a gate leading on to the beach, the signs to our ferry port nowhere in sight. Had we gone the wrong way? But there was nowhere else we could have gone. We wheeled our bicycles through the gate and fumbled our way across the dunes.

'Is that our ferry?' I asked, pointing towards a large boat that was resting in the water a few feet from the sand.

'Er, no, Anna, that's a classic yacht. Run aground by the looks of it.'

I peered closer. Its wooden deck was almost hidden by a confusing muddle of ropes and fenders, the anchor dangling uselessly at its side. The skipper was passing the time until the tide came in again by snipping his trousers at the knees to provide some relief from the heat. I hoped for his sake that the weather would last, or that those weren't his only trousers.

'Anyway, the boat we want won't be nearly as big as that.'

I looked around for a jetty from where the ferry might launch, but there was no sign of one; Graham must have it wrong, and there must be another, more obvious place. A lone seal bobbed near the bank as we waited.

'Look, there it is!'

I could hardly believe that the boat approaching could possibly be our ferry, or that the queue of people that had suddenly accumulated, including two other cyclists, would fit on to it. It looked little more than a RIB, those inflatable boats that take sightseers haring up and down the Thames. It beached itself gently and a plank emerged from the open bow, resting just above the waterline. 'Bags off the bikes!' ordered the captain, and we unclipped panniers and rucksacks, dropping bungees in our haste, then pushed up the ramp, trying not to barge into anyone as we struggled with our luggage. 'Hold on to your bikes!' was the next order, as the huge outboard motors were fired up and the RIB was swung around in the estuary. Off we went, powering across the mouth of the river, pitching lightly on the waves as salt water met fresh, pinned to our places by the shoulders of our neighbours. I smiled widely at Graham – despite the discomfort, the fear of capsize and the captain's unfriendly frown, this was brilliant: an old-fashioned, traditional way of crossing a river, how vehicles and foot passengers were transported before bridges were built, the water lapping at the hull mere centimetres from my feet.

Too soon we arrived at Point Clear and disembarked, making the journey down to Jaywick where, for the first time, there was the sea in all its glory. As the great expanse came into view, I stopped, struck dumb by its sheer size. The waves stretched seemingly forever. At last! This was what I had sought, the sea I would never tire of seeing. I lingered for a while; it was now Graham's turn to hurry me up, his growling stomach dictating that we continue. Our cycle route was perched on the edge of the sea wall and I couldn't help but turn to look every few pedals, my eyes drawn again and again to the horizon. What lay beyond that gentle curve? What lurked beneath those cool waves? It was easy to see why our ancestors had worked so hard to conquer the sea, the mystery of the distant shore utterly compelling.

Blue signs for the National Cycle Network frequently appeared beside the path; one of Sustrans' projects was to manage the NCN, and I felt a rush of affection for my old employer each time I saw one – for they were more than simply a signpost to the next town. Each sign brimmed with the promise of people unmet, destinations unknown and miles untravelled.

We reached the Georgian resort of Clacton-on-Sea, riding through the Seafront Gardens towards the pier, past theatres and white-fronted hotels, fish and chip huts and bingo halls, helter-skelters and roller coasters, exactly as it had been at Southend. I vaguely recognised it from our Sunday School outings, though it now looked drab and forlorn to my adult eyes. But better to stop here and be guaranteed supper than continue to Frinton, which was, in Graham's words, 'The land that time forgot.' The tatty cafes on the promenade were closing up for the night and I was secretly relieved. 'There must be somewhere open,' said Graham, leading the way up the streets away from the front. We settled down on the veranda of a hotel, leaning our bikes against the table, flopping into the chairs. The waiter came out.

'What would you like?'

'Fish and chips again, Anna?' said Graham.

'Definitely,' I said.

'Can I have some mushy peas as well? And also some coleslaw. Do you want some coleslaw? Two coleslaws, please. And a side salad. Make that two. And two glasses of water. Oh, and a Diet Coke!'

The waiter raised his eyebrows.

There was barely enough room on the table for all the food and for the second day in a row I wolfed it down; this wasn't just food, it was fuel. 'How many calories do you reckon we've just eaten?' I said, easily seeing off the last of my chips.

'Oh, I don't know. Far too many, probably. You need it, though! There's not that much of you to start with.'

Our stomachs bulging, we rode the final few miles to Frinton where we would part ways; sleep was beckoning, for Graham on the train home and for me in my guest house bed.

'Good luck, Anna,' he said as he gave me a hug. 'Don't worry about the trip. Just take it easy, and slow down a bit. Try to enjoy the journey rather than just riding to where you're staying each night. It would be a bit of a waste to make it all the way around Britain without really seeing anything.'

'Thank you,' I said. 'For the dinner, for hosting me last night and for helping me get this far.'

I took a deep breath as he rode away. Riding with Graham had helped distract me from the magnitude of the task I had taken on – it had simply been a day's ride with a friend. But now, left alone, I could truly contemplate what I was doing. I walked to the beach to dip my feet in the sea, gazing out across the water as it splashed against my legs.

For all my frustration, I knew that Graham had been right to insist that we sort out my bike, and that I should slow down and fully appreciate where I was. This was unlike any ride I'd ever done; I was heading out into the unknown, and if I wanted to make it back to Tower Bridge without it all going wrong I would have to start thinking differently. I'd assumed that, because I was a daily cyclist, I would step into touring with few problems. But just a few hours with Graham had suggested otherwise.

I used to hop on my bike and cycle the 40 miles to my dad's house without really thinking about it, but that was a familiar route, and even then I would stay close to the railway line just in case something went wrong. But there's no quick fix when you're on your own in the middle of nowhere. Despite my months of planning, did I honestly know what I was doing?

After only two days, doubts were niggling: doubts about the point of it all, doubts that I'd easily pushed to the back of my mind when riding with Graham. There was no reason to do anything unless it meant something, unless it had a use. And what's the purpose of just riding a bike? What good would it do? People had told me that this would be a life-changing experience, that I would 'find myself' on the road. But would I? Did I even want to?

I had given up everything for this: a job, a home, a boyfriend. Nick and I had met four months before I was due to leave and, though short, the relationship had begun to develop into something serious. But I had told him that he wasn't allowed to contact me while I was away; I was determined not to spend the entire trip thinking about someone else. But now, I felt wretched. Was breaking things off the right thing to do? What if he forgot all about me?

I stood looking out to sea, the surface turning to grey in the fading light. It seemed so impossibly vast that I wondered how I'd ever make it to Scotland, let alone beyond. Perhaps my friends had been right; perhaps this was too difficult. My feet sank deeper into the sand as the water washed repeatedly over them, my toes curled against the cold. I tried to push the doubts away and remember why I had started this ride in the first place, trying to recall the excitement I'd felt as I left Tower Bridge. Lights began to flicker along the shoreline, mirrored by a scattering of illuminated boats. I watched the waves for a while as they disintegrated in great foaming curves on the sand, twinkling in the final rays of the sun, then I turned and walked slowly up the beach.

DAY 3:
FRINTON TO LOWESTOFT

77 miles

The sea mist lingered, its thick white tendrils lying snagged on bramble bushes, the cobwebs spun among the hedgerows becoming detailed by dew. I rose early and emerged into the cool sunshine, the damp, crisp country air filling my lungs with delicious breaths as I pedalled through a world still asleep.

I was to meet my twin sister, Sarah, in Harwich, from where we'd be cycling together for the next couple of days. It felt like an age since I'd seen her (it was 48 hours) and I couldn't wait. I had never before spent more than a handful of days out of her company, and I couldn't imagine not seeing her for ten long weeks, my doppelgänger, my best friend, the person who understands me more than anyone. Having a twin sister meant that I had never in my life been alone – even when, in our formative years, this hadn't seemed like such a good thing. She had given unquestioning support as I'd prepared to go away, preparing a huge 'Good luck!' banner for the send off, and allowing me to sleep on her sofa once I'd given up my London flat. I wanted to soak up as much of her company as I possibly could.

A steady downhill slope drew me towards Harwich harbour, where the hulking giraffe-like cranes at the Felixstowe container terminal stood across the water, just visible through the mist.

I curved round Marine Parade, past the stark white 'low' lighthouse and the tall brown 'high' lighthouse, past the dinghies of the Yacht Club and the long arm of the lifeboat jetty, towards Harwich Old Town, where Elizabethan pubs and hotels lay scattered among the concrete port authority buildings, resting places for visitors who would arrive in this ancient port to travel to and from the continent. At the head of the ferry pier stood the wooden-framed ticket office, outside which sat Sarah.

'Sarah!' I was beaming widely. 'How was the train journey?'

'I really enjoyed it. It's so wonderful to be out of London,' she replied. 'The doors opened and I could hear birdsong.'

We wheeled our bikes along the pier, gazing across at the hazy shore on the opposite side.

'Wow! This is beautiful. Look at the sea!' She was just as excited by the water as I was. 'It's such a good idea for an adventure. There is so much variety on the coast – you're going to have a fantastic time.'

She fished out her camera, taking photographs of the cranes, the beach huts, the shadows of our two bikes resting against the railings. I smiled – Sarah loved taking photographs.

We ordered breakfasts from the cafe while waiting for the ferry that would cross the harbour mouth. I'd made the mandatory booking in advance, and with five minutes to go the ferryman stomped up to us, interrupting our last few bites of breakfast with, 'Are you two gettin' on this ferry or not?' We jumped up and struggled down the ramp, juggling bikes and toast.

This was the second ferry in as many days, and the third and fourth would soon follow, this section of coastline being dotted with rivers. A sign on the bulkhead showed that it was officially part of the National Cycle Network and was thus equipped with cycle racks; it made a nice change from sitting with my bike almost on my knees. We stowed our luggage and said hello to the other passengers.

'You must be sisters,' they said.

'Twins!' we replied as we sat there identically, our hair scraped back into matching ponytails.

'Are you cycling far?'

'Well, I'm just going as far as Cromer, but she's going around the whole coast.'

'What, of Britain? England, *and* Scotland, *and* Wales?'

'Wow. Terrific. I'm impressed!'

'And jealous!'

'So how far is it?'

'And how long will that take you?'

'Are you doing it for the challenge, or as a sightseeing tour?'

'Oh, you must go to…' A list of seaside resorts and pubs followed.

Riding with Graham had shown me not to rush, not to focus purely on the destination, but neither was this a sightseeing tour – I simply wouldn't have time to go to all those places! They were an organic part of the journey, though, a part that I could enjoy from the seat of my bike.

The boat crossed the border into Suffolk to arrive at the jetty at Felixstowe, and there we met Jon, another friend who would be cycling with me for a few hundred miles. It had been a chance meeting on the Regents' Canal the month before that had led to him being there; we'd known each other for a while through the Green Party but hadn't interacted much before stopping to say hello as we passed each other on the towpath. Our conversation had turned to my imminent departure and Jon had suggested that he might join me for a few days. I had unquestioningly accepted his offer, but afterwards had worried about what his presence would mean. He would be sharing potentially the most testing part of my journey, the part where I discovered what it was all about, where I settled into my new routine and explored the lifestyle I had chosen. I hoped that neither of us would find this a problem – we were both taking a gamble, having never so much as gone for a beer with each other before.

The tide was out as Sarah and I jumped down to the beach, and Jon helped us to drag our bikes across the wet sand.

He looked from her to me. 'Which one's which?'

'Very funny,' I replied. 'How's it going?'

'Well, I thought you said Tuesday, so I've been kicking around here since yesterday.'

'Oh, sorry,' I replied.

'Nay bother,' he said. 'It's nice to be out of London. Been working on my tan.'

I grinned. We'd get on just fine.

We set off, making our way along the NCN on traffic-free paths along the seafront and high up on the cliffs. It was glorious, lazy cycling weather and glorious, lazy cycling. Jon and I rode ahead on our streamlined tourers, the cleats on my cycling shoes helping to power me up the inclines, while Sarah dawdled behind, completely relaxed on her town bike, stopping frequently to reach for her camera. 'Come on, Sarah!' we would cry, itching to test our bikes and our legs. 'Let me take my photographs!' she replied. 'This stuff is really interesting. I want to remember this journey properly.' I was torn between wanting to do the same, to create a detailed document that I could then share with others, and wanting the journey to exist in the moment, my own memory of what I was doing document enough, not seen through the eye of a camera.

Our next river crossing, over the River Deben at Felixstowe Ferry, was in marked contrast to the previous – no harbour, no timetable or need to book; all that was required to hail the boat was the wave of a bat. We took up our place in the queue, wobbling down the pier between rows of children crabbing in the sunshine. The heat induced a soporific torpor among the crowds, from the locals wandering along the beach to the bare-footed ferryman, shuttling his boat back and forth across the river mouth. 'Don't you get bored, just driving this boat all day?' we asked him. 'Not at all,' he replied. 'There's always another load of passengers waiting; people rely on me. In the sunshine it's glorious and in the rain the river comes alive. The joy of it is in its simplicity.'

Once we'd been deposited on the opposite bank, the cycle route headed away from the sea, forced inland by the shingle bank of Orford Ness, through forests and villages towards Snape Maltings, where we would cross the River Alde. The pungent odour of cabbage replaced the smell of salt in the air as we pedalled through acres and acres of farmland, the low-lying fields offering no shelter from the sun, and it was three very sweaty and thirsty cyclists that arrived at Aldeburgh High Street, where the elegant Victorian buildings that had once drawn the upper middle classes to the area sat interspersed with shops, galleries and rows of fishermen's huts. Boats lay lopsided on the shingle having been hauled up away from the tide. The sea shimmered at the foot of the beach and we parked our bikes, torn between wanting lunch and wanting to run barefoot towards the waves. A couple of tentative footsteps on the scorching pebbles settled it – off we went to find a sheltered spot to eat.

Sarah had made sandwiches, but we both looked on in amazement as Jon opened a pannier that seemed to be entirely full of food and started to assemble his lunch: wraps, a bag of salad, salami, walnuts, a block of cheese... In went the red onion that he'd pinched from a field earlier in the day; Sarah and I had hoped that the farmer hadn't noticed him hurdling the fence.

'I've discovered a great way of slicing cheese,' Jon said, taking a credit card from his wallet and using it to cut pieces from the block. 'Means I don't have to carry a knife. Helps keep the weight down.'

Sarah looked at his overflowing pannier.

'Er, I'm sure that really helps.'

'What now?' I asked. The card was covered in cheese residue and wouldn't fit back in the wallet.

'Oh!' he laughed.

After lunch we braved the searing pebbles to sit on the beach, our bare toes soaking up the sun. A wedding party posed for photographs, champagne in hand. A little way back from the beach, above the forest, peeped the smooth curve of a huge white ball.

'That looks like a nuclear power station,' Jon said.

I checked the map. 'Yes, it is – it's the one at Sizewell.'

'Shall we go and have a look?'

We replaced our cycling shoes and ducked beneath the trees, several minutes later faced with the globe and the huge concrete buildings that surrounded it. We stopped still, silently looking; being in such close proximity to something so powerful created a certain unease among the three of us.

'It's horrible, isn't it?' Jon said eventually. 'What if it goes into meltdown while we're standing right here?' He made a face at the power station, which Sarah caught on camera.

There was an eerie quiet surrounding the site, the hustle and bustle of the operation kept hidden away inside one of the sterile-looking buildings. It was the newest of Britain's nuclear power stations and the first of many that I would pass on my trip, all of them built near the coast because of the need for a constant supply of water for cooling. I would never come to like them, the toxic by-product and potential for catastrophe outweighing, to my mind, any advantage in energy production.

Onwards through the Suffolk countryside we rode, passing through villages where square parish church towers peeped from behind thatched roofs, each village sign unique in its detail: the 'House in the Clouds' at Thorpeness; the thatched church in Theberton against which leaned the cage of a German airship shot down during World War One; the windmill at Westleton; a fishing boat at Dunwich. Stalls outside houses sold eggs and jam, and we stopped at the hedgerows to cram handfuls of blackberries into our mouths, the juiciest ones always just out of reach. Our final ferry was a tiny boat, the smallest so far, seeming almost too fragile to hold us and our bikes, the ferrywoman hauling on the tiller as we were plucked from the jetty by the racing tide and delivered to the opposite shore. From Southwold we journeyed inland to join the A12, which would take us the remainder of the way to Lowestoft.

I know the A12 well – it goes through Hackney, where I'd been living for the past few years. It was strange, after three full days of cycling, to have joined a road that could take us to London in a mere couple of hours. Thinking about it threatened to burst the bubble of my bike ride; I was suddenly anxious to put more miles between me and home, so I quickly led the way northwards, the others panting in my wake. The wide arc of the sea came into view as we freewheeled down to the Lowestoft seafront, and Sarah and I dashed straight into the blissfully cool waters, washing away the sweat and grime of the road, squealing as the waves splashed up to our chests, our shallow breathing abating as we grew accustomed to the delicious cold. At last! This was what I had wanted, to feel the rawness of the water after having gazed upon its surface all day. I kicked into the depths, the rising and falling carrying me as effortlessly as a cork, laughing deliriously at the sea's immense power. *Every day from now*, I promised myself as I swam long and hard, making up for lost time, staying long after Sarah had retreated to the shore.

DAY 4:
LOWESTOFT TO WELLS-NEXT-THE-SEA

70 miles

We awoke to the sound of rain drumming on the windows of our B&B.

'I knew that weather was too good to last,' Sarah said.

Covered from head to toe in waterproofs, we went to the seafront to meet Jon, who had camped nearby.

He had dressed for the day in his standard T-shirt and shorts. I wasn't surprised. I'd never seen him wear anything other than shorts, even in the winter: he was known as 'Shorts Jon' among our mutual friends.

'Won't you get wet?' Sarah asked him.

'Skin's waterproof,' he replied. 'At least it's warm today.'

We struck out for Great Yarmouth, the sky steadily dribbling around us. There's something so very English about a beach in the rain, that one lone stalwart with an umbrella a symbol of the British summertime. The few families who had persevered in their holidaymaking herded miserable children from the comfort of their cars, determined to enjoy their soggy fish and chips on the deserted pier.

The miles passed quickly, a tailwind speeding us along past holiday homes and caravan parks, and we laughed at the lonely village of California, looking like anything but its American namesake on this sodden day. The dunes seemed to glow beneath the grey skies, the Norfolk Broads vibrant even in the drizzle, picture-postcard boats sitting on narrow waterways behind banks of reeds and watermills dotting the horizon. 'Horsey!' 'Solar panels!' 'Windmill!' 'Potatoes!' we would shout, buzzing with the delirium that the rain invoked.

But good humour eventually fades, and once rain began to seep through our clothes it quickly seeped into our spirits. 'Can we stop for tea soon?' Sarah asked, her toes turning to sponge inside her canvas shoes. We found a beach cafe at Winterton-on-Sea and clutched at our mugs, the feeling slowly returning to our fingers, gazing through steamed-up windows at the drowned beach beyond.

We returned to the stubborn drizzle, which eventually gave way to a downpour, as if a sluice gate had opened in the clouds above. We squealed as water ran down our necks, our clothes quickly saturated, our hair plastered to our heads. Sarah removed her shoes and pedalled in her flip-flops.

'Just a few more miles,' I said as we left the Broads behind, the sea which had spurred us on earlier in the day now hidden from the coastal road by huge dunes, the squawking of seagulls and the sand that lined the road the only hints of its presence. Those miles were cold and wet, and we spent most of them staring at the road, avoiding overflowing drains, not talking, bemoaning our reversal of fortune from the sunshine of the day before. I felt desperately sorry for Sarah; I couldn't hope to avoid days like this, but for her, it must have been miserable. We trundled through the rivulets on the tarmac, our wheels kicking up the spray, muddy splashes covering our panniers. She soldiered on, quietly determined, refusing to moan.

'We're here!' I called as I reached the top of a hill, passing the town sign for Cromer, our dinner stop. Sarah slowly caught up then climbed from her bike to give the sign a kiss. 'The Gem of the Norfolk Coast!' she said, as I laughed.

Down in the town we dashed into a pub, discarding dripping clothes, the promised 'best sea views' obscured by the rain running down the windows. At least there was tea and peanuts behind the bar, so we warmed up and dried off, and once we'd mustered enough strength ventured to the chip shop below, leaving a large puddle behind. It was amazing how quickly our priorities had been reduced to the three basic things: shelter, food and rest.

'Three fish and chips please,' we ordered from the waitress.

'Would you like anything else?' she asked as she cleared the plates away shortly afterwards.

Sarah and I looked at the dessert menu.

'I'll have the sausage, chips and beans,' said Jon.

Sarah and I coughed in unison. 'What!?'

'I'm still hungry!' he said.

'I would be sick,' said Sarah as his second plate of food arrived.

'You'll never finish that,' I said. He did, perhaps just to prove us wrong.

We emerged from the restaurant to look down towards the pier half-hidden in the gloom. It was time for Sarah to head home, back on the train to London. She hugged me tightly.

'Thank you for being here,' I said.

'I've had a wonderful time; it's been brilliant, even today. I wish I could carry on!'

She took one final photograph of us, then pedalled off into the rain.

'Come on then, let's get this over with,' I said to Jon; we were still 20 miles from our destination. We clambered back on our bikes, shoving dry arms into wet sleeves, the cold material clinging to our skin, our joints reluctant to get moving. The slow curve of the Norfolk coast turned us steadily westwards until at last we arrived in Wells-next-the-Sea, pedalling quickly through streets lined with tiny shops and Georgian pubs to find shelter and dry off.

'Sea swim, Anna?' Jon teased as we settled by a pub fire.

'No way!'

I was as wet as I wanted to be, despite my waterproofs. My shoe covers had been utterly useless, soaking up ground water and keeping my feet wet rather than dry. I didn't use them after that. I was almost relieved when I lost one. We sat in the warmth, our clothes and bags gently steaming.

The two days riding with Sarah had been exactly what I needed; her presence for the past few days had made all the difference. She was now a part of my adventure, understanding it, feeling more included because of her cameo. She had enjoyed the sunny miles and endured the wet ones, swam and eaten and climbed hills and freewheeled down again. Everything I would do for the next ten weeks, she had done too. And though we had teased her, the pictures she had taken were fantastic. Later, I would spend hours poring over them – it was worth all the stopping.

Sarah had been able to see the journey for what it was, without the worry it would all go wrong: it was just a bike ride. We'd survived the rain. Nothing disastrous had happened. What did I need to know, really? Nothing that the road wouldn't teach me. I might not have it right yet, but in time I would. This was my adventure and I was doing it, and that was all that mattered.

DAY 5:
WELLS-NEXT-THE-SEA TO MABLETHORPE

121 miles

Just five days into the trip, my carefully laid plans had started to go awry. The pre-arranged accommodation in Skegness had fallen through, and the closest place we could find at the last minute was with a friend of a friend in Mablethorpe, a further 17 miles up the coast. With a budget of £10 a day I couldn't afford a hotel every night. It had already looked to be a long ride, but that extra stretch would take the estimated distance to 104 miles. We set off early, prepared to break our first century. We knew it would be tough, but had we known just how tough it would actually be, I'm not sure we would have attempted it.

In order to reach Mablethorpe, Jon and I would have to cycle around three sides of the Wash, that lopsided rectangle nestled into the coast of East Anglia. Our first glimpse of its massive expanse was at Hunstanton, 15 miles into the ride. It was immense. I gulped as we gazed across, glancing at Jon, suddenly guilty that I'd imposed such a long ride on him. This was ridiculous. How on earth would we make it that far?

'That's where we're aiming for,' I said, trying to sound blasé, pointing to a wind farm in the vague distance. 'Those turbines are just offshore at Skegness, then it's about fifteen miles further. So when we can see them from the other angle we'll know we're close.'

'OK then,' Jon replied, getting on his bike. He seemed utterly unfazed by the 400-square-mile body of water that sat between us and the opposite shore. I didn't want to reiterate that our ultimate destination lay beyond what we could actually see and that already seemed an impossible way off.

'OK then,' I echoed quietly, climbing on to mine.

Over the past two days we had established a good rhythm of riding, becoming accustomed to the other's pace and stamina. There was no need for me to have worried about sharing this section with Jon. I had thought I might become frustrated riding with someone else, my fierce independence demanding I do my journey my way. But Jon was easy-going and good company, happy to follow the route I had planned, and we had settled into a contented companionship.

We set off from Hunstanton, the initial vigour of the day and our nervous energy meaning we set an impressive pace, even though the headwind was strong. We'd take it in turns to lead, allowing the other to slipstream, trying not to be the one left behind. The Wash disappeared behind trees and towns, separated from the road by five miles of salt marsh. Through Sandringham forest, Castle Rising, North and South Wootton, we whizzed along tree-lined roads, enjoying the workout, the previous day's weather nowhere to be seen.

At King's Lynn we stopped for a snack; this was our first milestone, the first corner, 35 of our 100-plus miles ridden. This once coastal port now lay inland along the pinched estuary of the Great Ouse, the Wash's floodplains having been dried out for agriculture centuries earlier. We paused on the bridge over the river, the reedy banks long and straight and wide, watching the current catch in swirling eddies as we ate our apples. Jon was left holding only the stalk about a minute later.

I baulked. 'You've eaten the core!'

'What's wrong with that? It's only the same as the rest,' he replied.

Along the Wash's southerly bank we rode, crossing into Lincolnshire where every road was 'Marsh Lane' or 'Marsh Road' – how easy it would be to get lost around here. The fenland stretched into the distance, flat as far as the eye could see, only the spires of churches in scattered villages punctuating the wide open sky. We made our way along lanes short and straight and at sharp angles, constantly turning in and out of the wind, the map a grid of dykes, the roads guided by the embankments that were left when the area was drained. The sounds of human activity had almost completely disappeared; save from the odd vehicle, there was no sign of life other than the butterflies that spiralled up from the hedgerows and the deafening chorus of crickets.

We passed the 60-mile mark somewhere past Sutton Bridge; it was already further than I'd ridden the first day and we hadn't even had lunch yet. Those first 30 miles had seemed easy, but now we were flagging.

'Can we stop soon and buy some food?' I said. 'There must be a shop around here somewhere.'

The villages came and went: Gedney Drove End, Holbeach St Marks, Fosdyke, in each merely a handful of houses gathered around the road, huge stone houses where willows wept over immaculate lawns and white gates enclosed neat rows of chicken huts – but no village shop.

'Jon, I can't keep going,' I said; I was rapidly losing energy and my legs were starting to shake. The next town with a guaranteed shop was still ten miles away; there was no way I would make it.

'And you were laughing at how much food I carry! Come on. Let's share a wrap,' he replied, and opened that pannier. We settled on the kerb.

'Yummy,' I said, grinning. Processed sausage had never tasted so good.

The church at Boston came into view across the fields long before we reached it, the tower twice as tall as a conventional tower, giant-like on the landscape. We arrived and paused in the cobbled town square. This was the left-hand corner of the Wash: our second milestone. Seventy-five miles down, 25 or so to go.

'You OK?' Jon asked.

I nodded.

Once again heading north, the gusting wind was behind us. But we were soon losing momentum; 80-odd miles was taking its toll. There was no chance we'd be able to keep up the 15mph we'd been averaging at the beginning of the day. We pushed on, not wanting to be first to admit that we were struggling, passing by villages whos e names evoked another world – Old Leake, Hurn's End, Wrangle Lowgate, Friskney Tofts. I was desperately seeking out the wind turbines on the horizon that would signal we were nearing the end of our journey. The constant twisting and turning of the road denied us our tailwind, taking us in and out of the gusts, on and on.

'Shout at the wind!' Jon said, and we did, the vocal expression of our frustration making it easier to battle on, the sound being plucked from our lips as soon as it was uttered. Still, no turbines appeared.

We stopped for a break and some energy sweets by the side of the road, and I grew anxious that the route I had chosen would defeat us. We were running low on water and Jon's pannier was almost empty. The remaining seven miles might as well have been 70 for all the hope I had that we'd make it. But there was no alternative – we pushed on, pedal after agonising pedal.

At long last the tip of a wind turbine beckoned from the horizon; I cheered, exhausted but ecstatic, a renewed burst of energy speeding us on.

By the time we arrived in Skegness, we'd already covered the 104 miles I'd promised for the whole journey. My estimate had been out. I tried not to think about what was still to come, but headed for the beach, discarding my bike halfway down the sand and quickly changing into my bikini.

'Race you in!' I shouted. Somehow I still had the energy to swim.

'I really fancy a curry,' Jon said, as we dried ourselves off.

'We can't have a curry at the seaside.' I was a traditionalist when it came to fish and chips.

'But you've eaten fish and chips every day so far!'

'I know – I love them! Come on. I'm starving.'

He followed me into the restaurant and pointedly ordered a spaghetti bolognese.

The light was fading as we emerged from the restaurant. People were heading for the bingo halls and the bars, girls in short skirts and men in shiny shoes. We felt as if we were intruding on their Friday night, wandering along in our scruffy T-shirts and cycling shoes. We entered one of the garish arcades, the noise and whirr of the games overwhelming, trying our luck on the 2p machines. By the time we were ready for the final stretch to Mablethorpe it was dark.

We hit the road. It was miserable. After the bright lights of the Skegness seafront, the long, deserted, unlit country roads were a struggle. Our legs had already spent all that we'd asked of them. Every village we passed through reduced the number of miles to Mablethorpe excruciatingly slowly, and just as I was starting to become desperate, we were flagged down by a man shouting to us from the side of the road. We wondered what kind of odd people would be out so late around here. It was actually Dave, our host. Thank goodness he had come out of the house at that moment and seen us.

'Look at you two! You must be exhausted. Come in, come in!'

We crept inside the kitchen, cautious about wheeling sand through the house, but Celia brushed aside our apologies.

'How far have you come today?' she asked.

'From Wells-next-the-Sea. It was a hundred and twenty-one miles!' I said.

'A hundred and twenty-one miles? I can't believe that! Can you believe that, Dave? What an incredible ride. And riding through the dark just now. That must have been quite tough.'

'Yes, it was getting a bit much.'

'Well, you can make yourselves at home here. We have a room for you both, including an en suite bathroom each. This used to be a guest house so it has all the fittings. Unless you want to share a room?'

Jon laughed. 'No, thanks, that's OK!'

Celia smiled. 'Let me show you to your rooms then. You're welcome to stay tomorrow night as well if you want to have a bit of a rest,' she added over her shoulder as she led the way up the stairs.

Jon and I looked at each other and grinned. We didn't need asking twice.

DAY 7:
MABLETHORPE TO SOUTH FERRIBY
65 miles

The Lincolnshire plains stretched far into the distance as Jon and I rode north from Mablethorpe, with nothing to halt the wind as it hurtled across the fields towards the sea, bringing with it swarms of ladybirds which torpedoed our bodies and bounced off our helmets.

'Is it always going to be this windy?' Jon shouted, trying to keep his bike on course.

'We are on the coast I suppose!' I replied, gripping the handlebars to stop my front wheel from being repeatedly blown to the side. 'At least it's roughly the right direction.'

I tried not to think ahead to when I would reach the top of Britain and have to come back down the other side, into the prevailing wind.

For 30 miles or more we pedalled through farmland, passing fields upon fields of crops, the neat furrowed rows extending for miles in a striped blanket of pale green leaves and sun-baked earth. But the country lanes wound far inland and I was beginning to become frustrated. All I wanted was to be able to look out to sea with each pedal as I had along that cycle path at Jaywick. We approached Saltfleet, the name suggestive of the ocean, and just as we'd hoped, a signpost appeared: 'To the sea'. But at the end we were met only with wide saltmarsh and mudflats, a distant line of blue painting its far edge, a barrier of warnings preventing us from going further: 'DO NOT TOUCH ANY MILITARY DEBRIS IT MAY EXPLODE AND KILL YOU' and 'REMEMBER THE SEA CAN KILL'. Pools of water dotted the grassland, the lagoons constantly shifting with the flooding and receding tides. This was the Donna Nook National Nature Reserve, also used as an RAF target range. I doubted the seals had much peace. We turned back, greeted by an RAF biplane rolling down the road towards us. I caught my breath, then saw that the pilot was holding a walking stick, and that the engine was his mobility scooter. He'd actually given his mobility scooter the wings of a biplane.

Through Grainthorpe and Theddlethorpe we rode, finally reaching the seaside at Cleethorpes, where children took donkey rides on the beach. The town bustled with fairgrounds, ice cream vendors and al fresco diners, and we settled on the sand, the wind quickly adding the grains to our lunch. The estuary stretched out before us, the massive spit of Spurn Head engulfed in heavy grey clouds that seemed to melt into the sea, cargo ships caught in the downpour as they waited to come in to the ports of New Holland and Hull. We willed the rain not to travel inland as we bared as much flesh as possible, determined to soak up the transient sunshine despite the goosebumps.

From there it was a short ride up the river bank to Grimsby, along a narrow concrete track with railings to our left and nothing but a steep slope leading down to the water to our right. We'd stumbled across it by mistake, and didn't know if it was going to lead anywhere other than straight into the river, let alone if we were allowed to be there. But now that we'd found our sea view we were reluctant to give it up, so we persevered, unsure which to be more worried about – slipping off the edge, or being chased off the land by an angry Grimbarian. We kept going until the track spat us out in the middle of the docks.

Everything was eerily quiet. The thriving industry that had made Grimsby the fishing capital of Europe in the 1960s was now gone, the docks that would once have been bustling with trawlers setting out to sea or unloading their catch now deserted. Buildings stood empty, part demolished, the derelict ice factory and smokehouse hinting at a trade that once employed 6,000 people. The fish market was still operational, but most of the fish came from the continent or overland from Scotland, the battle over fishing territory during the Cod Wars of the latter half of the twentieth century causing a sudden and rapid decline of the main source of prosperity for the town.

We rode towards Grimsby's centre, the hush of the docks extending down the deserted streets, quiet even for a Sunday. The town seemed to be on pause, waiting for its turn in the waterfront regeneration programme of so many other ex-fishing towns. The name of the town's Viking founder, the Dane Grim, seemed to encapsulate the atmosphere of the place that day.

'That is a very cool boat,' Jon said, as we passed an old trawler that was moored alongside the Fishing Heritage Centre. He stood there, hands on hips, looking as if he'd just built it.

'Would you like a tour?' a man asked us, walking across the dockside. 'This is the Ross Tiger, one of the Grimsby fishing fleet. It's part of the museum.' The man introduced himself as Geoff, a fisherman who had worked on it for 18 years. We stepped on board.

He showed us the winches on the cluttered deck that would let the nets down, and the otter boards that held the net open underwater.

'We'd sort the fish into baskets and gut it out here on the deck, completely exposed to the elements. That was tough work. You'd have to throw back anything that you didn't want, probably dead; even though fish can survive out of water for a while it was unlikely to survive the lift up from deep water. There's always by-catch; it's unavoidable with trawling. Then we'd shoot the nets again, and send the baskets of fish down below through the hatch to be put on ice so it would be fresh when we came into port.'

We followed Geoff down the narrow steel staircase. It was hard enough walking on it when the vessel was stationary, let alone while the boat was pitching and rolling on the waves.

'These are the nets we used; the otter boards go here and here, either side, and these are the rollers along the bottom. The idea is that they bounce along the seabed rather than dredging it up, but it still causes some disturbance of course. That's how we catch the fish, actually – by churning up sediment so the fish come and feed on it. Then they get scooped into the net. The trouble is, over-fishing causes lots of damage to the seabed, with some trawlers breaking up corals and disturbing the sediment so much that it can't recover properly.

'Another problem is the decline of the fish stocks. We need to let the stocks recover, or use more sustainable practices like line-fishing. We've fished nearly all the species out of the water. Soon there won't be plenty more fish in the sea. It's really noticeable that fish is of a lesser quality than it used to be, especially cod. You should have seen the size of the cod we used to catch! The cod that ends up on your plate these days is tiny by comparison.

I don't eat cod anymore – haddock is my preference, not only because of the fish stocks, but us Grimsby lot are haddock men.'

He led us along a steel walkway above the roaring engines ('Think of the noise when that's going full pelt!'), through the galley and mess room, to the cramped quarters where narrow bunks were stacked on top of one another.

'This is where we slept. We went out in all weathers and sea conditions, so you'd have to strap yourself in otherwise you'd end up on the floor. We took it in turns on the beds – there's not space to have one each. It's a tough old life, working on these boats. Well-paid, though.'

We emerged back on deck, blinking in the sunlight.

'Any questions?' he asked.

'What happened to your finger?' I asked, indicating the stump on his left hand.

He told us how, as an 18-year-old just starting out on the trawler, he had been resting his hand on the railing when the otter board had swung back and crushed it. 'I learnt very early on not to put my hand there,' he said. 'It's a scary moment when you take your glove off and your finger's still inside!'

We left Grimsby, once more heading away from the coast; this time it was the great snaking Humber that forced us inland, deeper into the Lincolnshire Wolds as we traced the banks to the quiet Tudor village of South Ferriby. Earlier I'd phoned my host, Jan, a fellow Green Party member, to see if there was a campsite nearby for Jon to stay in.

'Oh, well he can stay here,' she'd said. 'There's a caravan in the garden that he's welcome to sleep in. Unless… How good a friend is he?'

I chuckled; almost everyone assumed we were an item.

'Not that good – separate beds will be fine!'

We arrived at the house and Jan welcomed us warmly inside. 'Dinner's nearly ready,' she said. 'But please, take your time to freshen up.' There followed the usual evening routine: a shower, a change of clothes, double portions of dinner and the expected conversation about my bike ride.

'We were really pleased to hear from you,' Jan said, once we'd settled round the table to eat. 'We're a family of cyclists, too. Ian did a tour with the boys many years ago, from the westernmost point of Europe to the easternmost point – Cape St Vincent in Portugal to Istanbul in Turkey. Alex was nine at the time. Will was only eight!'

'Gosh, that sounds incredible!' I said. 'How far was that?'

'It was about three thousand miles. It took us four months,' replied Ian.

'How did the boys cope?' Jon asked.

'They loved it,' replied Ian. 'Honestly, I found it more tiring than they did! We'd ride about thirty miles a day, then I'd put the tents up and find that the boys were haring around on their bikes. They just had so much energy.'

'Ian's just being modest about the mileage,' Jan said. 'I think their longest day was something like eighty-five miles.'

'Well, that's far, even for me!' I said. 'And you must have been carrying a lot of kit as well.'

'Yes, we had a huge amount of luggage: tents, sleeping bags, clothes, food and cooking equipment. I even took some Lego and a guitar! We put it all in a trailer which I pulled; maybe that was why the boys had more energy than I did at the end of the day.'

I found it hard to imagine what it would be like to do such a trip, so laden with luggage and spending so long on the road. And it must have been hard for Jan, waiting at home, constantly wondering and worrying where her family was. My journey seemed like a race in comparison, almost too easy, with a common language, one currency and no need for a passport. I'd found these things so comforting at first; now it seemed as if I were cheating. I said as much to Jan.

'Nonsense!' she said in response. 'You're going much further, and there are some very remote parts of the UK that you'll be visiting – it's not all going to be as easy as Lincolnshire you know! Many people would love to do what you're doing. Foreign travel is all very well, but there are so many gems right here on our doorstep, just waiting to be discovered.'

I smiled gratefully at her: that was why I was doing it, because I hadn't wanted to travel halfway round the world to have my adventure. This was about finding the unusual hidden within the usual, about seeking adventure from the things that we take for granted. The islands and creeks of Essex, the pretty Suffolk villages, the Norfolk Broads, the wide open skies of Lincolnshire – these were the things I had already treasured, and there would be so many more.

DAY 8:
SOUTH FERRIBY TO BRIDLINGTON
61 miles

The magnificent Humber Bridge dominated the skyline as we cycled along the Viking Way, a long-distance footpath that follows the banks of the river before heading south towards Rutland. We rumbled along the rough gravel track, the water that lapped at its edge brown and murky, the flooding tide swirling over the mudflats. The perfect curve of the suspension cables hung low in the distance and I paused to take photograph after photograph, utterly enraptured by its size, its symmetry, its strength.

'I thought you didn't like taking photos,' Jon said.

'But this is amazing,' I replied, pausing to take yet another. It seemed every pedal stroke brought with it a better view. But later, when I looked over them, I was disappointed: none of the pictures captured the true scale of the bridge, none of them could represent the real-life perspective, the ever-nearing views that had so captivated me appearing exactly the same in each.

Soon we reached the bridge and joined the track that would lead us across it; all at once the solid concrete deck and steel cables seemed vulnerable to the strong wind. I tried not to think about its apparent fragility as we rode out above the water, the heavy traffic rumbling past, spitting fumes on to our cycle path. The suspension cables seemed monstrous from up close:

thick as tree trunks, secured to the bridge with bolts as large as bicycle wheels, yet the tips of the towers looked worryingly wobbly as I craned my neck upwards, the clouds racing across the sky above them. I gripped the handlebars tightly, gritting my teeth as I followed Jon, who was already halfway across.

The Humber stretched towards the sea, and the wind that barrelled along the river pushed us towards the low railings with each gust, threatening to whisk us into the swirling water far below. The crossing seemed endless, this bridge the longest cycleable suspension bridge in the world, and my nerves were frayed by the time I joined Jon on the opposite side. After planting both feet firmly on the ground I took a deep breath and turned to look back, laughing out loud. It had been an exhilarating and terrifying crossing – and I had loved it.

We ducked off the bridge on the cycle route, twisting downhill back to river level, from where it looked harmless once more. It wasn't the last we'd see of it, glimpses of the distinctive towers still visible from miles away across the Yorkshire fields later that day.

The traffic became heavier as we drew closer to Hull, the roads growing busy as we rode through the village of Hessle and towards the centre of the city on the NCN. This was the first city I'd been in since London, its crowded streets a stark contrast to where we'd been cycling over the past few days. We'd swapped country lanes for dual carriageways, trees for office blocks, hedgerows for concrete pavements and metal barriers, and footpaths that wound across fields for neat lines of identical brick houses marching off from the main road at precise angles. Our wheels stuttered over the cobbles as we made our way towards the marina, seeking out the comforting familiarity of the waterfront, the gale that had almost swept us into the river now attempting to do the same with the row of national flags that lined the basin. The docked boats were alive with the wind that screamed through the rigging, halyards knocking, forestays clinking, weather vanes rattling. After nearly losing my map to the gusts I tucked it away, hoping that simply following the water would lead us where we wanted. But we soon became trapped among the docks, so retreated to the dual carriageway, thankful for the segregated cycle path that carried us eastwards, the strong wind an asset as we made our way back out to the coast.

Towns and villages became smaller and further spread out, steadily returning us to the unhurried pace of cycling to which we had grown accustomed. At last we reached the half-forgotten resort of Withernsea, perched on stumpy cliffs halfway between Spurn Head and Bridlington; it had an air of somewhere that had once been admired, but had slowly been abandoned, too far off the beaten track to have retained its popularity. The clouds had closed in, our sea view half-hidden in the gloom, the vast expanse of water murky and brown.

'I told you Jan would have been into yoga,' Jon said as we settled down on a clifftop bench to eat our lunch. She had mentioned her yoga class over dinner the previous night.

'I've never done yoga. I probably should, if only to help stretch my legs out.'

'Come on then, I'll show you some moves,' Jon said.

'*You* do yoga?'

'Yes, what about it?' he replied. 'The girls in my class are pretty hot,' he added with a sly grin.

So after we finished our sandwiches we each chose a paving slab and began. Upwards stretch – forward bend – left lunge and upwards stretch – right lunge and upwards stretch – cow pose – downward dog – right bend – left bend. The sea provided our calming soundtrack, the passers-by a surprise audience. We persevered despite my giggles.

The clouds eventually grew tired of holding their load and dumped it on us unceremoniously, the torrent sudden and heavy. We hurried to secure our bags against the rain, Jon picking out a large plastic bin bag and draping it over his head, me struggling to find my waterproof backpack cover, grabbing it and spreading it over the pannier rack. Water soaked my hat and ran down my neck, the rain bouncing from the pavement. A couple of minutes later it stopped and the sun came out, the footpath now blinding and the two of us looking as if we'd showered fully clothed. For the rest of the day the weather would play the same game with us; no sooner had we dried off from the last, another squall would come through and soak us thoroughly, the rain too sudden and powerful for us to bother with waterproofs in the end.

Up along the Yorkshire coast we rode, from Withernsea towards Hornsea and Skipsea, the roads deteriorating in quality the further north we travelled, victims of coastal erosion. We stubbornly followed roads that were marked as closed, hugging the edge, picking our way along tarmac that half crumbled down the cliff, leading through towns that had long since been claimed by the sea. This was perhaps where the sand spit at Spurn Head had been conceived, the clay and chalk gradually shifting southwards, the coastline constantly changing at the whim of tide and weather.

It was hard to imagine that these had once been normal main roads, and that to our right, where the dull water now surged and frothed, people had lived. Were the towns gradually abandoned, like some of the settlements we now saw teetering on the cliff edge, with nothing but a few empty barns and a couple of caravans remaining? Or was it more dramatic, the land collapsing without warning, tipping homes into the water? Perhaps that was why this stretch had lost its popularity, the unpredictable cliffs slumping and sliding on to the beaches below.

Eventually the tarmac disappeared straight off the edge, bringing our adventure to an abrupt end, forcing us to travel inland back towards the safety of the main road. The tiny villages that peppered the countryside almost seemed nervous that they might be next to fall prey to the hungry sea.

My nearly dry shorts were soaked again by the time we arrived in Bridlington and I quickly hurried to my guest house, desperate for a change of clothes. Jon had once more booked into a campsite, and I admired him without a hint of envy. Wandering down to the water's edge to meet him, warm and refreshed, having draped my sodden belongings around my room, I knew that even if it rained tomorrow at least I'd start off dry.

Down on the harbour, the tiny fishing fleet had finished bringing in its catch, the walkways strewn with lobster pots, ropes and nets, all watched over by perching cormorants hoping for an evening snack. The harbour walls stood tall at the low tide, deep green tidemarks long etched into the bricks. Lights from the few waterfront restaurants began to flicker on the shallow water as the day faded, and we stepped into one, desperate for dinner. I ordered the North Sea haddock. Geoff would have been pleased.

DAY 9:
BRIDLINGTON TO WHITBY

55 miles

The North Sea sat coolly under the crisp blue sky that morning, the only other creatures awake at that hour a large group of seagulls contemplating the water. We dumped our towels and quickly stripped down to our swimming gear. 'Race you in!' Jon said as he dashed across the dewy sand; I hesitated and then followed him towards the waves, bracing myself for what would certainly be a bitingly cold dip, shrieking loudly as I reached the water and splashed in up to my neck.

I lasted just 60 seconds before gasping my way back to the shore, struggling to breathe in the icy water. Shivering and smarting, I pulled on my clothes. This was only my third swim in nine days – the low tide in Southend, the rain in Wells and the river at South Ferriby had all conspired to make daily dips difficult. *Every day from now*, I promised myself.

'Amazing!' Jon said, joining me a few minutes later, salt water dripping from goose-pimpled arms. 'After you've got used to it.'

'I don't think I could handle that every morning!' I replied. 'Shall we grab a coffee and warm up? We have a bit of time before I have to meet my friend in Scarborough.'

Warm and full of hot drinks, we ambled up the coast, the cliffs giving the landscape a new dimension, a feast for our eyes after the sweeping flatlands of the past few days. Jon had been especially looking forward to this, wanting to test his legs on the inclines, disappointed that the four counties we'd ridden through had been so lacking in contours. He sprinted ahead, smiling and breathless. We climbed steadily to Flamborough Head, collapsing on to a bench high up on the cliff near the lighthouse, mesmerised by the waves that crashed repeatedly against the rocks. Then down again to Filey, through the crowded streets, dropping sharply to the beach where children played and surfers rode the breakers.

'This path goes all the way to Scarborough. Do you think we can ride on it?' Jon said, looking up the coast path that traced the cliff edge.

'I suppose so,' I replied. 'It's probably not meant for bikes but the surface looks OK.'

'This is brilliant!' Jon shouted over his shoulder once we'd squeezed through the gate and joined the path, the strong wind carrying us over the tops of sheer rocks, the cliff face rugged and wild. A few walkers were making their way along the precipice and gulls hung in the sky next to us, their wide-spread wings effortlessly riding the wind. But soon our path disappeared and we were left bumping across a dirt track, my poor bike rattling as we flew along the exposed clifftop, the thin tyres picking out each stone, the heavy luggage thudding with each bump. There was no shelter from the gusts and for the second time in two days I prayed that I wouldn't be sent tumbling into the water below.

Jon was in his element, pelting along the clifftop, while I followed more cautiously behind, envious of his recklessness but always mindful that my bike and I needed to stay in top condition – for us, there were still 3,500 miles remaining. I hoped to glimpse Scarborough, certain we must be nearly there, starting to worry that it was nearing the time I'd said I would meet Libby, a friend from university. The town appeared as we rounded a headland, still a long way off, minuscule white buildings sprawled out around the bay, the huge castle on the cliff just about visible. I decided to leave the coastal path and retreat inland to the safety of tarmac.

'You carry on, Jon,' I called. 'I'll meet you in Scarborough.'

Back on the smooth surface I frantically tried to make up the time, cursing myself for not accounting for wind and terrain when working out how long it would take us to get there. Sitting in that Bridlington cafe warming up after our morning swim, it had felt as if we had all the time in the world. But I was no longer in London, riding familiar streets on smooth surfaces. Here, the wind would blow, the hills would rise and fall, the road would meander. I hammered the pedals, my progress slow, my anxiety that Libby would be there already, wondering where I was, increasing the speed with which the minutes ticked by and decreasing the rate at which the miles passed. 'Sorry! Nearly there!' I texted at least twice, the final hill to the town steeper and longer than seemed possible. At last I reached the crest, the Victorian seaside resort spread out below, the Grand Hotel with its four towers built into the cliff and the long sandy beach curving round at its feet, with the endless wall of the castle perched on the headland like a crown. I descended through South Cliff Gardens, the path a zigzag of gravel through luscious and leafy flower beds, the delight that the Victorians took in holidaying by the sea evident in the careful landscaping of the town.

Down on the seafront I hurried to find somewhere to secure my bike, finding the cafe where Libby was waiting. It was over an hour past the time we'd arranged.

'I'm so sorry to have kept you waiting!' I said as I gave her a hug.

'That's OK,' she replied. 'I don't mind. I've been reading my book.'

We found a table, the summer holiday crowds causing the waitress to wear a strained look. I ordered fish and chips again, hoping that they would serve it to me in a giant Yorkshire pudding. The waitress didn't look too impressed by my request.

'Aren't you vegan?' Libby asked.

'Oh, er, yes. Well, about that…' I laughed nervously. 'I thought restricting my diet would make it difficult for my hosts. And I'm by the sea, so I can eat fish, can't I? It's more about cutting down on meat and dairy anyway…'

Libby laughed as I trailed off.

'Is this all of your luggage? It's hardly any!' My three bags were tucked neatly beneath the table.

'Most people say the opposite!' I replied.

'Well, I could never travel that light. Not for ten weeks anyway.'

'It's one of the things I like the most about being on the road. You quickly realise what you really need. If I haven't used it yet, it's just taking up space. I've sent a few things home already.'

'What about clothing? How do you keep things clean?'

'I do my laundry on my rest days. I have enough underwear to last me between those, and everything else I wear pretty much constantly – I've got two cycling tops which I alternate between, one pair of shorts and some trousers for colder days, and a cosy jumper and some leggings for the evening. It's quite liberating not having to choose what to wear each day. It's like a detox of possessions.'

We finished our lunch and Libby gave me a hug, wishing me luck for the coming weeks. I headed off to find Jon, who'd been snoozing on the beach in the quieter North Bay.

A disused railway line would take us all the way from Scarborough to Whitby: the Cinder Track, its name invoking the smutty trains that used to run along the route, with scattered remnants of the old railway in evidence – a station platform here, a signal box there. Part of the NCN, it was a classic example of a Sustrans route; the charity's first project was converting the Bath–Bristol railway line into a trail for walkers and cyclists, and with its success came many more, making use of the branch lines that ceased operation with the motor-car boom in the 1960s and Dr Beeching's cuts. We climbed steeply from the seafront to find the gravel track that stretched quietly northwards, hidden from the surrounding clutter of streets in a tree-lined gully. The path was rough, the gentle uphill tiring, but the solitude was delightful, our journey accompanied by a chorus of birds in full voice. I stopped to regain my breath after the exertion of bumping along the rough surface, nodding to a couple of cyclists as they passed. To the left extended the rich green vista of the Yorkshire hills, the trees to the right allowing snatched glimpses of the sea between their trunks. I squinted through them, trying to see the water which was by now far below.

Onwards we climbed, emerging high on the hillside to see the wide arc of Robin Hood's Bay, the scene hazy with the spray kicked up by white horses dancing over the water's surface. From our vantage point the track then descended, following the contours around the bay, and we zoomed downhill, freewheeling for 15 minutes or more as the gradient delivered us gradually to sea level. It was then a long climb back up the other side, and we huffed and puffed like the old steam trains to reach the top.

We followed the ridge of the hill, the river valley falling away beneath us as the path crossed a fabulous viaduct just inland from Whitby. The river sidled towards the ocean between huge cliffs, and from the vantage point of the viaduct we could just make out the town, the whalebone arch and the statue of Captain James Cook standing on a pinnacle on one side, and the high gothic arches of the ruined Abbey on the other.

I paused for a minute as Jon began the descent into the town. This would be the last evening when I'd have his company: tomorrow he would head home and I would continue my journey alone. Even though this was how I'd imagined I would travel, I'd be desperately sad to say goodbye to him. We'd set out on our journey together knowing just a fraction of each other, and we would part as firm friends.

With almost every pedal I'd spun since London I had been accompanied by someone else: Jon, Graham, Sarah. Perhaps it was a subconscious desire never to be alone. Alone, I would have nowhere to hide; I'd have to face up to what I was doing, dissect my motivations, think about the boyfriend I'd left behind. Jon must have been bored silly by all my talk of him. 'Nick did this, Nick said that, that reminds me of Nick...'

The day before I'd left Nick and I had sat cross-legged on his living room carpet and there he'd given me my parting gift: a small tube of lip salve. 'I love kissing you,' he'd said; it was the kind he used daily, his lips always tasting vaguely of the menthol contained in it. So each time I used it, it would be as if I were being kissed.

We'd spoken once since: the night of the London riots. He worked as a fireman and I was instantly terrified for him, but he'd been off duty that weekend, thankfully immune to the madness that was gripping the capital. From the safety of my Bridlington guest house it was hard to imagine what was going on back home. 'Are you calling to dump me again?' he'd teased, only partly successfully hiding the hurt underneath.

I was still unsure of whether I'd made the right choice, but I couldn't worry about it now. To think only of the people I'd left behind was not the point. From here, I would be by myself; that's what I had wanted, so I had to make it work.

DAY 10:
WHITBY TO WHITLEY BAY

77 miles

'Cheers for the ride, Anna,' Jon said as he hugged me.

'Thanks for coming. It's been brilliant having you here with me.'

'I wish I could've gone further but real life doesn't wait for long. Maybe when you get to western Scotland I'll come back again; it would be great to have some proper hills.'

I cycled off into the rain, my send-off committee waving from under an umbrella, the small huddle soon obscured. I'd groaned inwardly as we'd sat in the kitchen eating breakfast, wishing I could stay there all day rather than face the wet. But once I'd kitted myself out and headed off, it wasn't so bad. My baseball cap had turned out to be my most valuable item of wet-weather gear, keeping the rain out of my eyes so I could keep my head up. It was the invisible kind of rain that doesn't look particularly wet, but completely soaks everything, giving the landscape a greyish hue, the vivid Yorkshire moorland appearing dull and drowned. Dry-stone walls lining the road were slick with rain, farmsteads half-hidden through the drizzle, sometimes a forgotten outbuilding at the edge of the track. I took shelter in one and as I gazed from the blank windows I remembered how I'd explored this landscape as a child on family holidays.

The terrain was baring its teeth; long gone were the fens of Lincolnshire, and I was instantly caught up in the hills, toiling upwards then receiving a battering from the wind and rain as I freewheeled down. I descended hunched over the bike, fingers clutching at the brakes, reluctant to fully release them for fear of anything happening on the slippery surface. Hills rose ahead in the distance and I would see the narrow scar of a road rising up, hoping it wasn't mine. Then I'd get there and find that it was. I'd attack each one with determination, managing only a few pedal strokes at full power before the upward slope sapped my momentum and I'd have to click down the gears, cursing the road as my legs began to pull with the strain, muscles burning, lungs heaving, the slope never-ending. I'd grip the bottom of the dropped handlebars, pulling my weight forward to compensate for the rear-heavy bags. Even so, the front wheel would sometimes lift from the tarmac, only for a second, but long enough to cause me to wobble in the pedals. I reached the top of one and texted Jon: 'Those "hills" we climbed were nothing!' His reply beeped in: 'Ha ha! Good luck. Nice and dry having a pint in Whitby.'

From the wild abandon of the Yorkshire hills I approached Teesside, its industrial areas belching and dirty on the horizon. The dual carriageway from Redcar to Middlesbrough appeared almost from nowhere, bringing me sharply out of the reverie that the sleepy villages and meandering country lanes had created. I watched the trucks roaring past for a few moments, reluctant to join them, wondering why the map showed a cycle path. Then I saw it – a narrow strip of tarmac set back from the road, bumped with potholes and strewn with broken glass, the tendrils of bramble bushes creeping across trying to reclaim their land. This was one section of the NCN in dire need of upkeep. But it was preferable to being flattened by a truck. After six miles the track spat me on to a housing estate and I circled around for a while, trying to find my way out, wondering if any of the residents had seen me. *'Look, Mavis, there's a cyclist.'* *'Ooh yes, she's got a lot of stuff. Wonder where she's going?'* *'On holiday looks like. Or maybe she's just been shopping.'* What would they have said if they'd known I was part way through cycling round the coast of the entire country? Probably ask me what on earth I was doing on their estate.

Soon I spied a flash of blue girders in the distance. This must be the Tees Transporter Bridge. I headed off in its direction, the structure emerging gradually, the triangles of two cantilever arms seeming to float in mid-air, high above the water. I tried to see what they were connected to, but it didn't appear to be anything; how on earth would I cross? As I rounded the Riverside football stadium, four pylon-esque legs appeared, the bridge balanced on top. From the span dangled a carriage that was being shuttled back and forth across the water.

I stopped on the riverside to watch. It was as terrifying as it was fascinating, the gondola flying precariously above the water, suspended on colossal steel ropes. It looked like a giant Transformer robot. I joined the queue of cars waiting to load, entering the cage when it was my turn, cautiously squeezing myself to the front, paying my 70p for the privilege. I didn't dare look up, keeping my eyes fixed firmly on the approaching bank, the thin metal gates and water-splashed tarmac doing nothing to assuage my distress. 'DANGER, deep water,' read the sign. It was similar to that feeling you get on a fairground ride, not quite believing that it is entirely safe. I'm bad enough on solid suspension bridges, so this was almost too much. The two-minute crossing seemed endless, and once the gates had swung open to release me on the opposite side I pedalled away as quickly as I could.

The industry lining the north side of the river was a far cry from the rolling hills of the North York Moors where I'd been riding a mere two hours before. The coastline was obscured by a forest of oil refinery chimneys and an army of pylons that marched across the dull landscape. Dead trees protruded like broken bones from unkempt grassland, with the pipelines of a water-treatment works coiled high like mechanical snakes. Closer to Hartlepool I passed a landfill site, the stench of rotting waste making my stomach turn. It felt like another world, the scene from a science-fiction movie, desolate in the steadily trickling rain.

Soon I was back among houses but I had lost the trail. 'Excuse me, do you know where the NCN is?' I asked a passing man.

I grinned as he replied in a broad Teesside accent.

'You mean the cycle path, pet? Yes, it goes across that bridge there, and you can get on to it along this street here. Where are you aiming for?'

'I'm heading for Whitley Bay.'

'Aye, you'll get to Whitley Bay no problem, pet. Good luck!'

It was a nice change from the standard response that day, which had invariably been, 'Whitley Bay?! You're mad!' It was a common reaction that I eventually grew weary of, so instead I might say I was aiming for somewhere nearby, or if I was in a devilish mood I would say, 'London,' and wait for their eyes to boggle.

Five miles later I crossed the border into County Durham, once the heart of the coal industry, the old colliery towns that lay scattered along the coast exuding an almost audible air of abandon, rows of uniform grey workers' houses ingrained with the faint grime of coal dust. The very reason for their existence was now gone; the once peaceful rural villages that had exploded in size to accommodate the hundreds of thousands of workers who had descended into the mines each day were quiet once more. Through Blackhall, Easington and Ryhope I pedalled, feeling bleak.

From Sunderland, a traffic-free cycle path traced the wide sweep of the bay, following the path of the South Shields, Marsden and Whitburn Colliery Railway. It would once have carried the workers to the collieries and quarries and lime works, the area bustling and grimy. Now it was quiet, clean and spacious, with sweeping views of the huge harbour arms at both Wearmouth and Tynemouth. The cycle path led to the ferry terminal, where once the black gold would have been loaded on to ships for export. Now the river was quiet, the ferry to Amsterdam the only big ship departing the port.

On the north banks of the Tyne stood the ruins of Tynemouth Castle and Priory, beyond which lay the golden sands and lighthouse of Whitley Bay. I paused in front of a cluster of bright-blue marine buoys on the seafront; whereas once they had guided mariners to port, they now guided cyclists along the National Cycle Network, the numbers 72, 10 and 1 painted on their sides in 5 ft tall lettering. A signpost stood nearby and I leant my bicycle against it, looking up at the finger posts that pointed down each route: NCN 72, Hadrian's Cycleway, stretching the length of Hadrian's Wall to reach the coast in Cumbria; NCN 10, the famous C2C challenge, where cyclists dip their rear wheel in the Irish Sea and their front wheel in the North Sea 140 miles later; and NCN 1, its full length winding along the backbone of Britain from Dover to John o'Groats, this section named Coast and Castles. The names alone sounded salty, the fascination of cycling to the sea or riding alongside it clearly something that others shared. I looked at the sign: 'Irish Sea, 140 miles'. A mere two days' ride from here. It would take me at least another 1,500 miles to reach the same place; I had the whole of Scotland to make my way around first.

DAY 11:
WHITLEY BAY TO BERWICK-UPON-TWEED

84 miles

It was a miserable day. It rained all the way from Whitley Bay to Berwick.

Luckily I wasn't miserable, happy to trundle through the Northumbrian countryside, enjoying the spectacular bleakness of the coast. The sea was grey but the landscape vivid, grasses sprouting bright green from the dunes, and tiny crofting cottages that perched on the clifftops surrounded by fields that glowed in the rainfall.

I braved the conditions with a smile on my face, even though after a while I couldn't feel my hands and feet, and, when greeting a couple with, 'Lovely day for it!' found that the words stuck behind my numb lips. Still, I didn't envy the warm and dry folk in their cars, their primary view being that of the windscreen wipers. At least as a cyclist I was next to the coast, following the NCN through the National Trust park all the way up Druridge Bay – much better than being relegated to the road, a mile inland.

Castles loomed from the mist, the numerous fortresses that dominate this stretch evoking its bloodthirsty history. The ruins at Warkworth and Dunstanburgh rose starkly into the heavy sky, oppressive in the deluge. Then later came the nine acres of Bamburgh castle, its buttresses rising sheer from the hilltop, water beating against my face as I gazed upwards.

I pedalled through Seaton Sluice, whose name captured the weather perfectly, to Blyth, whose name didn't, then ambled towards Amble, 'the Friendliest Port,' and along to the colourful houses at Alnmouth that line the river mouth, full of character despite the sodden weather.

But once I'd reached Seahouses, I'd grown tired of the rain. I stood at the water's edge, unable to make out the Farne Islands even though they were less than two miles offshore. It was frustrating that I could not fully enjoy the Northumberland Coast Area of Outstanding Natural Beauty, shrouded as it was in clouds. I had become reduced to clock-watching, ticking off the miles, keeping my head down and my eyes glued to the road, trying to avoid the puddles that blocked my path and occasionally covered the entire carriageway so that I had to go through with my feet in the air.

I passed the end of the causeway that would take me to Lindisfarne, but with soaking wet feet and water running down my neck I was unwilling to make the journey, instead continuing northwards along the roads and bridleways that criss-crossed the East Coast railway line. A train clattered past, the long snake of carriages hurtling towards Scotland.

Finally, just south of Berwick-upon-Tweed, the rain stopped. The intense peace that descended at that moment made me stop, too; alone on the narrow cycle track among grasslands saturated with water, I began to pick out the sounds of the sea as they filled the space occupied moments before by wind and rain. The waves rolled somewhere in the distance, like the echo inside a conch shell, and a group of terns chattered in the sky. A pair of swallows flitted past, chasing each other in circles around my bike. I caught my breath, enchanted, and as I carefully resumed pedalling the birds kept pace with me; I hardly dared breathe for fear of scaring them away.

Soon I found myself leaving the low-lying bog and climbing up to the cliff edge, my bike struggling against the mud. The swallows abandoned their game as I approached my new companions: a group of cows, who didn't seem too happy about sharing their field with this unannounced visitor. I didn't know which to be more worried about – falling into the sea or being rammed by the herd, the headline Cycle Tourer Falls off Cliff after being Attacked by Bull suddenly stuck in my head. It didn't help that my panniers were red.

The town of Berwick emerged at last, tucked between a fold in the hills, the 28 arches of the viaduct carrying the railway importantly over the river. Huddled in its shadow sat the concrete road bridge and the tiny old stone bridge: an elegant trio of spans crossing the river Tweed to the last town in England.

I paused in a recess on the stone bridge, looking upstream to the viaduct. I'd been on that bridge before, travelling by train to Edinburgh. It would have taken a few hours from London and I had probably sat in the carriage drinking my tea, perhaps dozing as the detail of the coastline flashed by. By cycling, I had reached the same place, but this time I had worked for it, been actively engaged in the journey. I had gained an integral knowledge of my country with each pedal stroke, the path I'd taken from London filled with moments that would live with me for the rest of my life.

Eleven days seemed so little, 700 miles just a fraction of the total, but I had almost made it to that place that had once seemed so impossibly far off: Scotland.

PART 2:
EASTERN SCOTLAND

Days pedalled = 10
Days off = 1
Days to go = 61
Miles travelled = 726
Miles to go = 3,274
Punctures = 0
Ferries taken = 5
Days been rained on = 4
Sea swims = 3

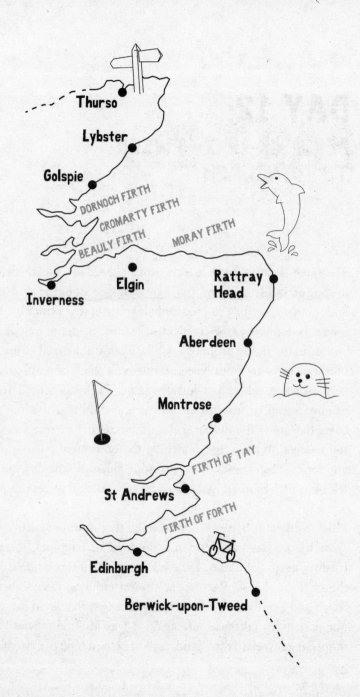

Thurso

Lybster

Golspie

DORNOCH FIRTH

CROMARTY FIRTH

BEAULY FIRTH

MORAY FIRTH

Elgin

Rattray
Head

Inverness

Aberdeen

Montrose

FIRTH OF TAY

St Andrews

FIRTH OF FORTH

Edinburgh

Berwick-upon-Tweed

DAY 12:
BERWICK-UPON-TWEED TO EDINBURGH

80 miles

The quiet country road stretched out ahead, patchwork fields leading off in all directions. Two hares lolloped along the roadside and, noticing my bicycle, suddenly leapt from the tarmac, their long ears flapping as they made their escape. 'Scotland welcomes you' read the sign. I propped my bike against the metal struts to take a picture, my front wheel resting on a patch of worn grass, perhaps where others had done the same. The hedge would need pruning soon; its leafy branches were already reaching out to cover the large capitals that spelt out the country's name. I stood for a while on the verge, watching the occasional passing car, and took a deep breath. I was just four miles into the day, but it felt like much more. It had been a bit of an ordeal to get this far.

I had awoken in Berwick-upon-Tweed that morning excited to cross the border into Scotland: the land of bagpipes, tartan, Irn-Bru, neeps 'n' tatties. I knew little of its culture aside from the obvious clichés. We'd spent several family holidays there, Sarah and I enjoying it so much after the first that we'd begged our parents to take us there again. I was looking forward to immersing myself in thwe landscape, it being a land of extremes:

the highest mountain in Britain; the highest road pass; the most
northerly and westerly points. I'd instantly be betrayed as a
foreigner as soon as I spoke. An immense sense of discovery
would surely accompany my journey.

From my hostel I had emerged into the town of Berwick, the
streets quiet as I explored the medieval fortifications, riding
around the town walls along the path that sat atop the giant
bricks, looking down on pink stone rooftops. Eventually I
arrived back almost to where I'd started, the looping ramparts
having led me in a large circle. While I enjoyed looking around,
I was really just trying to find my way out. Berwick was
amazingly well walled.

It wouldn't be the only time I would get lost that day.

Leaving Berwick on the NCN, I had become hopelessly
disoriented within a couple of miles. If I'd only known that the
cycle route initially goes west and south, I would simply have
followed the signs; I wouldn't have worried that I was heading
away from the coast, towards the centre of Scotland. I should
have enjoyed the scenery, the mountains that I'd been travelling
towards for the past ten days suddenly in front of me, but alarm
bells were going off: I hadn't seen a cycle route sign for a while,
and every turn of the pedals only increased my anxiety that
I was on the wrong track. Had I held my course for just one
more junction, I would have seen the red-on-blue route number
that pointed towards Eyemouth, but I lost my nerve and started
up a track across a field in what I assumed was the correct
direction. The rain of the past few days had left its mark: my
bike floundered in the mud, the wheels slipping and sliding until
I could ride no further. I dismounted and pushed, struggling
against the waterlogged ruts, finally emerging at the rear of a
group of farm buildings and realising that I must have come

along a private track. I smiled apologetically at a girl tending her horse in the neighbouring field, before wrenching open the farm gate and manoeuvring my muddy bike on to the road.

Relieved to be back on tarmac, but having absolutely no idea where I was, I approached the nearest house and knocked on the door for help. A few seconds later the door opened and a heavily pregnant lady stood there, looking at me enquiringly. 'Sorry to bother you,' I ventured, 'but I'm a little lost...' She welcomed me into her immaculate house; in the pristine living room I was only too aware of my appearance, sweaty and with shoes caked in mud. Perching on the arm of the spotless sofa I tried to orientate myself using a road atlas. Memorising as much of the map as possible, I thanked her and crept back to the road, soon reaching the sign welcoming me to Scotland. I'd left my hostel almost two hours earlier – it really shouldn't have taken this long to get this far. I tried to relax as I paused by the roadside, my much-anticipated arrival tainted by frustration.

Route-planning a circumnavigation of an island should be easy. I'd been tempted to do the entire trip just by following my nose and keeping the sea on my right, but was keen to avoid a similar situation to the man who ended up circling the Isle of Sheppey for 36 hours in a boat, believing that he could sail from the Medway round to Southampton just by keeping the land on his starboard side.

Maps would help me navigate cities, avoiding the docks and industrial areas that often line the coast, and prevent me from riding for miles along a road only to discover a dead end. So far I'd been making do with my route planner of Great Britain and the odd cycle map, together with the local knowledge of my hosts. But on that particular day, all I had was a set of instructions that I'd written down after looking on Google Maps: 'Follow NCN route through Eyemouth, Cockspurnbath and Dunbar, coastal road to North Berwick, NCN route to Edinburgh. Hospital, Colinston Road, Craiglockhart Terrace.'

Needless to say, it wasn't going well.

Thanks to the memorised road atlas I was back on track and I arrived at last at Eyemouth harbour, where a fleet of fishing boats clung to the harbour wall. I stopped to watch the Scottish flags fluttering at their mastheads, flags that would flutter whether or not I was lost. I tried to let the worry of the morning fade away. Now that I was on the NCN, all I needed to do was continue to follow it to the turning for North Berwick. But on leaving Eyemouth, the NCN dipped inland once more, prompting a return of those alarm bells. I followed it for a couple of minutes before losing all patience and returning to the coastal road. I was better off just following my nose.

I don't know what had possessed me to attempt an 80-mile ride based on five lines of written instructions, but they had made perfect sense when I wrote them down. It had looked so simple online. Three straight routes: all you need do is follow the signs. But I had quickly found out that on the road, everything looks different. It helps to know what's around the corner. The miles go so slowly when you're actually riding them that I quickly lost all sense of scale and distance compared with the map I had in my head.

And while I love the National Cycle Network, it helps to know whether it goes where you want to go. Sometimes it takes a detour around the houses only to put you back on the same road a little further on, or it signposts you left or right when you're flying downhill so sparks come off the brakes. Or you end up on the edge of Dunbar Quarry, no signs in sight, leaving you to carry your bike across a pile of rubble and over a couple of brick walls, drag it through a field and lift it over a barbed-wire fence until you reach the end of what was definitely not a cycle route.

Finding myself beside that quarry really was annoying. It had taken five hours to travel just 35 miles; I'd even resorted to cycling along a stretch of the busy A1 out of sheer impatience. I was hungry and frustrated, and ate my sandwich while riding, not wanting to waste any more time stopping for lunch. I just wanted to get there. Instead, I was getting lost.

Then, rounding a corner at the top of a rise, my frustration began to evaporate. It had been a tough climb and I'd spent most of it staring at the tarmac just ahead of my front wheel, lost in the steady rhythm of the pedals, but on reaching the peak I sat back in the saddle, straightening my shoulders and shaking out the tension in my limbs. As the road flattened out the seascape suddenly opened up: the headland curved away, revealing the silver channel of the Firth of Forth, beyond which lay mountains as far as the eye could see. I paused to take in the view. I was on the shoulder of Great Britain and there before me lay Scotland, its head. Across the water I tried to spot where I'd be cycling over the next couple of weeks, imagining myself crawling along that coastline like an ant on a map. If only I had actually had a map! The descent then began, my speedometer creeping to 40 mph, the rush of wind in my ears deafening. The thrill and fear focused me completely; I had taken flight.

At last I reached the turning for North Berwick, thankful that there was only one road and therefore no scope to get lost. The farmland stretched out on all sides, a ruined castle perching on the cliff, beyond it the chunk of Bass Rock rising from the sea as if a giant boulder had been accidentally dropped there. And mirroring it on land was the equally striking North Berwick Law, a 600 ft conical bump of a volcanic core sticking out at odds with its flat surroundings. At the end of the peninsula I rejoined the main road, this time persevering along the NCN when it signposted me on to the cycle track. But rainwater had flooded the bridleway, caking my wheels in the bog and I laughed wryly to myself: whichever choice I made today seemed to be the wrong one. The track hugged the shore, looping round old concrete piers towards Musselburgh and Prestonpans, from where I could just about make out the Forth Bridge in the distance, far beyond Edinburgh. Swans floated on the surface of the Forth, on whose far side sprawled the capital city, Arthur's Seat rising starkly from its centre.

Once I'd entered the city it would be a short journey to my home for the night, with my friend Eve and her mum. According to my instructions, I just needed to find a sign for the hospital, which I was certain would be obvious. I cycled around for a while, surrounded by 'Proud to serve Scotland' signs, but not the sign I was looking for. I sighed and guessed at a direction, my earlier frustration returning as I realised that, just because I'd visited the city in the past, it didn't mean I knew where I was going. Arriving in the centre by train was one thing. Trying to find a house I'd never been to in an area I wasn't familiar with was another. I pressed on in what I assumed was the correct direction. Two hours later I was grumpy, tired, ravenous and still nowhere nearer where I was aiming.

It took several phone calls to get me back on the right track, Eve having managed to pinpoint my position and talk me through how to get to her. As I turned into her road I had a word with myself. I should have made that phone call hours ago – there was no point in being so bloody minded that I got lost, exhausting myself mentally from the effort and physically from the extra miles.

'Silly Anna!' Eve laughed as I pulled up, amused that I'd spent so long rambling around such unsavoury parts of the city. She welcomed me with a hug and a much-needed dinner.

The day's ride had been unnecessarily stressful. I had most certainly learnt a valuable lesson in navigation and I vowed never to rely on such basic directions again. If I didn't have a map, I'd make sure to write down instructions that were actually useful!

DAY 15:
EDINBURGH TO ST ANDREWS
79 miles

I spent two blissful days in the Scottish capital, acting the tourist, visiting the castle and wandering the steep lanes with Eve. The city was buzzing with the Edinburgh Festival, the streets crowded with stalls taking advantage of the seasonal crowds, every available wall and postbox hidden by posters, unapologetically plastered on top of each other, vying for attention. Impromptu performances took place on street corners, drama troupes and comedy hopefuls handing out flyers, all competing for the favour of the fickle crowds. I'd planned to have one rest day there but after I'd spent one not-very-restful day doing chores, I needed another just to recover.

Was it really only a week since I'd been doing all this in Mablethorpe? Only two weeks since I had started the ride in the first place? So much had happened since then. But I had cycled only 800 miles. I still had so far to go.

My bike, which I had christened Randy (Sir Randy Mare Ridgeback Esq. to give him his full title), had been a wonderful packhorse so far, but there was no guarantee I would get to Thurso, the next rest point with a bike shop, before his rear wheel gave up supporting my heavy luggage. I'd serviced it before setting out, but the bearings were now grinding, the hub rumbling. The chain was also beginning to wear out and would grind the cogs down as I rode. My standard attitude would be to ride it into the ground, but it was not something I wanted to fix by the side of the road and, thinking of what Uncle Graham would say, I decided to replace the whole lot. The cost made me wince: new chain, chain rings, cassette and rear wheel for almost £200, a massive overspend on my £10 daily budget. But the alternative, of finding myself in the middle of nowhere with a collapsed wheel or a snapped chain, would be more costly. I handed over my credit card and tried not to think about it.

I had been contacted via Twitter by a fellow cyclist from Edinburgh, who'd offered to ride with me around the Firth of Forth. Thank goodness I wouldn't get lost leaving the city! Matthew and I met the next morning and weaved our way through the traffic towards Leith docks, soon zooming through woodland. Matthew led the way and quickly became swallowed up in the twists and turns of the path; with the benefit of familiarity aiding his speed he was soon hidden by the trees growing thickly on all sides. I plodded along behind, surrounded by piles of felled logs that lay half-hidden in the thick undergrowth, dappled light streaming through the canopy on to the twig-strewn ground. The path emerged at Dalmeny Park, the NCN allowing us what felt like exclusive access to the four-mile shoreline track through the estate, the Tudor Gothic house watching over us from its nest in the woodland. The trail took us along the sandy banks of the Forth, closer and closer towards the famous rail bridge.

A short while later we spied it through a gap in the trees and I stopped still, awed by the view, three gigantic rust-red diamonds poised above the water like a row of flatfish tied mouth to tail.

The bridge was huge beyond comprehension, defying gravity, so big that once the programme of touching up the paintwork has been completed, it's time to start again.

Each gap in the woods granted us a closer view, until eventually we passed underneath its railway tracks. The road bridge now dominated the skyline ahead, a fabulous suspension structure, yet easily overshadowed by its more iconic sister. We rode between the two, one stretching out behind carrying the rumbling trains, one ahead transporting the rushing motor traffic, a spectacular panorama. Through the quaint cobbled streets of Queensferry we rode, past the pier that had once served the ferry across the Forth, then we struggled up the short but steep cycle path on to the road bridge and bounced high above the water in the wind.

The Fife coastal path wound along the northern banks of the firth – the word used for the bays, straits or estuaries around the coast of Scotland. We picked our way round Inverkeithing and Dalgety Bay towards Burntisland (I said 'Burnt-is-land' and Matthew chuckled as he said, 'I think it's Burnt-island'), alternately through housing estates and off-road woodland trails, along secluded tracks and through tiny tunnels under the railway line. Back across the water lay the city of Edinburgh and the coastline I had ridden along a few days ago, with Bass Rock still just about visible several miles away at the mouth of the firth.

It was a pleasant ride with Matthew, but I was happy to be by myself once more after he departed at Leven. Matthew had been my first cycling companion since Yorkshire, and I had grown accustomed to being alone, with only myself to blame if I took the wrong route, only myself to consult over where to stop for lunch, only myself to determine the pace. I was utterly free to do what I wanted, when I wanted, to follow every whim, to suddenly stop without explanation and look at something, or take a picture, or simply enjoy being under the wide open sky. Now I had tasted all of those things, I was reluctant to have them taken away.

So I meandered around Leven just because I could, then carried onwards to the East Neuk of Fife, neuk the Gaelic word for corner, the promontory home to a cluster of fishing villages. The harbour at Elie was crowded with windsurfers, their multicoloured sails dancing across the water. From high on the clifftop near Pittenweem I watched seagulls mob the fishing boats that were bringing in their catch. I stopped on the Anstruther harbour front to gaze through the windows of the fish bar; friends and family had recommended it, but I had already had lunch and my dinner would be waiting for me in St Andrews. For the first time I felt resentful of my timetable and budget. I wondered if this fish bar had been on the sightseeing list that those ladies on the Harwich ferry had reeled off. It seemed a shame that I was missing it; I must already have missed so much. Why must I rush? The rows of filleted fish sat plumply on the other side of the glass, the sign 'Best fish and chips in Fife!' placed there as if to mock me. I shook my head to clear it. This was ridiculous. I could spend two years doing this journey and still not see everything that was on offer. This was how I had chosen to do it and that was that. I could always come back.

The coastal road north of Anstruther wove between fields and farms, the east coast maintaining its gentle undulation, the mountains that I had been fretting about since crossing the border far inland. I chose a comedy show to listen to on my iPod, laughing aloud as I made my way to St Andrews. Suddenly, the road ended. *That's not right*, I thought. Getting my bearings, I realised I had missed the turn-off and continued all the way to Fife Ness, a dead end on the peninsula. All I could see was the North Sea stretching into the distance. I turned to look back along the road down which I'd just ridden. I didn't recognise it at all; I'd been completely unaware of where I had been going, utterly distracted by what I'd been listening to. I stuffed the iPod back into my bag. Through the silence emerged the sounds that had become such an integral part of my journey. A bird called from the hedgerow, the breeze lifted the leaves, and somewhere just out of sight the waves continued their endless sigh. How could I have wanted to block this out?

I had thought that my iPod would be essential, that I'd get bored cycling all day. But this was no commute, no functional ride to be tolerated. 'It would be a bit of a waste to make it all the way round Britain without really seeing anything,' Graham had said. Perhaps this was part of what he'd meant. Listening to music is an escape; it puts you in a bubble, dulling your senses, taking you out of the here and now. Being able to hear was just as important as being able to see. And it wasn't as if I needed the distraction. There was always something to think about: where I had been; where I was going; when I should stop for lunch; the end of the day; the end of the trip; the beginning of the next. I was riding with subtitles, accompanied by a constant commentary that might later be written in my blog. Inevitably I started commentating out loud; it had taken only two weeks for me to start unabashedly having conversations with myself. I was doing fine.

Back on the correct road I made my way up the coast, soon reaching St Andrews. I was charmed by the small city, tucked away in a corner of Fife with no train station, its steep streets lined with a wealth of impressive architecture from the ruined cathedral and the tall church tower of St Regulus, to the castle and the ivy-clad walls of the university. I sidestepped the legendary 'PH' in the cobblestones, the site where a Protestant martyr had been burnt at the stake: it was said that any student who trod there was cursed to fail their degree unless they jumped into the sea at dawn on May Day. Though I'd already received my degree, I succumbed to superstition.

I walked down to the beach, passing designer shops, expensive fish restaurants and golf stores, this part of the city catering for the wealthy visitors who fly in from all over the world to play golf. I paddled in the sea, my first dunk in Scottish waters, but it was far too cold to go swimming. For the first time, I admitted that I wouldn't be sea swimming every day; I just didn't have the guts. All those excuses had simply been hiding my lack of resolve. Gazing out to the horizon with the cold water lapping at my ankles I decided that it didn't matter, as one day I would return to this corner of Britain and experience it again, in a different way: visit the Anstruther Fish Bar, swim in the sea, play golf, dine at expensive restaurants. Because all that could wait. I had a bike to ride.

DAY 16:
ST ANDREWS TO MONTROSE

57 miles

Over the following days I crept up the side of Scotland, the landscape becoming steadily hillier as I made my way towards the Highlands. From Angus to Aberdeenshire the inclines tested my legs – long upward drags where I could feel every ounce of luggage, thankful for my cleats, followed by wonderful freewheeling downs. The scale of everything took my breath away, each day bringing scenery even grander than the last. Just being outside under the wide open sky brought the ultimate feeling of freedom. There were no buildings to block the view, no boundaries to my panorama other than the mountains on one side and the wide open sea on the other.

The journey from St Andrews had taken me northwards through the famous West Sands links and towards yet another MOD firing range; passing signs warning of flying golf balls and flying bullets, I'd been glad to be wearing my helmet. Soon I had reached the sanctuary of Tentsmuir Forest, the trunks of the pine trees enclosing me like a protective wall, the dense canopy overhead creating a quiet in the air that was verging on spooky. Trails led away from the main path and I followed a sandy track, weaving among gnarled tree roots that tugged at my wheels, to the water's edge. I'd reached the mouth of the

Firth of Tay, the wide stretch looking so shallow at the low tide that I almost thought I could ride straight across it. As I headed back towards the main track I nearly collided with another cyclist emerging from the trees, tent in hand.

'Sorry!' we both exclaimed.

He laughed nervously. 'My fault. I'm not sure I was allowed to camp here.'

'I'm sure no one will mind. It's a lovely spot.'

'Aye, that it is,' he replied. 'Where are you heading with all that stuff?'

'I'm riding round the coast.'

'Oh aye. It's a bonny coastline down this way. I set off from Edinburgh a few days ago and have been pootling around, enjoying the sea view. I'm off to Arbroath today then I might head inland for some mountains tomorrow. Have you been on the road long?'

'Two weeks. I started in London.'

'Oh, my! The *whole* coast. Good on you. How have you found time to do something like that?'

I explained that I'd be looking for a new job after I returned home, so this was the perfect opportunity to have my adventure. 'It's only a ten-week trip after all.'

'Ten weeks! You must be shifting the miles.'

'I suppose so. I'm averaging about seventy per day.'

'Gosh, that's impressive. I'm happy if I hit forty!'

'Would you like to ride together for a little while? Although I am hoping to reach Arbroath by lunchtime…'

He looked at me for a moment, as if considering whether or not he could be bothered to keep up the pace, and then declined with a yawn. 'I'm going to go and find some coffee!'

I laughed and wished him well as I pedalled away.

The Tay Bridge crosses the firth, an unusual bridge for its sharp downwards slope from the towering cliffs of Newport-on-Tay to the city of Dundee on the low shores of the opposite bank. Between the two lanes of traffic runs a cycle path, raised above the road, its elevation allowing me uninterrupted views in both directions, and I freewheeled the whole way, being steadily drawn towards Dundee until I was deposited at a lift that returned me to ground level with a gentle Scottish accent.

The NCN winds through the docks and the Port of Dundee's strict controls demand photo ID of those who wish to pass through. I had been warned of this in advance, so was prepared to show my driving licence, but no one was on duty and the gates opened automatically as I approached. The docks were quiet, concrete paths leading me alongside once busy but now deserted railway sidings, passing a derelict and overgrown Tay Cafe, which I doubted still served meals all day, despite its declarations. The gate at the other end of the path once more opened without question, and I completed my uneventful passage through the docks wondering what all the secrecy was about. Signs hanging next to the CCTV cameras on the security fences warned 'ID needed' and 'No photography', so naturally I couldn't resist taking a photograph before pedalling off as quickly as I could.

Dundee is reportedly the sunniest city in Scotland, so perhaps it stood to reason that the rain began as soon as I left. I pulled on my waterproofs in the shadow of Broughty Castle, trying to dodge the droplets that hammered on the jetty. The days of rain had taken their toll; my waterproofs had lost their efficacy, the water seeping through instantly to the clothes underneath. I'd tried to scrimp on costs, but I should have invested in a better waterproof jacket. By the time I reached Arbroath I was utterly cold and wet.

The town sat huddled around its harbour, the yachts bobbing glumly on the marina with their hatches firmly closed. All along the waterfront fish and chip shops jostled shoulder to shoulder, 'Smokies sold here!' signs vying for my attention. I'd heard of the Arbroath Smokie, and was determined not to miss out this time. I pulled up at the Bellrock restaurant and hurried inside.

Arbroath is one of the few towns with a foodstuff named for it – similar to Champagne and Eccles, a Smokie is only a Smokie if it's from Arbroath. It's a whole salted haddock hot-smoked over a half-whisky barrel and served on the bone. According to local legend the dish was discovered by accident, when a fish store housing barrels of salted haddock caught fire one night and, upon tasting it, the townspeople found that the 'ruined' fish was delicious. I heartily agreed as I tucked into my hot meal, which tasted all the better since I was warm and dry, while steam clouded the windows.

Across the road from my snug spot sat the Signal Tower Museum, which had once housed the shore station for the Bell Rock Lighthouse after which the restaurant was named. There were pictures of the lighthouse on the walls and I imagined it now, 12 miles offshore, the rain pelting against its white stone tower, its light repeatedly sweeping across a grey sea, the rock on which it stood covered by the high tide and water surging around its base. What a feat of engineering that was, to construct something so far from the shore, on a piece of land that was only exposed for 12 hours each day. But it had been so vital a construction, warning mariners away from the hazards at the entrance to the Tay, rocks that had claimed six ships each winter. I shuddered as I looked out at the weather-beaten shoreline, sincerely grateful that I was captain of a bike and not a boat.

Two hours later I had dried off sufficiently to brave the elements again and as I pedalled past the last of the 'Smokies sold here!' signs, the rain stopped. I stopped, too, my face upturned towards the sky. I looked around for a minute, the landscape blanketed in droplets, noticing how utterly still and calm everything was. All I could hear was the sound of my own breathing. I watched a buzzard for a while, silently circling the hills. Leaves drooped heavy from the trees, bulging from their drink. The clouds hung low like a ceiling. Then a car came along and ruined it, so off I went.

It was raining again by the time I arrived in Montrose and my non-waterproofs were thoroughly soaked. I couldn't wait to have a shower at my hosts' house, aptly found through Warmshowers.org, a website for touring cyclists. The hot water seared my skin, the powerful jets massaging my aching body, thawing my numb fingers and toes and washing away the chill of the ride. I stood there for as long as I dared, hoping that the torrent I'd endured that day wasn't a sign of things to come. It was so easy to expect Scotland to be wet.

My host, Ian, had been out when I'd arrived, so it was his girlfriend who had let me in and made me feel at home.

'He's just gone for a ride. He thought he might see you on the way.'

'But it's raining!'

'He loves that bike – never misses an evening's ride,' she replied. 'In any case, you've been out in it all day.'

'Yes, but I have to. Otherwise I'd never have arrived!'

It was easy to have this conversation as we sat on the sofa with our mugs of tea. But even though I wouldn't choose to go out in the rain, once you're in it, it's not so bad. As Ian pushed his wet bike through the garden gate an hour later and struggled across the waterlogged lawn, rain dripping from his drenched Lycra, he was grinning from ear to ear.

DAY 17:
MONTROSE TO ABERDEEN

54 miles

The coastline stretched north, simple and beautiful; the sun had re-emerged, painting the day with its glorious tonic, splashing colour in every direction. I was no longer hiding my neck inside my collar, instead soaring along wide roads while across the fields the sea sparkled a rich blue. A tough climb took me from Crawton to Dunnottar, and as I rounded the ridge, I found myself looking down on Stonehaven and the prettiest harbour of any I'd seen. The perfect circle of the inner basin was framed by tiny pleasure craft that lay hauled halfway up the exposed sand on their warps, and an outer basin curved around it, the harbour arms flanked by the swaying masts of visiting yachts.

A sharp descent took me to the waterfront, the sun's reflection on the water blinding, the harbour surrounded by buildings of large grey stone, the churches adorned with spires that resembled the turrets of castles. Beside the harbour stretched the long curve of Stonehaven Bay, and I descended to the beach where myriad hues of shingle glowed in the sun, the pebbles becoming smaller and turning to sand as they reached the water's edge. Behind, the ruins of Dunnottar Castle stood on the cliff edge in silhouette.

I wandered along the shingle for a while, my steps uneven on the shifting ground, noticing just how much litter there was. Almost every step had something hidden beneath it – a fragment of a broken bottle, the corner of some long-discarded packaging, the disintegrating remains of a sun-bleached drinks carton. Where had all this junk come from? Perhaps from careless picnickers discarding trays of Dairylea Dunkers once the last had been gobbled up, or perhaps it had been washed up by the sea, originating from who knew where, travelling on the tides until it found its final resting place here on this beach. I collected the rubbish into a pile. Almost all of it was plastic. How ironic, I thought, that these single-use items are made from a material that lasts forever. I deposited it in the nearest bin. But even though that stretch of beach was slightly cleaner, the rubbish would only end up in landfill – a tidier version of this, but still, there it would sit, steadily becoming weather beaten, long past the duration of my life. We live in such a throwaway society, not truly conscious of the environmental impact of the products of our lives. 'Recycle' was such a buzzword these days; whatever happened to 'reuse' or 'reduce'? I returned to my bicycle with a heavy heart.

Shortly after leaving Stonehaven I caught up with another cyclist, his rear rack completely swamped by bags and bungees, the front wheel flanked by low-risers and a pack strapped to his handlebars.

'Hello!' I said as I cycled up alongside, the sedate pace necessitated by his heavy gear making my own load seem weightless by comparison. He smiled sideways at me, his eyes partly hidden by the short black hair that poked from beneath his cycle helmet, his face set in concentration. It was a friendly face, so instead of riding on as I often did, I slowed to match his speed. 'I'm Anna.'

'Patrick,' he replied.

'Where are you riding to?'

'To Aberdeen – I have a hotel booked for tonight.'

'I'm on my way to Aberdeen too. Do you mind if I ride with you?'

'Not at all.'

'Where are you going after Aberdeen?' His kit spoke of something more than the few miles remaining to the city.

'I'm riding the North Sea Cycle Route.'

I had seen signs for it as I'd travelled northwards, the route encircling the North Sea along the coastlines of England, Scotland, Norway, Sweden, Denmark, Germany and the Netherlands. The British stretch doubled as NCN 1 so I'd been following it on and off since Harwich. I wondered if completing that circle might be my next adventure.

'How far is that?' I asked.

'It's about six thousand kilometres – roughly four thousand miles. I'm cutting off the rest of the Scottish leg, though. The logistics didn't work on this occasion. It's a shame that I'll miss out on visiting Orkney and Shetland, but I can always go there on another trip.'

From quiet villages the view became more industrial as we approached Aberdeen, the NCN leading us past out-of-town warehouses and storage facilities. On the horizon sat dozens of tankers, waiting in the deep-water anchorage until they could collect their next cargo, and as we rounded the corner by the lighthouse the docks opened up, ships and cranes and huge drums crowding the dockside, the 'energy capital of Europe' absolutely dominated by the oil industry. Behind it rose the spires of Old Aberdeen and we made our way towards them, along wide streets lined with the silvery sparkle of granite.

Patrick's flight to Bergen would leave in the morning, several months of open road lying ahead of him as he slowly made his way along the coastlines of the five remaining countries that circle the North Sea. His bicycle would be dismantled and packed into a flight bag then loaded into the luggage hold of the aeroplane to be reassembled in Norway. Patrick was anxious that all the parts would arrive, having heard stories of cyclists whose wheels had been squashed or whose saddles had been lost. I thought about Randy, ready to ride in the morning without need for transits. How wonderfully simple it was to cycle! Randy and I had only to rely on each other, and together we could go as far as we dared.

DAY 18:
ABERDEEN TO RATTRAY HEAD

58 miles

The streets of the Silver City glowed under the morning sun as I made my way up past the Marischal College and towards the sprawling university. I was running late to meet today's riding companion, tutting at myself as I took several wrong turnings in my haste. I'd made friends with Bryan completely by accident; he'd been staying in the same guest house as Sarah and me in Lowestoft, and we'd struck up a conversation over breakfast, after the proprietress had handed him his plate saying, 'Here you are, Bryan,' and I'd followed it with a cheeky, 'Hello, Bryan!' Full of the initial excitement of my journey I had been more forthcoming than usual, wanting to talk to anyone who would listen, and Bryan had seemed a good candidate; similar in age to us, he looked like the kind of person I might get on with.

'Hello,' he'd replied with an amused smile.

'What are you doing here in Lowestoft?' I'd asked, ignoring Sarah's attempts to shush me and let him eat his breakfast in peace.

'I work on the oil rigs,' he'd replied, the gentle rolling of his 'r's giving him away as a Scotsman. 'But we've a day off because the weather is too bad today.'

'Do you live around here?'

'No no, I live in Aberdeen. But I'm here for a couple of weeks on a project. We haven't managed to do much work yet though and I think I've seen just about all there is to see in Lowestoft. Are you two just visiting the area?'

'Well…' I'd taken great pleasure in telling him about my bike ride, handing him my card with my web address on it.

'Oh aye, this sounds interesting. I'm into cycling too. I'll be sure to keep an eye on your progress.'

And he had, following my online updates as I'd steadily made my way northwards. I'd received a message a couple of days ago: 'It looks like you'll be in Aberdeen soon. My project has just finished in Lowestoft, so I'm heading back home – would you like some company?' What a coincidence! We'd met 800 miles ago and we would both arrive in Aberdeen on the same day.

As I approached our rendezvous point I couldn't help grinning. He was waiting by the side of the road, smiling widely in return. He was a lot taller than I'd realised.

'Hi!' I said. 'I should probably apologise for interrupting your breakfast that morning.'

'I was a bit taken aback, yes! It was quite early in the morning. And I didn't have my contact lenses in so for a second I was confused by there being two of you!'

Bryan's bike was lightweight and streamlined, unburdened by a rack or mudguards. I looked at it enviously. In contrast to my ride yesterday with Patrick, it looked as if I'd be the one working hard to keep up. We saddled up and headed off, Bryan leading the way through the north of the city, soon reaching the Bridge of Don.

'There's a colony of seals that nests here. Look,' he said, pulling over towards the railings and peering down to the river bank below. I stared for a while, unable to see anything, then noticed the movement of a flipper and the slow turn of a speckled grey head. There lay dozens of seals, camouflaged among the rocks that sat just above the waterline, their smooth long bodies blending effortlessly into the background.

'Wow,' I breathed, this encounter with wildlife long awaited. It had taken almost three full weeks of pedalling to see any creature in this number. I had imagined I would be surrounded by animals at every turn, that the countryside would be overflowing with deer, puffins, the odd eagle, maybe a few dolphins. So far there'd not been much beyond seagulls, buzzards and that one lone seal back in Essex. But here was a colony of them, in the last place I'd expect, peacefully oblivious to the stream of city traffic just metres away.

'How fast do you usually cycle?' Bryan asked as we rode away from Aberdeen.

'Faster than this,' I boasted, sprinting ahead. He easily caught up and soon I was panting along behind him, trying to hide my struggling. I shouldn't have boasted; I was no match for Bryan.

We passed through the town of Newburgh at the mouth of a large river. 'Let's go and see the Sahara,' he said, leading the way across the bridge and into a car park, past a signpost reading 'Welcome to the Forvie National Nature Reserve'. The car park edges were brushed with sand, a gravel track leading away from the tarmac. We rode along it until the track disappeared, the softly shifting sand beyond giving nothing for our tyres to grip, so we leant our bikes against a tussock and continued on foot. Thick and bristling grasses carpeted the ground and flowers sprouted against the odds from the dunes, until eventually the vegetation petered out and we were left facing a great mound of desert, the bald surface rippled by currents of wind. Beyond it lay another mound, and another topped with reeds, and somewhere beyond that the sea. I had never before seen so much sand in one place: peak upon golden peak stretching into the distance.

'It's incredible!' I said.

'Isn't it?'

We walked slowly back to our bikes and returned to the road, our shoes caked in tiny grains that ground into our cleats and stuck to our chains.

'This can't be good for the bikes!' Bryan said as sand cascaded in every direction.

'No. It's worth it, though.'

Further north, the dunes disappeared and cliffs took their place, wild and rugged, the same sea that had caressed the sand now surging against the rocks. We abandoned our bikes once more and walked out to the ruins of Slains Castle, its precarious position on the edge of the precipice reputedly an inspiration for Bram Stoker's Dracula. We snuck up one of the old towers, ignoring the 'No access' signs, and listened to the waves far below, hoping that the staircase wouldn't collapse while we were hidden in our perch.

Further still was the Bullers of Buchan, the remnants of a collapsed sea cave known as 'the Pot', the cliffs curving round haphazardly to where the cave mouth had once been. The water seethed and bubbled at the bottom, and all along the cliff face nested dozens and dozens of seabirds. Each ledge, recess and handhold had been inhabited, kittiwakes and cormorants and terns crowding the vertical rock.

We sat on the edge, gazing out to sea. These were the gems that I had been looking for: acres of sand; dramatic cliffs; seabirds in their nests. From seeing no wildlife, I now had a glut of it. I had Bryan to thank for all of this. Had I been riding by myself I would have ridden straight up the road, happily oblivious to all I was zooming past.

'My parents stay not far from here,' he said as we came away from the cliffs towards the winding country lanes. 'You're welcome to join us for dinner if you like.'

We rose and fell with the hills, our meandering through the countryside frequently accompanied by helicopters that buzzed above our heads.

'Why are there so many?' I asked.

'They're taking the workers to the oil rigs. I travel in them daily; it takes about an hour to reach the platforms. It's a very noisy, uncomfortable journey. Mind you, it's not much better when you arrive. Those things are like ticking time bombs.'

'I bet you get paid a lot for that,' I said.

'Oh, aye! Danger money!'

'What drew you to oil in the first place?'

'If you live in Aberdeen, you go into the oil industry,' he replied. 'It's not my passion. But it's good for now. I work in rope access, so it's tricky but good fun. I used to be a rowing coach, working with the national team. My current workmates don't believe me!'

Bryan's parents welcomed me warmly into their home in Longside, unperturbed that a strange girl had arrived with their son, an indication either of their Scottish hospitality or that they expected this of Bryan. While dinner was in the oven Bryan helped me stretch out my legs, his previous life as a sports coach put to good use, scolding me for the lack of attention I had been paying to my muscles so far – these, the most important piece of equipment I owned.

The ten-mile ride back out to the coast was painful: I'd eaten too much fish pie yet needed to cycle quickly in order to reach the hostel before 8 p.m. when the reception would shut. Bryan and his parents waved me off, wishing me luck. The food sat heavy in my stomach as I sweated towards Rattray Head, far from the bustling roads of Aberdeen and Peterhead, the single-track road becoming rough and potholed for the final mile. The small village of Rattray had long since been abandoned and all that remained was the lighthouse keeper's accommodation: a small house converted to a B&B and a large granite block housing the hostel I'd be staying in. 'Made it!!' I texted Bryan, arriving just in time and collapsing into one of the comfy chairs in the lounge. Next on the list was to have a shower but I hadn't packed a towel: usually my host would provide one. I thought for a moment then snuck into the kitchen and grabbed a clean tea towel. I might only be able to dry one toe at a time but it would do.

Refreshed and rested, I walked to the beach in the fading light. A lighthouse stood a couple of hundred feet offshore, and I looked up and down the coastline, revelling in the solitude of this remote place. The dunes were smooth and unspoilt by footprints, the endless sand soft beneath my flip-flopped feet, and once more I felt dwarfed by the drifts. I dipped my feet in the sea and marvelled at the fact that I was in the UK – why would I need world travel when I could have this?

Earlier that day, while munching the fried egg sandwiches that Bryan had bought for us at Cruden Bay, I'd realised that I'd clocked my first 1,000 miles. I gazed out to the horizon, running through in my head all of the places I'd been, tracing each creek and outcrop of the coast, all the way back to London. I remembered doing this near the beginning of the trip, full of doubt, worried about the point of it all. All of those concerns had utterly vanished. My daily purpose of cycling was the ultimate freedom; I had no need to be concerned about work or appointments or the endless things that creep into daily life. I turned to look northwards, towards the next unknown stretch of my journey, the map in my head blurry and uncertain. And instead of being scared, I felt achingly happy. The things that had guided my life before the ride were no longer relevant – all I had now was my bike and the coastline. I had already seen so much. And, as I cycled, I would slowly discover the rest of it, knowing that each day would bring a different experience, a different challenge, a different view of the same sea.

DAY 19:
RATTRAY HEAD TO ELGIN

78 miles

Riding a bike is a solitary thing to do, but it can also be very sociable. I flitted in and out of people's lives – a greeting to someone out walking their dog, an exchange with another cyclist, a chat with a shop owner. Being on a loaded bike in the middle of nowhere is a conversation starter. You almost feel obliged to get to know everyone you pass.

Surprised I was riding alone, people asked if I was lonely. It had taken time, but I had come to love those hours of solitude, the autonomy of my solo journey something that suited me. Being alone isn't the same as being lonely. Those days of ten or more hours in the saddle were filled with an endlessly changing landscape and a constant stream of thoughts, the company of my hosts each evening and the simple companionship of the open road.

Solitude was what I longed for as I passed through Fraserburgh Docks, finding the bustle disconcerting. At the tip of the headland stood a lighthouse, and I made my way towards it, the noise receding as I reached the cliff edge. It was just one of the hundreds I had passed, a family of guardians protecting vessels from our shores, tall and steady and reliable. But this seemed especially familiar, the squat white and beige column topped with a black light cage, and a weathervane perched on top of the domed roof. It was strikingly similar to the one offshore at Rattray Head, and that which had stood just outside Aberdeen.

The seascape stretched almost 360 degrees; I'd rounded the eastern bulge of Scotland and would now head west, following the coast of the vast Moray Firth all the way to Inverness, 100 miles away. I stood for a moment, breathing the salty air as the waves rushed at the shore far below my vantage point. The power and beauty of the sea once again took my breath away and finally, reluctantly, I turned my bike westwards.

Everything was suddenly different. The wind that had been pushing me steadily north for the past two and a half weeks was now against me. I sighed and pedalled harder, feeling the resistance increase as I did so. I had to force myself to relax and accept that I would be going slowly for the next day or so.

It was a sedate pace of life in this part of the world, the locals that I passed enjoying late breakfasts in deck chairs on the harbour, or hanging out their washing on the communal lines strung between rods on the shore, very publicly drying in the salty air. The road unfolded gradually before me, descending to fishing villages nestled among cliffs and climbing again through towns seemingly carved out of the granite of the hills. Thick white clouds covered the sky like a duvet.

From Macduff and Banff to Portsoy I rode, the Moray Firth gradually narrowing as I traced its shores, soon far enough along that the final part of the northern Scottish coastline began to emerge across the water. The land rose grey-blue on the horizon, merging into the sky so that I almost doubted it was there, becoming more solid and tangible as I crept ever west. Through Cullen, Portknockie and Buckie I followed a disused railway line, the Moray Coast line, a ten-mile stretch from the tall brick arches of the viaduct at Cullen to the cast iron Garmouth Viaduct over the River Spey. At Spey Bay I stopped to look across the water, the land on the other side now clearly visible. It seemed impenetrable, the mountains too high, the forest too thick, the terrain too tough. How would I ever be able to ride through such a place?

On the river bank stood the Scottish Dolphin Centre; this section of coast was notable as a habitat for dolphins, and I sat on a mound overlooking the estuary, hoping to catch a glimpse of the elusive creatures. The late afternoon sun illuminated the dunes that crowded the river mouth, the water dappled in the soft light, but there were no dolphins to be seen. I suddenly felt exhausted. Now that I'd stopped moving, I realised how hungry I was. I searched my pack. Two flapjacks and a few energy sweets were all that I could find. I scoffed them, but knew I was in trouble – my legs felt like jelly and my arms had started shaking. So this was what bonking was – the complete fatigue that hits an endurance athlete when they run out of energy. It wasn't nearly as fun as it sounded. 'Eat before you get hungry and drink before you get thirsty,' Graham had advised, but I hadn't done that and now it was too late.

I struggled back to my bike, shortly afterwards passing a sign: 'Elgin, 5 miles'. Usually this would be the point where I'd begin to relax, cruising towards my destination, knowing I'd be there in 20 minutes or so. But now, I was running on empty, unable to go at more than half my usual speed, my fuel tank utterly drained. It was agony. Each minor incline felt like an Everest, the headwind sapping my strength at twice the usual rate. I became desperate for a downhill, however slight, utterly distracted from anything but my hunger, each pedal movement a monumental effort. I gritted my teeth, crawling along, forcing my legs to keep going.

Elgin! I almost fell from the bike as I reached the town, but I still had to find Alex's house. A colleague from Sustrans, he'd given me instructions, but I'd no chance now of remembering them. After pedalling almost the entire southern length of the Moray Firth into a headwind I was exhausted. I phoned him straight away, having learnt my lesson in Edinburgh, and he talked me through the last mile or so, coming out to the road to make sure I didn't cycle straight past his house.

'Well done!' he said as I pulled up, too tired to even dismount. 'Come in and sit down! Welcome to my sardine tin of a flat. I bet you're starving. I'll apologise in advance – I've never made this before, so I hope it turns out alright.'

A few minutes later I was tucking into the most fantastic jumble of potatoes and vegetables that I'd ever had, Alex's skill with a frying pan enhanced greatly by my desperate need for food.

Alex worked in street design, making communities safer for cyclists, walkers and residents. 'It's about rediscovering some of the traits that streets were traditionally known for in the past – having a chat with your neighbours, kids playing outside their houses, being able to walk to the local shops,' he explained. He had moved to Elgin from Bristol when a good job with Sustrans had come up, even though it was in a remote part of a country with which he had no ties. I realised that his was a real adventure. At least I could go home at the end of the ten weeks. For Alex, this was home, 550 miles away from family and friends – an eight-hour drive or an 11-hour train journey.

Our conversation soon turned to my adventure and Alex congratulated me, which as usual I brushed off. But after dinner we unfolded my GB route planner, the first time since leaving that I had looked at the route in its entirety, and it hit me just how long this ride was. Simply rounding the great slab of eastern Scotland, that 100-mile shelf of rock jutting into the North Sea, was taking two days. We sat there for a while, just staring. And for the first time, I too was speechless.

DAY 20:
ELGIN TO INVERNESS

67 miles

Keen to avoid another lapse of energy, I started the day with a huge Scottish breakfast: bacon, sausage, egg, black pudding, mushrooms, tomato, baked beans, toast, Scotch pancakes and maple syrup, with extra black pudding (Alex couldn't manage his). Then I stocked up on snacks in the local supermarket: apples, flapjacks, the famous 'tablet' that Bryan had recommended (a deliciously crumbly Scottish version of fudge), malt loaf – I was pleased with my haul until it came to be added to my already full panniers. Apples, I discovered, are heavy. The rack groaned under the weight, and I was starting to groan under the weight of all that breakfast. It was with difficulty that I hoisted myself on to the saddle when the time came to leave.

I headed to the mouth of the River Lossie where the dunes of the golf course soon gave way to the long sweeping sands of Burghead Bay, sand spits and bleached white beaches lining the pinched head of the Moray Firth. Farmland stretched out on either side, plantations of next year's Christmas trees alternating with pig farms and chicken farms where hundreds of golden birds pecked in the muck.

The reedy strain of bagpipes floated on the air as I reached the village of Findhorn; a Scottish wedding was taking place, a crowd of kilted men spilling out from a church, with the piper standing by the door, welcoming guests with the most quintessential of Scottish sounds. I stopped to listen, reluctant to move on. Nine days in the country and these were the first I'd heard. When might I next hear such piping?

A few miles down the road I thought I caught a snatch of them once more. Then quiet descended, but a short while later, there they were again – louder this time and far less tuneful. In fact, it sounded like several sets of bagpipes, in different pitches, at different tempos: a cacophony of piping. I rounded the corner to see the Nairn Highland Games in full swing. Pipers piping at the entrance gates, pipers piping for the traditional Scottish dancing, pipers piping as they wandered around the large field. There was even a piping contest taking place, participants taking to the stage as others stood in line waiting in their kilts and sporrans. I stopped, delighted, the odd one out in a sea of tartan.

From there it was a short ride to Inverness; this was the end of the westward journey and the headwinds for this stretch, where the waters of the River Ness flow into the sea, the landmass above it once more heading north. I entered the ancient Pictish stronghold, the northernmost city in the United Kingdom, the roads overflowing with vehicles. I was a city girl at heart, happy in my adopted home of London, accustomed to holding my own among city traffic, but three weeks on the open road had seen to that. A driver pulled out in front of me. 'Moron!' I screamed as his tail lights disappeared around the corner. I was breathing heavily, flustered and frustrated, and pushed on for the docks and the calm of the water. There before me stood the Kessock Bridge, huge, immense, a fan of cables crossing the Beauly Firth, the fourth firth of the journey. Funny, I'd crossed the Firth of Forth so long ago.

As I left the city behind the roads became more welcoming, the sky more spacious, each junction returning me to the rural solitude to which I'd grown accustomed. A single-track lane took me the final stretch to my host's house: Andy, another Warm Showers find. His family lived in an expansive farmhouse where each room seemed to lead to yet another; I almost had an entire wing to myself. From large windows I gazed out on uninterrupted views across the fields and forests, with a sliver of the Moray Firth just visible at the foot of the valley.

At dinner time, seven people squeezed round the table, Andy's already sizeable family made larger with the addition of an exchange student and me. We passed round baskets of garlic bread and salad, hungry forks diving repeatedly into the spaghetti bowl while Andy recounted stories of family cycling holidays, the two girls groaning with embarrassment as he told tales of snapped chains and punctures and the kids getting lost.

'I think the worst was when I was cycling in Exmoor with my nephew, the kind of terrain where you're either at a forty-five-degree angle pointing up or a forty-five-degree angle pointing down. It was raining quite hard so it was slippery, and I had reached the bottom of a hill and was waiting for him, but ended up waiting for ages. The longer I stood there the colder I was getting, but I couldn't face going back up the hill to see why he was taking so long. About twenty minutes later another cyclist came past and told me to go back because Jack had fallen off. Turns out flies had flown into both eyes and he had slipped off and broken his collarbone. He was almost hypothermic by the time I reached him!'

I listened in horror, aghast that he could talk about the incident so casually, and now even more nervous about reaching that part of the country, making a mental note to keep my sunglasses on to protect my eyes from injury-inducing flies. I hoped his nephew hadn't been scarred for life by that experience. But then I thought back to my own family cycling holidays as a child, as young as five, where my three sisters and I would ride in convoy between my parents, through the tulip-crowded gardens of Holland and along the turbine-strewn waterways of Denmark. There, a lorry had passed too close and I'd fallen – I have vague memories of gravel and broken glasses. But that didn't put me off. Perhaps it was those trips that had given me this insatiable appetite for cycling.

DAY 21:
INVERNESS TO GOLSPIE

64 miles

The Black Isle, jutting into the Moray Firth just north of Inverness, had been growing less and less black the closer I'd drawn; as the detail of the land had become clearer I'd seen forests and flower-filled fields, and now I stood on its southern shore, surrounded by luscious ferns and fallen pine needles. Across the water I could see the coastline along which I'd already ridden; somewhere along that shore lay Lossiemouth, Findhorn, Nairn. The land, grey-blue on the horizon, seemed impenetrable, the mountains too high, the forest too thick, the terrain too tough. But when I had been there, it hadn't been like that at all. Each hill had come and gone, each road passing as the last had done. Heading towards where I now was, looking at these shores that I now stood upon, it had seemed impossible. Now I was here, and it wasn't scary at all. Why had I worried?

Soon I reached the ferry that would carry me across the Cromarty Firth, the fifth firth, passing the now familiar lighthouse with its squat tower nestled among the houses on the peninsula. Water splashed over the ferry's loading platform as I wheeled my bike on board, joining the few cars that had already embarked and been spun around by the turntable on the tiny deck. With space for just four cars the queue of traffic on the shore would have quite a wait. But it would save them and me a 40-mile detour – crossing firths and sea lochs by ferry and bridge made the 6,000-odd miles of the Scottish coastline a little easier to cope with. The boat crept across the water, dwarfed by the cargo ships powering to their terminals.

After a short hop over the next peninsula I reached the Dornoch Firth, my gateway to the top of Scotland, where I'd join the A9 that would be my guide for the remainder of the journey north. The road sign read 'Golspie (13), Wick (68), Thurso (74), John o'Groats (85)' – all places I'd eventually be going to, some still a couple of days' ride away. A bubble of excitement caught in my throat: this was it, the final stretch north. These names on a road sign would soon become places, fed to me one by one as I devoured this single road. I set out on to the Dornoch Firth Bridge, seeing with fresh eyes the peaks stretching inland, the road ahead lined with gorse, the corrugated surface of the loch rippled by the wind.

The road crept steadily northwards through farmland and across trickling burns. I passed an old mill house where two chairs made from redundant mill wheels sat at the bottom of the garden. Highland cows lay in the fields, rusty brown and unmoving, contemplating me from under their great flops of hair. A road sign warned of deer, but no deer appeared. Maybe the sign would be the closest I came to seeing one.

My host lived in Golspie Mill, one of the few remaining traditional water-powered mills in Scotland. I turned off the main road on to a stony track through the woods, following the rushing water of the Big Burn that feeds the mill wheel on its way from Dunrobin Glen to the sea. I emerged from the trees to see the sturdy building, ivy covering its sandy bricks, the wooden wheel tucked in close to the south wall. Piles of firewood were stacked to the windows and old millstones rested against the bricks. Opposite sat the miller's house, a chimney stack perched at either end of its whitewashed walls, sash windows gazing from underneath the roof tiles like heavily lidded eyes.

Michael the miller strode round the corner, welcoming me to his home in a broad Antipodean accent.

'Which part of Australia are you from?' I asked.

He looked at me for a moment, then replied, 'The New Zealand part.'

'Oh, sorry.' I laughed in embarrassment.

'Would you like a tour of the mill?' Luckily he wasn't one to take offence. We stooped through the low door, the afternoon sunshine flooding the interior and bouncing from the walls and floor, the bricks and slate ingrained with decades of white dust. Flour-encrusted overalls hung by the door, bags of oats sat neatly under the hopper waiting to be milled and wooden staircases led upwards into the rafters where hoisting lines dangled, ready to lift the sacks of flour. The giant cogs and belts that were driven by the mill wheel were nestled high in the loft, their intricate mechanisms precisely balanced, turning as reliably as they ever had. Draped over every ceiling and every wall, at every level and in every corner, were hundreds upon hundreds of cobwebs, the fine coating from the floury clouds that filled the air preventing them from hiding in the shadows.

Michael lived with his Scottish wife and young child in the old mill house, where the floorboards creaked and the staircase was wonky, but the bath was huge, the water hot and, later, the wooden kitchen table laid out with as much food as I could eat.

'You'll be passing into Caithness tomorrow,' he said as we tucked in. 'Watch out for those Caithness clans. There've been a good few battles between them and our lot.' He winked. It seemed that the Scots had a deep loyalty to their home and a mistrust of everyone else – even Scots who weren't native. He assumed a Scottish accent. 'Oh aye, it's pretty barren. But nae you worry. Soon enough you'll be back to bonny Sutherland.'

DAY 22:
GOLSPIE TO LYBSTER

41 miles

Back on the A9 I continued to make my way northwards, cruising along wide roads carved into the mountainside with fields towering above me to the left and falling away sharply to the right where they met the sea. The road followed the contours rather than crossing them and the cycling was easy, apart from one descent so steep and quick that it made my ears pop.

A few miles north of Helmsdale I passed into Caithness. Almost instantly the landscape changed: the mountains disappeared, leaving in their place open rolling fields and windswept moorland, interrupted with ramshackle collections of buildings and scattered settlements. Rusting farm equipment lay abandoned in fields empty of crops, filled instead with tufts of grass waiting to be grazed. The absence of trees was noticeable. Across the bleak landscape the bracing wind roamed freely, wind turbines spinning furiously under the cathedral-like skies. Grey cairns, rugged coastline, exposed hills, the burnt red colour of sandstone seeping from the sparse landscape. Was it only because I had been told it was barren that I found it to be true?

The tarmac beneath my wheels stretched hypnotically ahead, becoming indistinguishable from the surrounding landscape. It was almost a surprise to arrive in Lybster, my final stopping point on the east coast, a small fishing village consisting of one straight street and a very steep descent to the harbour. It had once been the third busiest fishing port in Scotland but it was almost impossible to imagine the rush of boats coming in and out of its tiny harbour, where only a rusty lighthouse and a handful of fishing vessels moored alongside the harbour wall remained.

It had been a short day; relying on people's generosity meant that I took accommodation where I could find it. I settled in a cafe to wait for my hosts, Mano and Louise, to return home.

It was dark and raining by the time they pulled up outside in their car, their headlights piercing the intense blackness and illuminating lines of driving droplets as I followed them back down to the harbour. They had just returned from a week's camping in another part of Scotland and seemed completely nonplussed that I was there, though they must have been exhausted. Louise and I sat in the kitchen demolishing a large pile of Kit Kats until I too was desperate to turn in. She ushered me off to bed, waving away my offers to help clear up. They were accustomed to adventurers passing through, having hosted a large number of people through Warm Showers. I was just the latest in a long line. What an interesting lifestyle, I thought, meeting so many people from different walks of life. And out here, where there aren't many places to stay, they must get hundreds of LEJOGers and JOGLErs, and tourers and travellers. How exciting! As I went up to bed I handed her my card, saying 'This is the website address for my blog.' She took the card and looked at it for a moment, then replied, almost wearily, 'Another blog!'

DAY 23:
LYBSTER TO THURSO

56 miles

The bleakness of Caithness seemed to become more profound as I pedalled away from Lybster, acutely aware that I looked like a regular LEJOGer to passers-by. A couple of children playing in the street had wished me luck as I left that morning, assuming I'd be finishing my ride today, and I'd thanked them – it was easier than explaining what I was really doing. As I cycled through Wick, however, I felt embarrassed to be on my bike. I was just one more of the many riders who pour through the town, reaching their moment of glory 16 miles later. The locals must be sick of it. I kept pedalling and avoided catching anyone's eye.

About five miles shy of John o'Groats, I caught up with a man who was walking along the side of the road. It seemed unlikely that anyone would be in this remote corner unless they were on a journey from end to end, yet I approached him with incredulity – who would walk from Land's End to John o'Groats?! It must have taken such a long time. He must be mad!

'Have you walked here from Land's End?'

He smiled shyly at me. 'Yes!'

As I spoke to him, I regretted how quickly I had judged him. He was just like me, someone who wanted to do something challenging and original. He had been making his way steadily towards the far north-east of Britain, sketching and painting as he went, for two months – less than the total time I would be on my journey, yet I had been so quick to think his plan ridiculous. I could now appreciate why some people had such trouble understanding what I was doing, why my friends had been so worried.

His journey had been tough, much tougher than mine, the effort of carrying all his possessions on his back compounded by the constant blisters. I felt a renewed surge of affection for my bike, taking most of the strain for me – I could go far and fast with little effort with the help of this simple machine. I wondered why Frank hadn't done the same.

'Because I don't know how to ride a bike!'

I wished him luck and continued on my way, after reassuring him that he was nearly there. Later, I would hear a joyful yell echoing over the hills; I assumed it was him, celebrating the completion of his exceptional journey.

I reached the final turn-off with three miles remaining. There was just one road ahead and it would lead northwards until I could go no further. The fields around were empty, the windswept landscape appearing barren under the oppressive grey skies. I felt as if I were cycling off the edge of the world. All this time I'd had the sea on my right hand side and very soon it would also appear directly in front of me. Slowly, I inched my way over a rise and suddenly there it was, the very top of Britain. No more north.

'John o'Groats, a welcome at the end of the road,' read the sign. I wondered how many people had passed that sign and relished those words. For me, it was just one more day in my long bike ride. I rode through the sparse village, passing the few scattered hotels and guest houses and crofting cottages, then continued up to Duncansby Head, a few miles beyond John o'Groats and the true top right-hand corner of Britain. I ate my lunch in the shadow of the lighthouse, gazing out to Orkney, the wind blowing hard around me. For just over three weeks, I'd been slowly accruing the miles, 50, 60, 70 at a time. The landscape had shifted so gradually, from the concrete jungle of central London to this windswept pinnacle on the top of Scotland, that I had hardly noticed. Each day had simply been a small ride to the next stopping point. But, thinking about it as a whole, it was almost unbelievable that I'd actually cycled here from London.

Perhaps even more unbelievably, on the tip of Britain there was a mobile signal, so I called all three of my sisters, telling them where I was, sharing with them my first big milestone, my first turning point, my first significant moment.

Back down in John o'Groats I headed towards the tourist area, where a signpost indicates that it's 874 miles to Land's End. My Land's End was still 2,000 miles away so I declined to have my picture taken under it (for £12) but instead sat down outside one of the cafes, meeting a couple of students, Sam and Mike, who had just finished their end-to-end ride. They had been riding with Mike's uncle, who had only intended to accompany them for the first couple of days, but had ended up coming all the way. He didn't seem the least bit fazed at having ridden the length of Britain by accident. They had set off from the bottom left-hand corner of Cornwall a mere ten days ago, at around the time I had entered Scotland, and had been covering around 100 miles per day, aided by the tailwinds but struggling in the first few days with weather and the fearsome Cornish hills. Their final stage had been from Inverness, in less than half the time it had taken me to travel from that city; their bikes were set up perfectly for speed, the aluminium frames unburdened with pannier racks or mudguards, a small pack suspended over the rear wheel luggage enough. If you're only on the road for ten days, you don't need much more than a change of clothes and a toothbrush.

By coincidence the two boys were staying in the same hostel as me in Thurso, so after their break we rode to the town together, the undulating road weaving past clifftop fields packed with grazing sheep and leading round the wide curve of Dunnet Bay. The wind had swept away the gloom of the morning and the sun glowed on the water as we passed Dunnet Head, protruding like a giant thumb into the Pentland Firth. I had wanted to go to its tip, the most northerly point on mainland Britain, but settled for taking pictures of its giant sea cliffs as we passed by, knowing that my companions would not appreciate the extra miles.

We rode at a steady pace, Mike anxious not to do any further damage to his rear tyre, which had worn through in patches after 1,000 miles of riding. The tyre had held out just long enough, and the same was true of the boys; now having passed their point of completion, the adrenaline was fading and the final few miles dragging. I had already ridden further than them and was still less than halfway, but not remotely tired. It's not about the distance, it's about the expectation: you go as far as you've set yourself up to go. Had this been my final day, I'm sure I'd have felt as exhausted as they did.

In Thurso we raided the local Co-op for their celebratory feast, piling our basket high with pasta and garlic bread and plenty of beer; toasting the completion of Mike and Sam's journey with them seemed appropriate, especially as I'd be taking the next day off. After nine straight days of riding I needed a break. I had almost run out of clean underwear, and I was not yet one for turning my knickers inside out.

Full to the brim we walked down through the town, past the museum, the bike shop, the steak house, the castle, the fish sheds that lined the harbour – all places to explore the next day. As the evening drew to a close we paddled in the bay, the moon glowing in the lingering light of these northern skies. The wide beach was deserted, the waves gently lapping at my toes and it struck me how strange it was to be standing here, my feet in the same sea that I'd been dipping them in all this time, but now on the very top of Britain.

I gazed out to the horizon. No more going north. It was downhill all the way from here.

PART 3:
HIGHLANDS AND ISLANDS

Days pedalled = 20
Days spent resting = 3
Days to go = 49
Miles travelled = 1,360
Miles to go = 2,670
Counties pedalled through = 21
Punctures = 0
Ferries taken = 6
Days been rained on = 6
Sea swims = still only 3

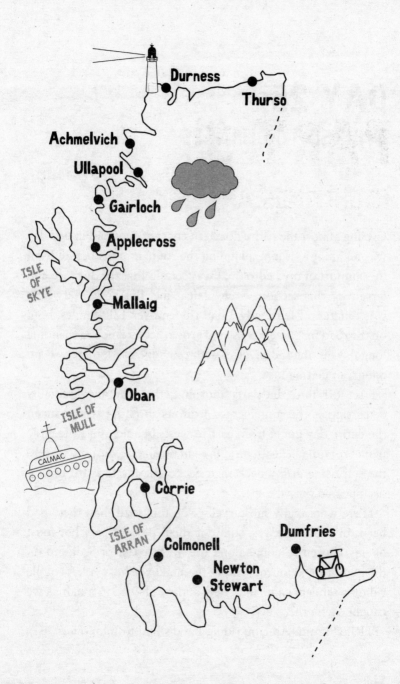

DAY 25:
THURSO TO DURNESS

78 miles

Cycling almost the entire northern coast of Scotland in one day was an ambitious aim; planning the route months before from the comfort of my bedroom, I was certain that the distance and terrain of this section would defeat me. But now, everything was different. I felt ready. I had ridden over 1,000 miles, been on the road for three weeks, and grown accustomed to spending long days in the saddle. And with only one road, there was no danger of getting lost.

I set off into the early morning, the sea mist gradually dispersing as the sun emerged from its shroud. I would spend the entire day going from east to west; I could almost feel the planet rotating beneath me, the road turning against my wheels, the sun rising at my back then beckoning me forward until it disappeared over the sea.

There were many more cyclists on this road than there had been on previous days, some of them day trippers but most having chosen to come along the north coast of Scotland on their end-to-end journey rather than take the busy A9. A couple riding a tandem came into view and we slowed to a halt as we caught each other's eye.

'Hello,' I said. 'Are you riding Land's End to John o'Groats?'

'Yes,' they replied, bursting with smiles. They looked happy and healthy, completely at ease with the road and with each other. For a moment I envied them their bicycle, for the companionship, absolute trust and synchronicity one must use on such a bike.

'How has it been riding the tandem?'

'Not nearly as difficult as we thought it might be. We've had a fantastic journey. Coming along the glens through the Highlands has been a wonderful way to end.'

'How are you going to get home?'

'That's one of the things we've been wondering about! It's unlikely our bike will be able to fit on the local trains, so we'll probably have to cycle down to Inverness. Not just yet, though! We'll stay in John o'Groats for a day or so to recover, and take a little holiday. Perhaps visit Orkney. What about you? Are you riding down to Land's End?'

'I'm actually riding the coast. So I will eventually get to Land's End, but probably not for another two thousand miles or so.'

'Looks like you have a few visitors,' said the man with a smile.

I glanced down at my arms. Midges! Every inch of bare skin was covered with black specks, and I hastily bid farewell to the couple as I pedalled away from the swarm, brushing them from my skin as I rode. I'd been warned of this: the midges of western Scotland are particularly vicious, and once they've caught wind of a stationary human being they show no mercy. I hoped that I would be able to out-fly them on my bike.

As I rode west, the undulating coast began to give way to mountainous terrain, the steady inclines and gentle slopes that typified the east coast now replaced by sharp descents and angular precipices. This was the moment I had been waiting for: it had finally become difficult. But the more the hills began to bite, the more the scenery compensated for it. I had left the moors of Caithness behind and was once more in the rich vista of bonny Sutherland. There was so much to admire, so much variety, from the gorse-covered cliffs and the jigsaw of mountaintops to the tumbling valleys that harboured beautiful bays, the bright-blue water accentuated by endless heaps of sand.

From Bettyhill to Tongue the road weaved away from the great sea cliffs whose faces were peppered with waterfalls and caves, nearby which eileans, the Gaelic for islands, floated. Sea lochs reached inland with long fingers, their shores overlooked by ancient crofting cottages and the bright-purple heads of thistles. This was the 'A' road, the main road through this part of the country, where sheep were more plentiful than cars. It rose and fell, twisted and turned, keeping the path ahead hidden until the last minute, the sense of remoteness increasing with every bend. This part of Scotland was deliciously wild. Meandering among the mountains that for days had been a distant view, I felt glad that, as a cyclist slowly creeping along, I had the time to fully drink in my surroundings, not needing to stop to appreciate it in the same way that a motorist would. And I could see so much from the vantage point of my saddle, often a head and shoulders above the drivers, the vista open wide, not blocked by walls or hedges or a tin box.

The roar of an engine caused my head to turn, briefly distracting me from the hill I was climbing. It was only a motorbike. It zoomed off ahead, making short work of the incline as I returned to my task, the interruption having caused a stutter in the rhythm of my ascent. Then another passed, and another. Soon there was a long line of motorbikes passing me, spewing clouds of petrol in deafening unison. I had no choice but to stop and wait, slightly intimidated by these souped-up cycles, my own machine looking pathetic in comparison. It took a while for the fug to clear from the hillside. My only engine was me. My moment of envy was brief; I resumed my toil, connecting with each mark in the road, each degree of the rise, the sound of birdsong and the smell of the fields intensifying the experience in a way that was inaccessible for motorists.

I have often been asked, 'What about the hills?' as if hills are a reason not to do it. But hills are an integral part of any journey, an unavoidable obstacle, fundamental to the challenge, and while they will cause the cyclist to curse, reaching that hard-earned crest makes the ride mean more somehow: you've earned the view. Physical pain can be overcome. It's the mental process that will get you to the top. I would set myself targets – how many pedal strokes until that tree? How many more until that rock? I would save my lowest gear until I couldn't hold out any longer, then realise with a sinking feeling that I'd already changed to the lowest gear and there was no further help my bike could give me. I'd then stand up in the pedals, the last resort, sometimes zigzagging across the road just to sustain enough momentum to keep moving, knowing it wouldn't be much easier pushing. Then with lungs heaving and legs burning I would hang on for the last few painful moments, gritting my teeth, before pausing at the top to catch my breath and look behind at the land that had been conquered. The pain would then fade and be forgotten, so it was easy to say that the hills were nothing. I had made it this far, hadn't I?

The daylight was fading as I reached Durness, my hostel perching above Smoo Cave at the top of a large rise. I sprinted up the hill, feeling every bit the athlete, the countless climbs that day the perfect warm-up. Across the peaks to the east arched a rainbow, the distant rainfall transformed into technicolour by the dying rays of the sun. I watched until the colours dwindled and the air became cold, unwilling to retreat indoors. This was one of the moments I savoured, glowing with the satisfaction of a hard day's ride, with a scene of breathtaking beauty laid out in front of me. I was as far from home as it was possible to be on this island, yet felt utterly content, with nothing for company but the road, the sea and the wide open sky.

DAY 26:
DURNESS TO ACHMELVICH

85 miles

Cape Wrath is the extreme north-westerly point of mainland Britain, a peninsula stuck on the top left-hand corner of Scotland. Though part of the mainland, no roads traverse the bleak and unwelcoming terrain; the cape is accessible only by boat across the Kyle of Durness. An old track struggles for 12 miles across the rough and windswept landscape, through a naval gunnery range, leading eventually to the most remote lighthouse on the mainland. There are scattered shacks along the route, some used by the MOD, some abandoned, the only one still permanently occupied that which houses the lighthouse keeper and his wife, who together run the small cafe for visitors. The location of the lighthouse is unique; despite being physically part of the mainland, it has 'rock' status because it's so difficult to access, relying on a helicopter for supplies.

I'd been wondering whether or not I should go out to the Cape. It would make the already long ride to my next hostel even longer, and it was a dead end – I wasn't keen on having to follow the same road out and back. And I knew that the rough track wouldn't do my heavily laden bike any favours.

'Cape Wrath? Oh, you should definitely go across!' said the gentleman that I'd been talking to over breakfast. 'Now that you're here, it would be a waste not to.'

'Why don't you leave your bags in our car?' his wife said. 'That would make the journey slightly easier. We're planning on walking back from the lighthouse so you won't be holding us up. It's no bother at all.'

'We'll leave the car keys on top of the wheel, so you can unlock it when you need to. I'm sure it will be perfectly safe.'

I gratefully accepted, silently reminding myself that petty theft didn't exist in this corner of Britain, so leaving my worldly possessions inside a car with the keys casually resting a few feet away would be no problem.

We arrived at the ferry stop and watched the tiny boat make its short trip across the water with the first cargo of passengers. The return journey brought back a cyclist who had camped overnight, and I was reassured about my decision. His pannier-laden bike had tyres thinner than mine – if he could do it, so could I.

On the opposite shore, the couple wished me luck as they joined the other passengers departing for Cape Wrath in the minibus. I set off in their wake, smug that I'd not have to pay £10 to get there, but could instead enjoy the sunshine and desolate beauty of the Parph as I bumped my way across it.

My smugness did not last long. The track was uncomfortable at best and downright terrifying at worst: the once-smooth tarmac was broken and pocked, moss growing from the cracks, the layer of stones beneath causing my bike to rumble and stutter as we made our passage. The land rose and fell, and I came to dread the downhills, my fingers firmly gripping the brakes and my wrists jarring as I tried to control my speed enough to keep the bike from bucking and vibrating. Uphills were a relief; at least my progress was slow so that the ride became smoother, but I didn't have much of a chance to enjoy the view, my eyes firmly fixed on the stony track ahead. Randy complained loudly and I suddenly became anxious when I realised that though I had a puncture repair kit in my saddlebag, my pump was in the bags in the car. This was the worst road that I'd ridden yet and the most likely to give me a flat tyre. I hoped that Randy would hold out.

Over an hour later, with shredded nerves and sore fingers, I glimpsed the black dome and the familiar beige and white column of the lighthouse, which signalled that I'd reached the tip of the peninsula. Puncture-free but exhausted, I limped towards it, greeted by the passengers of the minibus who were about to make their return journey. The site was soon deserted and I entered the tiny snack shop, asking the owner if I could use the toilet. 'Och, we dinnae have any plumbing here,' he replied, chuckling. 'Ye'll have t' find a bush!'

I stepped inside the museum, the collection of buildings quiet but for the wind. Pictures on the walls showed the great Robert Stevenson, lighthouse engineer, whose stepfather had been one of the first members of the Northern Lighthouse Board, and whose sons Alan, Thomas and David had followed in their father's footsteps in the engineering trade (his more famous son, Robert Louis Stevenson, going on to be a writer). Thus the Stevenson family had had a hand in building or designing almost all of the lighthouses in Scotland. So that was why they had looked so similar! I thought back to those at Aberdeen, Rattray Head, Cromarty and Fraserburgh, with their unmistakeable features. It really was a family resemblance.

The lighthouse was perched near the edge of the cliff, the surrounding scrub enclosed by a low whitewashed wall that might once have prevented the keeper's sheep from wandering too near the edge. I clambered over it and carefully crouched on hands and knees as I settled on a ledge with my legs dangling over the side. The wind howled across the plateau, rustling the stubby vegetation and whistling between huge bald rocks. I took a deep breath to steady myself, gripping the earth beneath my fingers, and leaned out to look down at the water. The seagulls circled far below, mere dots from this height, the deep blue punctuated with foaming ripples. The ocean stretched into the distance, powerful and beautiful. I tried to imagine what landfall lay beyond that gentle curve of the horizon: the Arctic Circle, Canada? I felt as if I were gazing out to the edge of the earth, but it was a different edge to that which I'd discovered at John o'Groats – wilder, more terrifying, more raw and elemental.

It was time to return. I sighed as I set off again back to the boat, reluctant to have to follow a path that I had already taken. But as I started down the track, I realised that everything was different. Just as the Nordic sailors had named the tip of this isolated peninsula Cape Wrath, from the Norse word *hvarf*, meaning turning point, I, too, had turned a corner. I had started my southwards journey, even though I was on the same road. The lighting was different, the scenery was different and I felt different.

Unfortunately, this didn't make any difference to the terrain, so I gritted my teeth as I cycled the hour-plus back to the boat.

I had almost arrived back at the ferry pier when the minibus passed me going along the road in the opposite direction, heading back to the lighthouse with its fresh load of passengers. This was not a good sign. John, the ferryman, had told me that he would only make the journey with several passengers on board, not for me alone. Looked like I'd just missed them. I sat on the end of the jetty, the tide out and the Kyle of Durness now almost completely drained. I could almost have walked across the exposed sand that lay before me. Half an hour passed. Then another. The tide came in, slowly creeping its way up the paving stones of the jetty. All I could do was wait.

I dragged my bike higher to avoid the rising tide, willing the minibus and the boat to return – I was hungry and lunch was in the bags in the car. Suddenly I felt nervous. I hoped no one was making off with my bags as I sat there helplessly across the water. As I waited my thoughts began to run wild: someone would find the keys, surely they would, and not only would my panniers be gone but so would the car... How idiotic to have left them like that... It would have been better if we'd left the boot unlocked, then at least if someone opened it and took the bags, the owners would still have the keys and their car... As I reached a state of mild panic the sound of an engine broke the silence and the minibus reappeared, followed shortly by the boat. After two hours of waiting, it took a mere two minutes to cross the now full loch. I approached the car, found the keys and retrieved my panniers – safe, of course.

It was already 3 p.m. and I had 60 miles yet to travel. As I cycled away from the ferry it began to rain. I'd heard that the west coast of Scotland was wet, but I hadn't expected it to be so prompt. A few miles down the road there was a resounding crack of thunder, as if the clouds were clearing their throats, preparing for a downpour. This duly came, the sky turning to charcoal as it filled with clouds, the mountains in the background suddenly sinister as they blackened under the weight of the water.

Despite the rain I made good progress. The land was not as hilly as the mountains suggested and the warm air was still – perfect for cycling. Unfortunately, it was also perfect for midges. Hundreds of black specs were collecting on my wet T-shirt and shorts, being scooped up as I rode, and no sooner had I brushed them away than more had taken their place. I passed through a village and quickly darted into a shop.

'Those dratted things,' said the shopkeeper as a couple squeezed through despite my best efforts.

'At least you're away from them in here!' I said.

'Not if people let them in,' she replied pointedly.

The cool stream of air conditioning circulating the shelves made me shiver in my wet clothes, so as soon as I'd made my purchase I stepped back outside, dashing across the road to the bus stop. But I wasn't the only one who thought this made a good place to shelter. After a moment I was back on the bike again, wiping midges from my face and out of my ears.

The rain stopped as abruptly as it had started and all of a sudden I was cycling through bright sunshine, lost in a world of mountains. The road took me over passes where rocks burst from soft purple heather, then beside crystal clear lochs with mirror-like surfaces un-rippled by tides. One loch was covered entirely in water lilies. It looked pretty as a picture – although I had given up taking photographs, thanks to the constant war with the midges. I'd almost perfected the art of keeping the bike moving as I reached for my camera, turning it on and positioning the shot while riding, holding my breath as I stopped (isn't it carbon dioxide that midges are attracted to?), taking the photo as quickly as possible then pedalling off again before they realised I was there. It was a hilarious but ridiculous routine and one that I couldn't hope to keep up.

Soon I reached the Drumbeg Road, the single-track lane wiggling its way around the peninsula that would eventually take me to my hostel. The hills of western Scotland were now truly living up to expectations, my ride a roller coaster: up after down after up after down, each dip hiding me from the next dip, each peak revealing dozens more. They were short, but steep, with only two speeds: painfully slow and dangerously fast, my brakes squealing against the twists of the road as I descended. I'd creak slowly to the top of a rise, then demolish the down in a matter of seconds. I found out later that this is renowned for being one of the most difficult roads in all of Scotland, two ladies that I met in a cafe one day disbelieving that I'd actually cycled it: 'And with all that luggage!'

My five-hour jaunt to Cape Wrath was taking its toll: I'd been on the road for 11 hours and still had ten miles remaining. It was growing late, the sinking sun casting elongated shadows and turning the sky a deep gold. The still of the evening air had encouraged great clouds of midges to gather, hanging low in my path, so that I had to constantly duck and dodge to avoid them. This strange dance was exhausting, the road relentless, the warm evening sapping my energy. I was tired and thirsty, running low on water, and it made me think back to one of the talks I'd given at a school for Sustrans, where one of the younger pupils had asked, 'What if you get thirsty?' I'd smiled and shown her the water bottles that I would be carrying. 'But what if you get so thirsty you fall off your bike?' she had insisted. I had told her confidently that wouldn't happen, but I was starting to feel that it might.

The sun soon settled on the tip of the mountains in the west, a deep yellow painting the clouds above, a rose colour stretching eastwards towards the bulbous peak and sharp ridge of the Suilven and Canisp inselbergs ('island mountains') that rose starkly from a landscape shaped by ancient glaciers. All of a sudden I felt very small, dwarfed by the sheer scale of my surroundings, a tiny creature creeping through this awesome terrain. Despite being exhausted, I loved it: this was a real adventure.

Finally I reached the turning for Achmelvich, where the hostel sits right on the beach. It was perfect – vast silver sands with the sun resting on the water. I wanted to sit and watch it disappear over the curve of the earth while listening to the waves gently splash against the shore. There was no one else on the beach, and I quickly found out why, hastily retreating to the hostel as I batted midges from my bare arms.

With the ride over and my focus gone, it took all my strength just to unpack my belongings and shower. I'd been on the road for 12 hours and had eaten very little, and my heart sank as I realised I'd not thought to buy food for my evening meal. The adrenaline had faded; I desperately needed food and I needed lots of it. Searching the hostel kitchen's 'help yourself' shelf, I found some old pasta that someone had left behind. I cooked a huge plateful and smothered it with olive oil, then sank into a chair, gobbling every last bit. It was the most delicious thing I have ever eaten.

DAY 27:
ACHMELVICH TO ULLAPOOL

35 miles

It was under fairly unremarkable circumstances that I met a remarkable man – both of us killing time, waiting for the next phase of our journeys to begin. Mark was attempting the ultimate adventure: to cycle around the world. Yet here he was, riding back and forth along the Ullapool waterfront, seemingly with no agenda. The events that had brought him there were unfortunate. Thirteen countries and almost 9,000 miles into his trip, Mark had been knocked from his bike, breaking his leg and forcing him to return to England. His method of resting his broken bones was questionable – less than six weeks after the accident he was back on his bicycle, on a 1,500-mile ride around the Western Isles of the UK, keeping in shape until he'd recovered and could continue. I could feel his frustration. When I departed Tower Bridge that first day, I assumed that when I next saw it I would have cycled around the whole of Great Britain. To have my trip curtailed, before I'd finished, because of an accident, was unthinkable. But the whole world? The dreams and anticipation that must accompany an adventure of that scale were unimaginable. I couldn't conceive of the helplessness and disappointment of having to go home and start again.

Mark and I eyed each other a couple of times as we cycled up and down the main street. It seemed appropriate to approach this other cyclist who, judging by his laden bike, was probably on a similar ride to me. I was looking for something to do while I waited for my youth hostel to open, having arrived early, the ride that day a mere 35 miles. And, so far, it had been underwhelming. After the epic effort of yesterday's ride, it paled in comparison; I had lost my verve for cycling. The landscape hadn't changed, but my outlook had. No longer did I feel like the magical traveller, tiptoeing through the giant's lair. I was just riding a bike, not noticing the scenery, finding the road dull. I had to keep reminding myself to enjoy it. I was bored with steadily trundling up and down hills – from feeling invincible for the past few days, I was now weary, tired and irritable. My legs didn't seem to be working. Each small incline was a monumental effort, every steep hill nigh on impossible. I didn't want to do it. Why couldn't this be easy? I longed for a day off, an easy ride, and a cup of tea.

Part way through the morning, a foreign car had passed me on the way up a hill, a family on holiday packed into the back. I moodily followed in their wake, bemoaning my slow progress, irritated by holidaymakers in vehicles. As I neared the top I saw them again, leaning on their car to take a photo and admire the view. I grizzled as I kept pounding away at the pedals, but as I passed, they surprised me by bursting into a round of applause. I grinned and attacked the hill with renewed vigour, and as I reached the top I paused, took a deep breath and tried to accept that not every day would be easy.

So it was just before 3 p.m. that I pulled up in Ullapool and even though there were plenty of cycling hours left in the day I was happy that this was where I'd booked my accommodation. Sometimes you just can't hit a rhythm. The town was busy for its size; though remote, it's the port for ferries to the Outer Hebrides. I rode slowly along the waterfront, the water crowded with yachts and fishing boats, a buzzing street market hidden away in a back street, the whitewashed guest houses glowing in the dull light of the day, windows displaying locally made soap, tea towels, tartan and shortbread.

It was then that I saw Mark doing the same thing. He had the look of a seasoned traveller, his skin suntanned, his chin stubbled from weeks of being on the road. His jet-black hair was covered with a Rapha cycling cap and his smile was accompanied by permanent dimples. I tried to place him – Eastern Europe, perhaps? I rode over to say hello.

'Hello,' he replied. Aha. Oxfordshire.

'Where are you cycling to?' I asked.

'Stornoway. My ferry leaves at six o'clock. What about you?'

'I'm cycling round the coast of Britain.'

'Fantastic! I want you to tell me all about it. Let's go and get a cup of tea. Do you like tea? I love tea!' His speech was delightfully expressive, his enthusiasm infectious. 'This place looks good,' he said, leaning his bike against the glass window of a cafe.

'Ah, brilliant, cake,' he said, an array of tray-bakes and sponges piled high on the counter. 'Let's have some. I love cake.'

I laughed. I was going to like this man. 'Tea and cake! The joy of simple things!'

'Isn't that why we are cyclists?' he replied.

We settled down in a couple of comfy chairs; usually I'd be in the saddle at this time of day, and having nothing to do but talk for a couple of hours was a rare treat. Although it was more a question of listening with Mark – a constant stream of conversation tumbled from his mouth as if the world would end before he had said all he wanted to.

'So, you're cycling the coast. Where did you start? How are you finding these hills? Have you been attacked by the vicious midges yet? What bike are you riding? What spec are your components? Is that the original headset? I've heard they're not very good.'

I glanced outside at Randy leaning up against the wall; I had no idea of the answers to his questions. Luckily he didn't give me much time to answer before the next came.

'Have you seen many other people on the road? I always stop people when I see them and write down their names and where they are going in my little book. Here it is. These are all the other cyclists I've met.'

I looked at the scrawl of names and places, watching as he wrote down 'Anna. Coast of Britain'.

'How heavy is your luggage? I invested in a Hilleberg tent – cost a bomb but it's worth it. Where are you camping?'

I almost nervously admitted I wasn't.

'What? You can't do a bicycle tour without camping!'

'Why not? I hate camping. Anyway, I'm on a cycle trip, not a camping trip.'

Mark looked unconvinced. 'Where are you staying then?'

'I arranged my accommodation in advance. I emailed the entire Sustrans staff team before I left and asked if anyone could help me out with a place to stay. Out of several hundred cycle enthusiasts placed around the country I was bound to find something.'

'So have you managed to space it evenly? How far are you riding a day?'

'It's worked out really well actually – most of them are a good day's ride apart. Sometimes a bit less, sometimes a bit more.'

'So what's your daily average?'

'About sixty or seventy miles a day. But today has been quite short – there aren't many places to stay around here. I don't mind though. I'm feeling a bit lethargic.'

'It happens. You should try riding for eleven months.'

'Is that how long you were on your trip for?'

'Yes, before that bastard knocked me off. Although to his credit he did take me to the hospital and then arrange for me to stay at his cousin's house.'

'Wow! He must have felt terrible about it.'

'Not as terrible as I felt. It's pretty tough when you see the bike you spent so long getting perfect mangled by the side of the road. And knowing I was injured beyond being able to continue. I just sat down on the verge and cried.'

'So what now?'

'I'm going back to the exact location of the accident so I can carry on with it. It won't be until early next year now, so I need to keep in shape. The doctor didn't say I couldn't cycle so I set up my turbo trainer the day after I arrived back in England. I had to lie to my mother saying the doctor confirmed it was all OK, but fifteen minutes on the trainer was fine. Then I was doing thirty minutes and after a week or so I was riding my bike again, about two or three hours a day. It's healing well. As long as I don't fall off!'

Soon Mark's boat was on the pier, loading. We went outside and compared the weight of our loads, as is customary for cyclists to do. Gave the tyres a quick squeeze. I don't know why we do that. No matter how experienced a cyclist you are, it's hard to resist the urge to check someone's tyres. Mark's bike was fully weighed down: panniers, bags, tent, maps, water bottles, bar bag. Mine looked like a toy in comparison.

I gave him a hug, this whirlwind of a man who had crash-landed on my miserable day and cheered me up. I would take his resilience and relentless cheer with me in the days to come, and it was a genuine smile I wore as I cycled to my youth hostel. I hoped I'd see him again.

That evening I sought out a restaurant with Wi-Fi so I could catch up with some blogging. It had been two days since I'd posted anything online, having been unable to pick up a signal in that corner of Scotland, and I had embraced the enforced separation from technology, feeling like a true adventurer out in the wilderness. As soon as I'd arrived in Ullapool and my phone had started beeping, the bright-red phone boxes that I'd seen scattered incongruously throughout the landscape had suddenly made sense. One text arrived from my aunt: 'Well done for turning south. You'll now have the sun in your eyes rather than on your back,' and another from my dad: 'No tweets, no blog – are you alright?!' Given that my last tweet had been: 'Cape Wrath – I hope it's not as angry as it sounds', I needed to reassure people that I hadn't fallen over the edge.

Before I went to bed I checked the weather forecast, groaning as I saw the line of black clouds with raindrops on the screen. The only variation was that one of them had a lightning bolt coming out of it. I sighed as I anticipated a wet day. At this stage, I didn't know what I was in for.

DAY 28:
ULLAPOOL TO GAIRLOCH

58 miles

The youth hostel kitchen was busy that morning, teeming with people making fry-ups and toast, preparing for their day's adventures. I hovered by the microwave waiting for my porridge to cook, catching the eye of a couple of guys about my age.

'Are you that girl who's cycling round the coast?' one of them, Cristobal, asked. 'The receptionist mentioned you.'

'Yes!' I replied, enjoying the brief feeling of fame.

He and his friend Jake were in Scotland for a short cycling holiday and were heading down the west coast towards Applecross. 'How about we ride together for a couple of days?' Cris asked, inviting me to share their bacon and eggs with them.

Company and breakfast were two things I would be foolish to turn down, especially on such a miserable day. We settled down to eat, exchanging nervous comments about the weather.

'So how long have you been cycling around up here?' I asked.

'A couple of days – we took the train to Inverness then hired bikes. We were going to head north from here but the weather forecast was too bad! Although I'm not sure it's going to be any better heading south,' Cris replied.

'Cris has been to Applecross before and he said it was beautiful, so we decided to go there instead,' said Jake.

'What about you?' I asked. 'Have you been cycling in Scotland before?'

'No,' he replied. 'Cris promised me it would be amazing. I hope he's right!'

Once packed and ready, we emerged from the hostel and retrieved our bikes from the shed, the rain almost impossibly hard. I was wearing as few clothes as possible – skin is waterproof after all, as Jon said. My trousers would only become soaked through in rain this heavy. I tried to convince myself that I would warm up once we got going, as I looked at what the boys were wearing – waterproof trousers, jackets, two pairs of gloves, shoe covers – the whole deal. My bare legs shivered in my cycling shorts.

We set off into the downpour, the wind blowing us southeast along the main road. The heavy rain had transformed the landscape overnight, the tranquil roadside waterfalls and streams of the previous day now great columns of water, rampaging down the mountainside in angry torrents. Rivers had burst their banks and the previously calm surfaces of the lochs were alive with waves. Mountains disappeared into the haze. We could barely see across to the other side of Loch Broom, less than a mile away.

'This is the full Scottish experience – this is what you risk!' Cris said, grinning even though the weather was atrocious.

Jake looked a little more dubious. 'Well, not much we can do about it now.'

'So do you ride much?' I asked Jake.

'Only to work. Cris is more the cyclist. He competes in triathlons – he's a nutter! He did an ironman recently!'

An hour into the journey, we reached the turning on to the coastal road which would take us out of the shelter of the trees and up on to the exposed land of the moor. All of a sudden we were battling the wind, which whipped across the plains with nothing to halt its progress. It was instantly colder, the rain now smacking into our faces. This was horrible. I took a deep breath as we pedalled into it.

The joviality that my fellow travellers and I had been enjoying was instantly quenched. The uphills became slower and the journey bleak as the hammering rain drained us of energy. The road took us over a pass, at the mercy of the elements, the wind now impossibly strong, water blowing horizontally across our path as the road crept higher and higher.

Soon all conversation had stopped, our concentration fixed purely on keeping going through the relentless downpour. We took it in turns to lead, every so often checking on each other. 'I'm OK,' I managed to stutter through chattering teeth. An hour later I was frozen – I couldn't feel my hands or my feet and my legs were starting to shake.

I cursed my foolishness for not wearing more clothes. The others must be soaked but at least they'd be warm. It was far too late to put on another layer now. To stop and fumble with my bags would just make me colder and, in any case, I was doubtful as to how much my numb fingers would be able to grip. I was desperate to stop riding but pausing in the middle of this wilderness would not be wise.

Each bend in the road I prayed would reveal a town, or some kind of shelter. Each corner came and went, revealing nothing but the barren road stretching ahead. Another hill, another stream rushing past. We cycled past a derelict house and I fantasised wildly about stopping inside, but the dilapidated walls did not offer much hope of warmth.

Finally we saw a sign for a craft shop and gallery. Surely they would have tea! We drew close enough to see the 'Sorry, closed' sign banging against its frame and my heart sank. I wasn't sure how much longer I could hold out. My legs were shaking hard, my teeth chattering violently, my numb hands and feet growing painful.

All sorts of thoughts go through your mind on a day like this. My first thought was, Please, please don't let me get a puncture. I could not imagine anything worse than trying to wrench that tyre off with numb hands in the pouring rain. Second: Am I going to get hypothermia? What would I do if I did? What if the phones don't work out here? I imagined waiting for hours for a car to pass that could help us. Third: What happens if we don't pass a town soon? How much longer can we keep going? Could we stop that passing camper van and ask them if we can come in? And if we did pass a town, what if there was nowhere to go? Could we knock on the door of a stranger's house and ask them for help? Fourth: a happy picture of us all talking and laughing over a steaming cup of tea. This scenario was getting more and more faint with every pedal.

It was an hour and a half after joining that road that we reached a sign for Dundonnell, and the welcome sight of houses. A man who'd just passed us in his car indicated up the road to where there was a hotel. I giggled deliriously as we approached it, gasping with cold and almost hyperventilating as we pulled up to the kerb. Jake unclipped my helmet for me as my numb fingers were unable to release it. Those 90 minutes had been by far the most horrific of the trip.

It took a full two hours of sitting by the fire in the hotel bar to stop shivering. I'd huddled in the bathroom for ten minutes trying to gain the strength to change into my dry clothes and compose myself. In the warmth, by the fire, full of hot squash, tea and chocolate, we laughed about our ordeal and compared notes about what had been going through each of our minds as we had journeyed along that bleak stretch of road.

'I couldn't believe that craft shop was closed!' I said.

'I was looking at that house with no windows to see if we could stop there,' Cris said.

'I was trying to work out if we'd all fit in my Bivvy Bag if things got really bad,' said Jake.

Soon another cyclist joined us beside the fire, someone we recognised from the hostel in Ullapool, his Lycra dripping and his hands shaking as he tried to rub the feeling back into them.

'Have you just come along that road too?' we asked him.

'Yes. What a day!' he replied. 'I stopped in that run-down house. It wasn't very warm!'

I wondered how he had coped. Our day was bad, but at least we had each other to keep us going. Had I been by myself I knew it would have been much worse.

Putting our wet clothes on and getting on the bikes again was really tough; we almost had to coerce each other to get back out in the wind and the rain, but once we resumed riding it wasn't so bad. And this time I was wearing my waterproof trousers. The road soon came off the moor and the wind died down, and we finally arrived in Gairloch, soaking wet but warm. We dashed into the first hotel we saw, draping our sodden clothes around the bar, ordering nuts and more tea and hot squash. The rain had penetrated through my layers, my skin damp and my fingers like sponges.

'We made it!' I exclaimed, hugging my fellow riders.

'I can't believe you convinced me to come here!' said Jake, and Cris laughed. 'I had this idea that we would be wild camping in forests, cooking on open fires and swimming in lochs. This is torture!!' But he was smiling as he said it. I felt sorry for him – this was by far the worst weather I'd come across, and it was unfortunate that these were the few days they'd chosen to come up here. I had been prepared to encounter a bit of rain, but at least I would have many more good days to make up for it.

For the second night in a row, Cris and Jake's camping plans were rained off, so they headed to a B&B while I went to find my host. It was wonderful to stay in a house after five nights of hostelling. Anne fussed over me in her motherly Scottish way, making sure I was warm and dry after hearing of my day. A hot shower, a soft towel and the first time I'd used a hairdryer for a month. Then a huge bowl of homemade Cullen skink – a fantastic Scottish fish dish that I'd been curious about ever since cycling through Cullen ten days ago. The scalding soup warmed me to the core, the memory of the day's struggles evaporating with every mouthful. It was one of Anne's specialties, and she was glad to have the excuse to make it, along with the rich toffee sauce that she'd made for dessert, winking as she served me my second portion. She was apologetic about the weather, but conceded that enduring a bit of rain is part of the west coast experience. I didn't doubt she was right, but I was glad the day was over.

DAY 29:
GAIRLOCH TO APPLECROSS

67 miles

The rain refused to let up as I met Jake and Cris on the Gairloch seafront, drizzle seeping into our clothes. But it didn't seep into our spirits, the rain not quite so hard as it had been the previous day, the weather warmer, and the route more sheltered. We slowly made our way through Wester Ross along lochs and glens, round headlands scattered with eileans, beneath the leaves of forests and over moors, surrounded by mountains, either panting as we climbed or laughing as we descended, singing as many songs about rain as we could remember. Had this been our only wet day we would have struggled. But we felt invincible, this nothing compared with what we had endured the previous day.

The scale of everything was immense. Loch Maree stretched alongside us for ten miles, the water wide and grey and alive with the rain. Streams and waterfalls descended from the rusty mountains that crowded the peninsula. We turned away from the loch to trace the River Torridon, the huge National Nature Reserve of Beinn Eighe (pronounced 'ben-ay') filling the sky with a mass of ridges and spurs, their tips a mixture of white scree and pink sandstone, slopes blushed with heather, a rich forest of Scots pine crowding their feet.

'This is incredible,' Jake said as we pedalled through the glen, dwarfed by the peaks surrounding us on all sides.

'I knew you'd like it,' Cris said, racing past.

I let the two of them ride on ahead, watching as they reached the top of a hill then were tipped over the edge like a rollercoaster carriage. I pedalled alone for a moment, smiling to myself. Being alone, earning my challenge, doing it all for myself was all very well, but to have others sharing in this was wonderful. For days I had been rendered speechless by the panorama of mountains, constantly catching my breath to see the ever-changing skyline of peaks, yet they seemed more real somehow, simply because others were there to share the view. Together we marvelled at their awesome height, together we sweated over the passes, together we coasted along the valleys.

It was three very bedraggled cyclists who fell through the door of the Applecross Inn that evening, tired and wet but happy. Even in August, the pub had an open fire roaring in the corner, so we huddled close to it, drying out our sodden clothes and feeling the glow seep back into our numb fingers.

There was a couple sharing our table who had been out that day exploring the famous Bealach na Bà pass. I knew it was not to be sniffed at, this pass, the highest road ascent in the UK, going from sea level to over 2,000 ft. I would be riding it the next day and was apprehensive about how difficult it would be, having already heard rumours about its slopes, its hairpins, the elusive summit that teases you with each bend. My host in Applecross had written me an email when she had heard of my intention to cross it, saying, 'Do you know how crazy that is?!' Truth be told, I didn't know how crazy it was. But this old cattle drovers' road was the most direct way to Mallaig, so that's the way I would be going.

I felt reassured talking about it with this couple. The man had ridden over and back that day, his girlfriend following in the car; to do it twice in quick succession must mean it couldn't be all that bad. By all accounts the driving sounded just as difficult. I knew it would be hard, but I'd been doing well with the hills so far and, as long as I knew how long it was likely to take, I felt prepared.

The rain eased off, enough so that Jake and Cris could finally use that camping equipment and justify having lugged it around with them this whole time. It wasn't quite the wild camping they'd been dreaming of, the forest too drowned, but there was a campsite nearby which was good enough. The next day, they would head eastwards back towards Inverness and their train home, and I would continue south. I hadn't realised how close Inverness was; the centre of Britain was a gaping hole around which I tiptoed, and though it had taken me over a week to pedal from Inverness, it would take them only a day to get back there.

I waved them off; they had been terrific cycling companions, turning up at just the right moment and helping me through the hardest day of my ride so far. Two days ago I hadn't known anything about them and now they were my heroes. I felt sure we'd see each other again, as they also lived in London; they might even come to my welcome home party.

As they headed off to set up their tents, I continued to my accommodation that night – my aunt had contacted the local school and one of the pupils had offered me a bed in the family home. I thought about what Mark had said about my missing out on a 'proper' adventure by not camping: the sunsets, the stars at night, the hooting of owls, waking to birdsong, the lullaby of rain pit-patting on canvas. Relaxing in the bath that evening after two days of cold, wet cycling, I didn't mind one bit.

DAY 30:
APPLECROSS TO MALLAIG

66 miles

The Bealach na Bà, which translates as the 'Pass of the Cattle', is the Holy Grail of hill climbs, the 'toughest and wildest in Britain', appearing regularly in top ten lists of the UK's hardest climbs. From the edge of Applecross Bay I cycled to the start of the road that would take me over the pass, a sign by the roadside warning 'Road normally impassable in wintry conditions', the 'Road closed' sign tossed casually to one side.

I began my ascent.

I could see the mountain ridge from near the bottom, partly hidden by the clouds, although in my optimism I refused to believe that the road would go right over the top of it. My eyes searched for an alternate route, a safer one round the edge, my hopes dwindling as I thought about what this ancient road was constructed for – taking cattle to market required the most direct route, regardless of height. A white van, just a speck at that distance, emerged from the cloud, confirming my suspicions. Onwards I climbed.

The rough tarmac snaked up the hillside, the gradient sometimes lurching upwards to cross a tussock, sometimes relaxing on a gentle slope, but always gaining height. Settling into the climb, the rhythm of the pedal strokes induced a mild hypnosis; left, right, left, right, on and on. It was simple: all I had to do was keep pedalling and keep going up. The greenery surrounding the bay was soon left behind, rusty moorland turning to rock as I climbed above the tree line; left, right, left, right, on and on.

The road zigzagged up the mountain, a succession of gradually narrowing Zs, my body soaked in sweat even though the day was grey. I sometimes paused to catch my breath, refusing to look back but focusing instead on each hairpin as it came and went, the pointed corners giving something to aim for, aiding my progress as my legs rotated steadily, powering me upwards.

Suddenly I found myself in the cloud that I had thought was so far beyond me, and I stopped to pull on my coat and trousers against the instant chill. I could barely see the road ahead and started to worry that I would miss the summit, the low visibility having robbed me of all sense of perspective. Flagging down an approaching car, I asked them how far it was to go, the reply of 'Nearly there!' causing me to babble at them about my bike ride in exhausted relief. 'I'm cycling round the coast of Britain!' I exclaimed before they'd even asked. They smiled politely, waiting for me to continue riding, and soon a row of cars had accumulated, so I waved and continued the climb.

At long last I reached the summit, having ascended a total of 2,053 ft; it had taken one hour of steady climbing to get to the top. I clambered from my bike and pushed it over to the viewpoint, leaning it against the tiny cairn as I studied the plaque. Broadford on the Isle of Skye lay only 13 miles away, but in the heavy cloud there was no chance of being able to see it. I looked around, adrenaline coursing through my veins, my breathing slowly returning to normal, unable to stop smiling. Even though I couldn't enjoy the reportedly stupendous views over Skye, the mist created an eerie and tranquil experience that was just as thrilling. I stayed for a while, bewitched by the haze, not wanting to return to the land far below.

Eventually I remounted my bicycle, descending into the murk. A few minutes later I emerged from the cloud, staring with trepidation at the route that snaked its way down the other side of the pass. Barriers would stop me hurtling off the mountainside but, even so, it looked treacherous. I descended with the brakes firmly on.

Every so often I glanced behind me, very glad that I wasn't doing this the other way; the switchbacks on the southern face looked more vicious than the side I'd ascended. Thirty minutes later I arrived back at sea level, my nerves frazzled but my spirits soaring with the sense of accomplishment. For the remainder of the day I devoured the miles, glowing from my Bealach experience, feeling invincible. The long dragging hills near to Lochcarron didn't faze me at all, and I sped through the Kyle of Lochalsh, the road lined with pines, my only companions the sheep on the verge and the Highland cattle grazing next to burbling streams.

The hump of the Skye Bridge hove into view, arching over the water like a giant caterpillar. I'd originally decided not to visit any islands, to stick to the mainland and maintain some kind of purity in my circumnavigation – western Scotland is so littered with islands, would I only have completed my trip if I'd gone to every one? But the road on the mainland would weave far inland, cutting off great swathes of coast, travelling right up to the Great Glen and Fort William, by-passing Knoydart and Ardnish and the west-reaching finger of Ardnamurchan. I had to accept that I couldn't ride every inch of coast; I'd tried many times to seek out a coastal route where no route existed. But to go so far from the sea, and to miss out the most westerly point of the mainland, was not something I wanted. It was better for me to hop across the base of Skye, using it as a stepping stone, and rejoin the coastline 15 miles later.

I crossed the bridge, feeling a little guilty as I looked back, the mainland soon out of sight. The road was wide, flat and deserted, and hills rose behind gorse hedges, their reflections in the still waters of roadside lochs almost as clear as the real thing. I pictured the island's feathered fingers stretching northwards, feeling as if I were floating in the middle of the ocean, an outsider to the land that I had been tracing for so long.

I arrived in Armadale and wandered into the cafe at the Clan Donald visitors' centre, realising with a jolt that I'd been there before. The upper-level gallery and the shields and flags hung around it were unmistakeable – we must have come here on our family holiday when I was a teenager, all piled into the car, and we would certainly have driven along that road, it being the only one. But no part of the route had been familiar. It was as Ernest Hemingway wrote: 'It is by riding a bicycle that you learn the contours of a country best.' I had worked to summit each rise, had coasted down each hill, and the slow rise and fall of the land was now ingrained in my memory.

The ferry departed for Mallaig, a remote fishing port perched on the edge of the mainland, seeming to cling to the mountains for fear of being dropped into the sea. A criss-cross of peaks and ridges stretched endlessly behind the village. The ferry rounded the starboard-hand marker at the end of the harbour arm, a statue of a fisherman guiding us into the port, his blank eyes gazing out to sea, a stone child clutching his hand. The harbour was crowded with fishing boats of all shapes and sizes, their decks stacked high with crab pots and buoys in chaotic technicolour. I instantly loved Mallaig, the bustle a refreshing change from some of the other ports I'd visited whose prosperity had dwindled. I watched a seal eat fish from a fisherman's hand.

A few paces back from the harbour front was the Fishmarket Restaurant, whose kitchens were served by the very boats that were unloading their catch. This was fish at its most local and fresh. I ordered rope-grown mussels, Dover sole and a cranachan to finish it off – a delicious traditional Scottish dessert made from oats, cream, raspberries and whisky.

The light had faded by the time I emerged, stuffed to the brim. Mallaig was just coming alive. Those boats heading out for the night were now a Christmas tree of lights, the flashing of navigation buoys that blinked in the oily blackness guiding them on their way. Lights glowed in the houses built into the hillside as if hanging in mid air, their rows of matching windows gazing out to sea like the eyes of the town.

DAY 31:
MALLAIG TO OBAN

81 miles

From high on the hill I looked down towards Mallaig and beyond, back to Skye where the Cuillin mountain range dominated the skyline, its black ridges specked with snow even in August. As the terminus for trains up the west coast from Glasgow, and the end of the road from Fort William, Mallaig was the place to which people would journey in order to catch a ferry to the islands that sit prominently on the horizon: Skye or one of the Small Isles, the spiky crown of Rum and the gently slanting plateau of Eigg appearing as cardboard cut-outs in the haze that morning.

I was in high spirits as I pedalled southwards towards Arisaig: I had conquered the Bealach na Bà, the rain had stopped, the air was fresh and I was full of a delicious breakfast. The road lay at the foot of mountainous precipices, stark grey and brown above the tree line, but rich in greens and the purple of heather below. This stretch was the prettiest of any I'd seen; lost in the crinkles of the coast I zigzagged around each inlet, the shoreline peppered with tiny eileans, the beaches appearing bright white, the rough sand edged with huge purple thistles. The water rippled under the breeze, the occasional boat the only sign of life.

The road came away from the shoreline, weaving through the forest-clad Moidart peninsula, and eventually I reached the turning for Ardnamurchan Point, the most westerly point on the British mainland. The road became single track, tracing a route between and around mountains, the forest now replaced by moorland, only the heather that grew among the rocks lending colour to my surroundings. Sheep lined the track, grazing on the bracken, lifting their heads to fix me with a steady gaze as I approached, before scattering across the hillside, bolting from the silent threat of my wheels. A herd of cows sat far below on the beach.

I followed the road as it weaved ever west, enjoying the isolated beauty, the magic of this peninsula. I savoured these extreme points, the most easterly, the most northerly, the most westerly. The sea appeared between a V in the hills, the perfect line of the horizon stretching between the mountains. Then I spotted the black domed roof of the lighthouse and as I drew closer the tower emerged, the unpainted stone distinguishing it from its brothers and sisters, but its style unmistakably Stevenson. I stood quietly in its shadow, my feet inches from the water that splashed against the rocks, the most westerly person on the British mainland.

The ferry to Mull departed from Kilchoan, five miles back along the peninsula. This was a much more modest version of that which had carried me over the sea from Skye, its single cargo, a campervan, taking up almost the entire deck space. It was simply a piece of road enclosed in a boat, for passengers to drive on one end and drive off the other.

So I cycled on one end and cycled off the other in Tobermory, instantly captivated by the pretty village with a long row of buildings lining the harbour front, each painted brightly in different colours, radiating cheerfulness. The usual lobster pots were piled high on the harbour arm, a sturdy clock tower marking the village centre, the church spire rising towards yet more colour on the hill. The gentle curve of the harbour was flanked by rocks protecting the town from the rough seas, hundreds of boats bobbing on their moorings or sitting in the tiny marina, waiting to explore the islands and sea lochs of this stretch of coast. The Western Isles Hotel sat regally on the cliff edge and guest houses crowded the harbour front. The town clearly relied on tourism for its prosperity but it wasn't a rowdy type of tourism – there was a calm, friendly buzz about the place. I walked slowly up Main Street, past trinket shops, cafes and bakeries, and jewellers with necklaces carved from local stone, before passing the final painted building and climbing the steep hill away from the village.

The wide and hilly road descended through the island, the huge mountains in the north covered by forests, occasional glimpses of streams sparkling as they cascaded down the steep slopes. The road soon became single track, twisting and turning between the hills. There was thankfully no sign of the local lads who reportedly use these lanes as their own private racetrack. I passed through Salen and after that the road was flatter, hugging the coast next to sandy inlets with abandoned boats resting on the beach, flashes of the mainland visible across the Sound of Mull. I looked across to the forests and hills that crowded the water's edge, feeling that twinge of guilt once more – that's where I should have been. But I knew that the road would have taken me miles inland; at least this way I was by the water.

'Please watch the eagles from here', requested a sign by the side of the road. I knew the islands were an excellent habitat for wildlife of all kinds – red deer, otters and the fabulous sea eagles. Here on Mull, there was an abundance of sea eagles since their reintroduction in the 1970s, after they'd been hunted to extinction in the early twentieth century. I had assumed I'd see at least one on my trip, but racing along on a bike is not conducive to birdwatching. Back in Wick I thought I'd seen one – I'd heard they are impossibly huge, but not as huge as the small aircraft I'd actually been looking at. Now, apparently, all I had to do was stand by this sign. But as I took up my spot, I noticed the fluttering flags of the Craignure golf course behind the fence. Perhaps that's what it meant.

I reached Craignure, and had a look around the Visitors' Centre. There was a wildlife-spotting chart, where tourists wrote down what they'd seen that day, but I was unable to add anything to the list. It had been a quick dash down Mull's backbone. I stood on the deck of the second ferry of the day, watching the island recede into the distance. The wash of the boat spread like a fan behind us, the glow of the setting sun framing the lighthouse that guides seafarers through the Sound of Mull.

The boat rounded the Isle of Kerrera that shelters Oban from the Atlantic, the ruins of Dunollie Castle sitting on their rock, this ancient stronghold of the McDougalls standing guard at the harbour mouth. Grey-brick hotels lined the shore, their large windows overlooking the bay. McCaig's Tower sat above the town, a huge circular folly that crowned the hilltop, appearing more and more prominent as the boat pulled into the shore. A distillery chimney loomed above the waterfront, and the masts of Tall Ships swayed in front of the waterfront restaurants, docked alongside the fishing boats that had delivered their catch to the restaurant kitchens. Oban is known as the 'Gateway to the Isles', a bustling port, with at least six ferry routes operating between here and the islands. As I disembarked the strain of bagpipes came floating across the water. I'd visited before with my family and it felt comfortingly familiar.

I was ravenous, even though it seemed as though all I'd been doing that day had been eating. My enormous breakfast of cheesy eggs, four slices of toast and cereal had quickly been followed by two bananas and two Kit Kats; then there were two sandwiches and three doughnuts for lunch, a cereal bar, some shortbread and an apple on the first ferry, some dried apricots, half a malt loaf and a cherry-and-almond flapjack on the second, and I'd just scoffed the remainder of my fudge. And now I was desperate for my dinner. It seemed fitting that in Oban, the 'Seafood Capital of Scotland', I should sample some of the local fish – all this time in Scotland and I hadn't yet eaten smoked salmon. But I only had a few nights left in the country and I didn't want to miss out on the haggis, neeps and tatties either. I stared at the menu for a while, then decided I couldn't decide and chose both. 'Hungry?' the waiter asked as he wrote down my order. They didn't go at all well together.

Even after all the food I'd consumed that day, I left the restaurant still hungry. So I went to get that other Scottish classic: chips. By the time I had wolfed those down, I was absolutely stuffed.

I stood on the waterfront, the harbour lights twinkling on the water, the deep orange glow of the floodlit McCaig's Tower a beacon over the town. I gazed into the darkness, listening to the gentle wash of the waves against the harbour wall, before turning and wandering back to my hostel through the now dark streets, the strains of a ceilidh in full swing floating across the water.

DAY 32:
OBAN TO ARRAN

73 miles

It was the first day of my second month on the road, and I woke that morning in my comfy hostel bed, with bright sunshine pouring through the windows. I did not want to go cycling. Oban was lovely and I wanted to see more of it – at least go up to McCaig's Tower and sit where I had sat as a teenager, looking out across the water and discovering Scotland for the first time. I had been travelling through unfamiliar lands for so long, it was nice to be in a place with which I had a connection. I didn't need a rest day, but I could certainly have a late start.

I dragged myself out of bed and broke my first rule: tea. I'd not been drinking any caffeine during the trip, except for on my days off. I love tea but it goes straight through me, something I could do without while riding my bike. And it's not as if I needed the pick-me-up – wide open skies and fresh air tend to do that for you. I was happy for the enforced detox – one cup of tea always leads to another.

But I was feeling lethargic. 'All I want to do is drink tea and eat cake!' I wrote on Facebook.

I settled in the lounge with my steaming cuppa, wrote some postcards and caught up on the past few days of my blog. Time ticked away but I wasn't worried. I only had a 60-mile ride to reach the ferry that would take me across to the Isle of Arran –

a mere walk in the park considering some of the distances I had been covering recently. With my average speed of 10 mph and the last ferry departing at 5.45 p.m., I had a couple of hours before I needed to set off. It was mostly one road that I'd be following so I was sure I'd make it in time.

At 11 a.m. I finally left the hostel, ambling down to the waterfront. There were six and a bit hours before I had to catch the ferry. Just as I was checking the map, I heard a shout. 'Hey!'

It was Mark!

He'd just arrived in Oban, fresh from his Hebridean trip. Since I'd last seen him we'd both been making our way southwards from Ullapool, him over the islands, me along the coast. Despite having spent only three hours in his company, it was like seeing an old friend.

'How wonderful to see you!' he said. 'I saw on your blog that you were here but I thought I'd missed you. Shall we have a cup of tea?'

'Well...'

I looked at my watch. I really had better be going. But I could squeeze in one cup.

We found a quayside tea room with a view over the harbour and swapped stories about our respective cycle trips between Ullapool and Oban, almost not letting the other finish before jumping in with the next anecdote. I was happy to sit there, swept up in Mark's verbosity, chatting away. But time was getting on, and that ferry wouldn't wait. At 12.15 p.m. I finally pedalled away. I had five and a half hours to cycle 60 miles.

The first 20 miles or so were easy; I attacked the undulating road with vigour, and managed a healthy 15 mph average. So far so good. At Kilmartin, 30 miles into the ride, I stopped and had some lunch in a tea room, pleased with my progress.

The sun was shining and the road had so far been kind. I was halfway and I still had three hours left. I was enjoying the fast riding, pushing myself more than usual. I felt good and strong.

Back on the road after lunch, the gentle headwind that I had vaguely registered in the morning had picked up, and soon the steadily building hills were adding to the equation. I reached the Crinan Canal where the towpath would lead me to Lochgilphead, just 20 miles from my destination. I'd been looking forward to this part. It was the first canal that I'd ridden beside on the whole trip, one of my favourite types of route – calm, flat and a lovely respite from the rush of the roads. But being on a gritty and rutted path meant that my average speed dropped substantially. I started to panic – the five-mile long canal path seemed never-ending, the reliable tarmac of the roads suddenly much more attractive.

I returned to the road at the top of Loch Gilp at 4.15 p.m., suddenly worried that I wouldn't make it. I was exhausted. Four hours of flat-out cycling, hauling my 16 kg of luggage, was beginning to take its toll. I had 20 miles yet to travel. The wind wouldn't let up. And the hills were starting to become steep.

I persevered, at last reaching the turning that would take me to the ferry port. I had five miles to go, and I had 25 minutes to do it. It seemed that I would make it after all. Then, bam! MORE hills. Up, down, up, down, constant, relentless, tough, too steep for my tired legs. And now I was riding straight into the wind. I almost cried with frustration. I was so near – I couldn't believe that after all that pushing I would miss the ferry. The ladies I'd been chatting to in the tea rooms at lunch had described this road to me, telling me there's a terrific view of Arran and the ferry port from the top of a hill, then it's downhill all the way.

Each crest I prayed would be the one. But each time another hill rose up beyond. I kept on going.

Hill after hill after hill. I was standing in the pedals, pushing, pushing, racing against the clock. I couldn't contemplate missing that ferry, trying not to think about where I would stay that night if I couldn't get on to the island. I didn't have anything left, but forced myself to give it. I would not fail, after all this!

The minutes ticked away. Ten minutes to go. Five. Another hill. And another. At last, when I was perilously close to the time of the ferry's departure, I reached the top of a hill and there it was – the island of Arran across the water and the little ferry waiting in the dock, loading its cargo.

Loading!! I raced down the hill, the cars that had just disembarked passing me on the narrow road. I reached the bottom, red in the face, out of breath, my panic subsiding as I approached the boat and slowed to a halt. I snatched a quick photograph of the ferry with the island rising up behind it, then dashed to the loading platform. I lashed my bike to the railings then flopped on the deck, completely finished.

I had learnt my lesson. No more tea for the rest of the trip.

DAY 33:
ARRAN TO COLMONELL

65 miles

Having zoomed through Skye and Mull, I loved being able to spend a full night on Arran, becoming a part of that island community for a short time, knowing that the only way of getting anywhere was across the sea. Mountains rose starkly from the island's centre while the road circled the perimeter, climbing and falling between the glens. It was a long upwards drag from Lochranza in the north, followed by what felt like an endless descent towards Brodick through steep mountainside fields in which red deer grazed – the first I'd seen.

I walked to the water's edge, hopping over the rocks at the shoreline. The seaweed glistened in the sunlight, drying as it clung to swirling red boulders, its edges touching the surface of seawater pools where fish darted, waiting for the tide to wash them free. Across the water the Scottish mainland curved away in the distance, the sparkling expanse of the Firth of Clyde the final firth to cross.

Arriving in Ardrossan by ferry was something of a culture shock – I'd grown accustomed to the sleepy fishing ports and deserted roads that I'd been riding through for the past week or so, and seeing the town sprawled out ahead was unnerving. This was definitely a different kind of Scotland, with Glasgow just up the road and the traffic becoming heavier as I made my way southwards. It hadn't been this busy since Edinburgh.

I joined the NCN, which would lead me all the way from Ardrossan to Ayr, the mountains of Arran slowly fading from view as I cycled for 25 miles along the sweeping banks of the Firth of Clyde. The coastline was much straighter and flatter than that which I'd been following for the past week – no more sea lochs, no more mountains, just the wide curve of the west coast. It felt good to have the open water as my constant once more. The trail through north-western Scotland had held such beauty, such variety, but I had missed this, the expansive sea view in which the water stretched ahead undisturbed for miles and miles.

The cycle route eventually took me away from the seafront path and into the hills. I rounded a corner, a steady downhill leading into woods, but I found myself pushing hard against the pedals. How could that be? I checked my rear tyre – no puncture. There was no wind either, yet somehow I was struggling to cycle down a slope.

Confused, I spotted a stone by the side of the road: 'The Electric Brae', it read. Looking more closely, I discovered that this quarter of a mile of road, while appearing to slope downwards, actually slopes upwards, an optical illusion caused by the configuration of the land on either side of the road. It was named 'Electric Brae' because of an ancient assumption that magnetism caused the bizarre effect. I made hard work of it, thinking how much better it would be to be going in the opposite direction and freewheeling uphill!

I continued along the coastal road through the small village of Maidens and to Girvan, where I was welcomed to the town by a boat made of bricks asking 'Whit's Yer Hurry?' For once, I wasn't in a hurry – no more ferries to catch, no curfew to meet and a day off tomorrow to look forward to.

I was almost at the end of my fifth week on the road and I had travelled 2,000 miles. I was halfway.

DAY 35:
COLMONELL TO NEWTON STEWART
102 miles

Since the beginning of the trip, each pedal revolution had taken me further and further from home. But now, the return journey had begun, with more distance between me and my starting point than there was to the finish. From now, I'd be heading home.

Thirty days of cycling six, seven, eight hours a day had transformed me; I had never been so fit. Every part of my body was primed for the job of powering my bicycle to the next destination, each muscle working at the peak of its efficiency. Not an ounce of fat remained, despite my eating twice as many calories as usual. My sole purpose was to ride a bike. This is what our bodies were built for, after all: physical activity. To run, to hunt, to walk for miles to gather food and water, to carry wood for fuel and rocks for shelter, to build and chase and toil. I was born to do nothing more than cycle.

I set off into the dewy daybreak, droplets sparkling on the hedgerows and mist hugging the fields. Shortly into the day's ride I passed a sign saying 'Newton Stewart: 17 miles'. I ignored it and headed in the opposite direction, knowing that it would take a full day of cycling to get there: I'd reached that section of the coast where peninsulas hang down like stalactites, taking me miles out of my way with each outcrop of land. As I pedalled away from the sign, my optimism faded. This seemed pointless: why cycle over 100 miles when my destination lay just beyond that hill? Although I'd questioned my island hopping, now I almost wished there were some islands strategically placed to bridge the gaps between the peninsulas. It's not the destination that counts, it's the journey, I tried to tell myself, but the further I travelled, the more I felt as if I were cycling for the sake of it. Why do something if there's no pleasure to be gained? My day on the sofa had instilled a laziness that I couldn't shake, and had also allowed a cold to start brewing. Motivation was not at its highest.

A quick loop around the anvil-shaped Rhinns of Galloway gave me a brief glimpse of Northern Ireland across the Irish Sea, and then it was down to the Mull of Galloway and up again to trace the vast shores of Luce Bay. Part way down its eastern side I reached Port William, where a signpost indicated that if a straight line were drawn between the two most extreme points of mainland Britain – Land's End and John o'Groats – I would be almost exactly halfway along it. The day was becoming rapidly greyer, the sky clouding over, making me even less keen to travel all the way down towards Burrow Head only to have to retrace my steps up the other side. But there I was to be joined by my host Phil, who had assured me that the Isle of Whithorn, a hidden gem, would be worth it.

'You cycle really fast!' Phil said to me as we pedalled, the hills coming and going with ease.

'Sorry. We can slow down if you like.'

'No, no, it's OK. You must be super fit! I bet you love being able to cycle all day every day.'

'I do love it, yes. It's a very simple lifestyle. But some days don't work as well as others and today is one of those days.

It might be because I've passed the halfway mark, so I know exactly how much there is remaining. It seems an awfully long time ago that I left home.'

'I can sympathise with that,' Phil said. 'Come on, I know something that might make you feel better.'

We had reached the foot of the peninsula and the small harbour of the Isle of Whithorn, where folks hauled wooden rowing boats away from the tide. A rocky stretch of land peeked from behind the edge of the bay.

'What's that?' I asked.

'That's the Isle of Man,' Phil replied. 'And if you look the other way, you'll see what I wanted to show you.'

I looked to the east, where the next peninsula sat, grey and hazy across the water. Beyond it the land rose high with the mountains I had come to expect from this part of the world. I frowned, unsure of why Phil had thought that would impress me.

'What am I supposed to be looking at?'

'England! That's the Lake District.'

'No!' I peered closer. He was right – these peaks were too far south to be anything but. England! My home! I felt a jolt of excitement, a surge of longing in my stomach. Home. It's a strange concept for a traveller, especially as 'home' in the traditional sense for me no longer existed: I would be finding somewhere new to live when I returned to London. But, looking at that landscape, although miles from anywhere with which I had any association, I felt a tug, an itch for the familiar, a desire to be surrounded by people whose culture was similar to my own. The draw of home is hard to resist.

From the Isle of Whithorn we rode north, through large country estates set behind long brick walls and mature trees, following the creases and folds of the River Cree to Newton Stewart. Herds of cows wandered nonchalantly across the road.

'This is us,' said Phil as we pulled into a small housing estate on the edge of the town.

'Thanks for showing me those places,' I replied. 'It was a good ride in the end.'

DAY 36:
NEWTON STEWART TO DUMFRIES
79 miles

England inched closer as I repeated the game of tracing the coast in great U shapes, down and up, down up, down and up. Once again it was tempting to take the direct route, so as each loop curved south I would stop and find something unique, telling myself, If I hadn't come this way I would never have seen... From the top of the ruined walls of Carsluith Castle I looked down into fields where Belted Galloway cows grazed, a distinct pale cream stripe around their middles separating black heads from black rumps. I stopped to peer inside the Galloway Smokehouse, the counter laid out with rows upon rows of fish, fresh from the huge smoking bins in the rooms behind. The long loop round Kirkcudbright Bay took me past huge wrecks of wooden sailing vessels, their rotten hulls slowly disintegrating, and up to the harbour where dinghies sat squat on the dry banks, those who'd neglected to raise their centreboard pitching to one side. I rode beneath the thick pines of the Galloway Forest Park, the sun's light trickling through with a deep green glow, and then away from the shelter of the trees where I was blinded by the sun's reflection from tarmacked roads slick with the overnight rainfall. Closer to the coast, trees grew permanently bent over, victims of the prevailing winds, their branches and leaves extending parallel to the ground even though the air that day was still.

At last I rounded the final outcrop and traced the River Nith towards Dumfries, my last overnight stop in Scotland. I paused on the town bridge, watching the water flow beneath the bricks, wondering where in the country it rose. The ride for the past month had been hard work, but I knew I would miss Scotland when I crossed the border the next day, from the detail of the coastline to the immense scale of everything, for being able to ride for hours without seeing another person, for being as far north as I ever had, for the islands and the culture and the wildness of the landscape. It had been an extraordinary experience.

I had asked friends what I should do before I left the country, and one of the suggestions was to have a deep-fried Mars bar. I wasn't sure if it was a good idea or not, but as I'd never had one and as I'd be sure to cycle off any impending heart attack, if ever there was a right time it was now. It would be the culmination of the gastronomic adventure I'd had as I'd journeyed around Scotland: smoked salmon and Aberdeen Angus steak, haggis, neeps and tatties, shortbread, butter tablet, porridge, Cullen skink, freshly caught fish, cranachan, rope-grown mussels and Arbroath Smokie, and now a deep-fried Mars bar.

I set out to find somewhere that would sell me the famous snack, but chip shops in Dumfries were surprisingly scarce. I cycled round the town for half an hour trying to find one, eventually spying a flashing neon sign: 'New to Rob's – deep-fried Mars bar! 99p!' Thank goodness for that. I ordered one, trying not to show my nerves as the boy behind the counter dunked my chocolate bar in batter then chucked it in the deep fat fryer. I was tempted to ask him to take my picture with it, but thought better of it, instead sloping off with my hot battered Mars bar clutched in my hand. Just round the corner, I stopped and took a bite. Before I knew it I'd gobbled the whole thing. It was delicious.

PART 4:

NORTH-WEST ENGLAND AND WALES

Days pedalled = 31
Days spent resting = 5
Days to go = 36
Miles travelled = 2,149
Miles to go = 1,881
Counties pedalled
through = 27
Countries pedalled
through = 2
Punctures = 0
Ferries taken = 12
Days been rained on = 10
Sea swims = still only 3

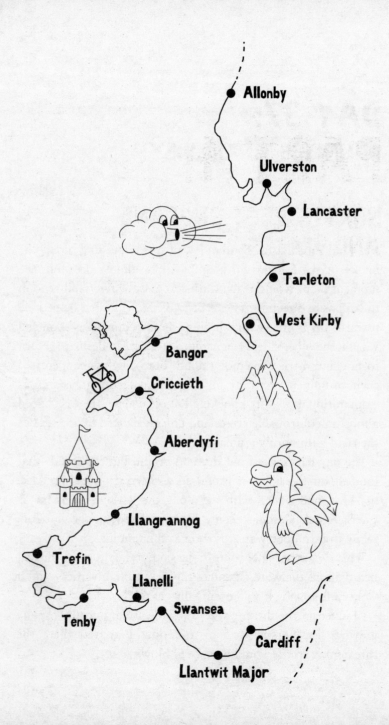

Allonby

Ulverston

Lancaster

Tarleton

West Kirby

Bangor

Criccieth

Aberdyfi

Llangrannog

Trefin

Llanelli

Swansea

Cardiff

Tenby

Llantwit Major

DAY 37:
DUMFRIES TO ALLONBY

82 miles

My final morning in Scotland was spent speeding along the banks of the Solway Firth at 25 mph, almost dreading the moment that I would reach Carlisle, cross the river and head in the opposite direction. The ferocity of the wind that helped me towards the border would become an impediment as soon as I was on the other side, bringing into conflict my desire to return to England. I tried to enjoy the lift, but being at the mercy of such an immense and invisible force was terrifying as well as exhilarating, the gusts knocking me off course, the easy speed almost uncontrollable. Trees and grasses danced by the side of the road with unruly animation.

The day had started out dry and bright, but the clouds that loomed on the horizon promised a thorough soaking. Alec, my host, had ridden with me along the River Nith as far as Caerlaverock Castle, keeping his eyes fixed on the horizon, ready to turn homewards as soon as the rain hit.

'This is part of NCN route 7,' he said, trying to make himself heard above the wind. 'It comes this way from Inverness, and if ye keep following it ye'll eventually get to Carlisle.'

I looked in the direction he was indicating, into the rapidly greying sky, hoping that by the time I arrived there the threatening storm would have been blown away.

'Come on, I'll buy ye a cup o' tea and some cake,' he said. 'Ye'll be glad of it later if the weather breaks. Especially with tha' cold,' he added.

We entered the castle tea rooms, the triangular battlements of the medieval stronghold standing imposingly behind their moat. 'That's where you're heading,' he said, pointing across the water, my destination that day a mere handful of miles away across the Solway Firth. 'It's quite a ride. At least ye'll have the wind helping ye along this bit. I'll leave ye here and start heading back. Good luck – I hope it stays dry!'

I stopped to look across the water after he'd gone. The corrugated skyline of the Lake District was blurred with rain, my home country looking less and less welcoming the longer I stood there.

Through Bankend, Powfoot and Annan, drawing ever closer to the border, I hurtled along with the gusts, the clouds kept at bay by the wind. Perhaps I was right and the storm would continue eastwards. But Scotland wouldn't let me leave without a farewell shower, and as I arrived in the border town of Gretna the heavens opened. I quickly sought out a bus stop in which to shelter, watching the torrents collect in huge puddles in the road. Then, as abruptly as it had started, the rain stopped, leaving behind soaking wet streets that glistened in the bright sunshine. It was almost as if the weather had put on the show especially for me, marking my final moments in the country.

Buses swung in and out, dropping off passengers and picking up new, old ladies shuffling home with their shopping trolleys and mothers scolding young children as they splashed in the puddles.

'Looks like quite a load you have there! Need a lift?' called a driver as he rounded his bus into the stop.

I smiled. 'I don't think I'd fit!'

'Going far?' he asked.

'Just to England.'

'Och, nearly there,' he said as the doors closed and he swung away.

Nearly there, I echoed. I wondered how an invisible line could be so significant. But a border crossing represented so much: a different culture, a different language, a unique set of laws.

Nowhere was this more relevant than in Gretna Green, the place to where young couples desperate to be married had once eloped, following a change in the English law which demanded parental consent for anyone under the age of 21, and for the ceremony to take place in a church. The village had become a hotbed for quick marriage ceremonies in the middle of the eighteenth century; on the old coaching route from London to Scotland, it was the first settlement that lovers would encounter beyond the border and the blacksmith's shop had become the location for the ceremony, the blacksmith conducting the marriage in a simple hand-fasting ceremony before announcing the union by striking the anvil.

I had seen a sign for the Anvil Hall as I'd dashed for shelter, so now that the rain had ceased I followed the arrows and crept inside. It was just one of the dozens of marriage venues in Gretna and Gretna Green, and most likely the grandest – a renovated church, lavishly decorated and filled with cut flowers and candles. At the head of the nave stood the traditional blacksmith's anvil, with 'The Anvil of the Old Marriages' written in bold lettering. Outside the venue stood a sign saying 'Gretna Green'. It seemed a far cry from the simplicity of the humble blacksmith's shop.

I pedalled towards the edge of the town, past the wedding shop, the wedding photographers, the wedding car hire centre, the wedding makeover shop, towards the first and last marriage rooms and the First and Last House in Scotland. Then, crossing the river, I reached the signpost welcoming me back to England.

I couldn't decide how I felt. I had cycled round an entire country and had spent 25 of the 36 days that I'd been on the road in Scotland. I would now have to leave this place that had shaped so much of my journey; so much had changed since I'd reached that sign that said 'Scotland welcomes you' 1,300 long miles ago, disorientated and exhausted. That little lost girl had been left behind. I had learnt to read the sky, the weather, the road, as well as the map. I now had an instinct for direction, an uncanny ability to pick out the blue NCN signs, even knowing if they were pointing the right way. I had gone from touring novice to confident traveller, the plains of the east and the mountains of the west having made me strong. I was able to demolish hills in minutes, riding 80 or 100 miles in a day without blinking. I had made friends with the road, had embraced my routine: eat, sleep, cycle.

And from not knowing much about Scotland, I felt that now I knew it intimately – the landscape, the changing sea, the countryside and the cities. I'd met some lovely people, made some friends and endured some really tough stretches of cycling. Every place I'd been through I'd said the name to myself in my dreadful attempt at a Scottish accent.

But now, here I was, back in England. Home. I wanted to climb from my bike and hug the tarmac.

Traffic zoomed northwards along the nearby M6 and I imagined the drivers sitting at the wheel, stony-faced and purposeful, all of them unaware of me and my journey. Would they feel the same significance as I did when they crossed the border? Would they even notice?

The constant traffic rumble grew steadily fainter as I approached Carlisle, skirting the edge of the city to reach the floodplains of the Solway Firth. Signs appeared beside the road warning of high tides and quicksands, counting down to disaster: 'If the water reaches this point it is 2 ft deep', 'If the water reaches this point it is 3 ft deep', etc.

This was where Hadrian's Wall had once stood, that famous line of stones marching from the Solway Firth through Cumbria and Northumberland to the east coast. I remembered those giant blue marine buoys that I'd seen in Tynemouth, marking the end of Hadrian's Cycleway. I must be level with Whitley Bay.

But here, there wasn't much of a wall to look at, instead a few uninspiring signposts marking out its path, inviting visitors to trail through boggy fields and across marshland in search of its remains. My romantic vision of cycling in its shadow had been thwarted by the passage of time.

Back across the firth, the land that I'd been racing through that morning receded into the distance. But here, as predicted, the wind was against me, so once I'd reached Bowness-on-Solway and found the words *Ave Terminum Callis Hadriani Augusti Pervenisti* ('The End of Hadrian's Wall path'), I took a shortcut to Silloth. The tide was high by the time I reached the coastal town and the weather had begun to deteriorate; the grey horizon had finally caught me, the sky dull and heavy. At the waterfront I watched waves crash against the steps, the brown water seething and frothing, barely able to see the mountains of Scotland through the haze. It was as if the clouds had drawn a curtain – the Scotland show was over. The morning's ride already seemed like another world. Since then I'd crossed a border, changed direction, and everything was different.

I stood at the top of the road to Allonby and sighed. '8 miles' the sign said. With such a fierce headwind, my average speed would be substantially reduced. Better let my host know what was going on. 'I'm just in Silloth,' I yelled into Nikki's answering machine, 'but you can probably hear that the wind is quite strong! So I'll be at least another hour.' I clambered on to the bike and set off.

A couple of miles along the road, the rain I'd been dreading began. I tucked my neck deep into the collar of my coat then managed a snivelly sob. It hadn't taken long for the glow of being back in England to disappear. I suddenly felt anger towards the weather. The Area of Outstanding Natural Beauty on the opposite coast in Northumberland had also been masked by rain, these two flanks of Britain leaving nothing in my memory but Outstanding Rainfall and Wind. I crouched low over my bike to stop the droplets from bashing into my face while I tried to ride in a straight line. A couple of times I almost ended up in the hedgerow and it took all of my concentration to keep from being blown into the path of the passing traffic.

After an hour of this, I arrived in Allonby, soaking wet and exhausted. I stopped in the middle of the tiny village trying to get my bearings, the rows of houses on either side of the road looking sorry for themselves in the downpour.

'Well done!' a man called as he hurried to his front door. 'I passed you down the road. You're doing well!' This cheered me up, and I knocked on Nikki's door smiling.

'There's a bath run for you,' she said as she opened the door. My smile widened. She bustled me into her home, her two dogs almost knocking me flat.

'Oh dear, sorry about this!' I said as a trail of mud and water followed me in.

'Don't worry about that,' she replied. 'The dogs bring in much worse! Now, would you like a tea? Or a brandy?!' I followed her into the kitchen, greeted by a delicious smell. 'Dinner's nearly ready. I've made you a veggie curry. I hope you like curry. This is Stuart,' she added as her husband came down the stairs.

'Hi, Anna,' he said as he extended his hand. 'Didn't look so nice out there this evening.'

'Go on then, get yourself in that bath before it gets cold,' Nikki said, opening a door to let loose a cloud of steam. 'Take your time!' she added as I quietly shut the door, the struggles of the day evaporating as effortlessly as the water from the bath.

I smiled as I caught snatches of their chatter. Like most of my hosts, Nikki was unknown to me apart from a brief exchange of emails. I imagined the conversation that had led to me being there:

Stuart: 'You've done what?'

Nikki: 'I've invited someone to stay in our house.'

'Who is she?'

'I don't know. She works for Sustrans. But I've never met her before.'

'You've never met her?'

'No.'

'But you've invited her to stay in our house?'

'Yes.'

'Well, what's she like?'

'I don't know.'

'Surely you've spoken to her?'

'No!' (cheerfully)

The hot water thawed out my fingers as I lay submerged among the bubbles, breathing in the steam in order to clear my blocked head, my mug of hot lemon balanced on the side, glad I wasn't trying to set up a tent on the rain-lashed coast. On a day like this, it was truly wonderful to arrive somewhere with a hot bath ready run, a hot meal waiting and new friends to be made.

DAY 38:
ALLONBY TO ULVERSTON

85 miles

'It really is a stunning stretch of coast up here,' Nikki and Stuart had told me the previous evening, trying to convince me that Cumbria deserved its Area of Outstanding Natural Beauty accolade. But as I stood on the beach that morning, I found it hard to believe – the sea looked so angry, the heavy clouds robbing the landscape of colour, both ends of the bay lost in the murk. 'You must visit again, when the weather is better,' Nikki had said as she'd waved me off, the wind plucking the cardigan from her shoulders. 'Ooh Anna, I don't envy you! It's howlin' a hoolie!' and with that she'd disappeared inside.

As I rode southwards I caught glimpses of what Nikki and Stuart meant: stone walls harbouring wild grasses from the wilder sea; beaches dotted with huge seaweed-covered slabs of rock; fleeting views of the water from beneath stone arches as the cycle route traced the railway line. But my head was down most of the time, bowed by the wind. I stopped at the Flimby Pie Shop, the door banging loudly on its hinges as the wind snatched it from my hand. 'I recommend the breakfast pie,' Nikki had said. 'It's a breakfast, in a pie!'

'One breakfast pie, please,' I said to the lady behind the counter.

'You're lucky there, lass,' she replied. 'It's my last one.'

I sank my teeth into the crumbling hot pastry, biting into sausage meat, scrambled eggs and beans all jumbled together inside. Delicious.

Soon the sprawling mess of the Sellafield power station emerged from between the hills, the fifth nuclear site I'd passed. The buildings scattered around the site looked tired and worn out, the place scruffy and chaotic, and as I drew steadily closer to the perimeter fence I held my breath; the very air seemed radioactive. It felt dangerous to be cycling in such close proximity, though a herd of goats grazing in the neighbouring field looked unfazed. I remembered having visited as a child, the visitors' centre extolling the benefits of nuclear power, and even at that young age I had the feeling they weren't telling the whole story. There'd been a fire there in 1957, and a leak in 2005, so I hoped that there wouldn't be another disaster while I was within range. I cycled a bit quicker after that.

Approaching Millom I stopped to look out to sea, seeing the Isle of Man for perhaps the last time, its profile having been a constant feature on the horizon for the several days that I'd been circling southwards from the Rhinns of Galloway. I would have been happy to stop riding there. It was 40 miles earlier that I'd waved goodbye to Nikki and it had been utterly draining to ride against the wind all day, fighting the gusts to keep my bike on track, unable to rely on downhills for respite. My throat hurt and my nose was running. But there were a further 45 miles to ride in order to get through all the Furnesses (Broughton, Kirkby, Askam, Lindal, Dalton and Barrow) to Ulverston where I was booked into the Walkers Hostel. After being glad the previous night that I'd arranged to stay with Nikki, I was now resentful of my timetable: it would be much easier just to head for the nearest B&B.

This was another section of coastline riddled with peninsulas and I was tempted to ride straight to Ulverston; I knew it would technically be cheating, to miss out a section of coast, though suffering the long way round when I was beginning to reach my limit wasn't very appealing. But I had long wanted to stand at Barrow-in-Furness at the foot of the peninsula and look across Morecambe Bay, that famously treacherous and immense body of water, knowing that the next day I would be doing the same from the opposite side.

Come on, Anna, stop moping, I told myself, setting off for the foot of the peninsula. *This is a coastal cycle. No cutting corners.*

But before long it began to rain and, dashing for shelter in Broughton-in-Furness, my resolve to go to Barrow began to fade. Now I was tired, ill and wet. I just wanted to be there so I could rest. I was sick of cycling, sick of the weather, sick of the hills. I set off up the hill out of Broughton, the road slippery in the downpour, unable to breathe properly through my bunged-up nose, and began to sob with self-pity.

I put my bike down and sat at the side of the road, head in hands. 'I – can't – do – it,' I gasped, my back heaving with big weeping breaths. I took out my phone and dialled Sarah's number, desperate for the comfort of speaking with my twin.

'Sarah,' I said, trying to control my voice. 'I'm ill and… I don't want to cycle any more. It's horrible… out here and it's… raining… and it's windy and… I can't… do it!'

'Oh, Anna! You poor thing. How much further is there to go?'

'To Ulverston, which is… about ten miles away, but there's a huge… pass between here and there which I don't want to cross, and I should really go… down to the bottom of the peninsula to Barrow to see Morecambe Bay.'

'Well, the best part of Barrow is the nature reserve, and it sounds like it will be getting dark by the time you get there so you wouldn't be able to see it anyway.' Sarah had been to college in Lancaster, so was familiar with this area. 'Why don't you head down as far as Dalton or something? That's part way down the peninsula so you'll still be able to look across the bay.'

'I suppose I could do that. But that would be cutting corners.'

'Well, not really. You can't possibly cycle every inch of the coast; you can only do what you can do. If you're not very well then there's no point in dragging yourself through it and making yourself so ill you can't continue.'

'I suppose so.'

'Honestly, try not to be so hard on yourself. You don't have to prove anything out there. No one will criticise you if you change your mind en route.'

'OK. I'll aim for Dalton.'

'Good idea. I hope it doesn't take too long and you get a good view across the bay. Call me if you need to!'

I instantly felt better, Sarah's reasoning coaxing me from my misery, and as the showers subsided I freewheeled down to Dalton-in-Furness and onwards to Bardsea where I could finally stand on the banks of Morecambe Bay.

I stood there in the twilight, watching the lights of the towns twinkling across the vast water as swans floated on its surface. The light was fading fast; each day that passed brought with it fewer cycling hours. By the time I reached the hostel in Ulverston it was 8 p.m., and dark. Summer was well and truly over.

DAY 39:
ULVERSTON TO LANCASTER

50 miles

At the top of a hill just outside the Walkers Hostel in Ulverston stands the replica of a lighthouse. I'd fought my way up the steep grassy slope, bike-free, and stood there at the top, looking. The 120 square miles of Morecambe Bay sat below, Morecambe and Heysham on its far side. I had been tempted to ride on one of the footpaths that cut across the bay, but I knew it was a bad idea; I had heard the tragic story of the cockle pickers who had been caught out by the racing tides and had drowned. The water shows no mercy to those who might play with it.

The bay was grey and murky on this overcast day, the view obscured by clouds that hung low from the sky, pregnant with rain. It seemed unfair; I'd been looking forward to reaching this point, looking forward to the novelty of circling such a huge bay where at each stage I could emerge at the waterfront and see where I'd come from and where I'd be going, learning how everything connected. But forcing myself down to Bardsea the previous evening now seemed a waste, as surely I wouldn't be able to see anything when I looked back across from the other side.

My cold had now developed to its worst point: my throat burnt with each breath, my head felt dizzy, my sensitive skin shivered uncontrollably one minute and poured with sweat the next. I decided that enough was enough – taking the direct road to Lancaster would cut off the whole of Morecambe Bay, but I didn't care.

I managed five minutes on the A road among the spray kicked up by lorries before I headed for a more sheltered route. There was no way I was going to follow that road for 37 miles. I'd rather take the long way round. I ducked down a woodland track, emerging next to a river which bulged with the recent downpour. The rush of water replaced the rush of traffic and the twitter of birdsong replaced the roar of engines, the blustery wind all but disappearing now I was off the exposed tarmac. This was much preferable. For a couple of hours I meandered through villages, slate roofs shining with drizzle, the thick ceiling of trees providing enough shelter that I needn't worry about being out under a downpour.

At Grange-over-Sands I descended to the banks of the bay, between grey stone buildings that lined the road, doorways hung with ivy and front gardens spilling over with pink hydrangeas. I had already cycled 37 miles. If I'd followed that main road I would be there. But I would much rather be here, in this village, eating Kendal Mint Cake and watching the world go by.

I continued through Arnside and towards Silverdale, every so often emerging at the water's edge, trying to glimpse Ulverston and even Barrow, but the clouds were stubborn, the bay almost featureless at high tide, the grey water stretching endlessly into the distance. Then at Carnforth, I joined the Lancaster–Morecambe canal, and as I heaved my bike up to the elevated towpath, the clouds scattered and the sun emerged. Glimpses of the bay appeared between rooftops as I sailed past the villages on the way to Morecambe, with only herons and narrowboats for company.

The canal eventually delivered me to the front where I was able at last to look across Morecambe Bay in its entirety. The tide had beat its rapid retreat and the bay, full the last time I'd looked, was completely drained. It seemed impossible that all of that water could have disappeared so quickly, leaving behind an immense saucer of sand. But instead of the lacklustre pit that I had expected, it was a vibrant collection of hues: silver veins of channels meandering through the rich brown, patches of seaweed and grasses springing from its surface, and scarlet hulls of boats lying aslant under the now blue sky.

I could clearly see the towns I'd cycled through that day – Arnside, Grange, Silverdale, even Bardsea – and I gazed across, the mountains of the Lake District as distinct on the horizon as when I'd looked in their direction from across the Scottish border. I wondered which peak was which, hoping that there might be a skyline map on the seafront to tell me. Then I saw it – and what a skyline map! Not content with a drawing, Morecambe Council had placed a huge metal silhouette on the waterfront, almost as tall as me, every crag and settlement labelled on its bright copper surface. I laughed in surprise. I sat for a few minutes on the waterfront, looking at where I'd been, glowing with the satisfaction that I'd stuck it out and made it round the bay.

From there, I headed for Lancaster along NCN 69, a disused railway line, the Way of the Roses. I'd ridden that line years ago with Sarah, so for once I knew exactly where I was going. As I neared the town, the sights that had been so familiar during Sarah's student years emerged: the Millennium bridge, the Water Witch where we used to drink, the green dome of the Ashton Memorial high on the hill, and the castle, all peeping from within a sea of sand-coloured buildings. I'd visited her frequently from my own university town of Manchester, and to be somewhere so familiar, and to be staying with a close friend's mum, was a comfort to my tired, aching, ill body. I couldn't wait to take the next day off and I fully intended to spend most of it in bed.

DAY 41:
LANCASTER TO TARLETON

54 miles

It's amazing how much the weather can dictate one's mood. At no time did I feel this more keenly than the day I cycled from Lancaster to Preston with Richard.

Richard had contacted me via Twitter and we'd met for the first time the previous day. I'd spent most of that day sipping hot lemon, recovering from my cold, but had ventured into the town as my bike needed some minor repairs: the three-week-old rear wheel could do with some attention, having done over 1,000 miles in its short life, and I wanted to treat Randy to a new rear tyre, hoping I could uphold my zero-puncture record.

Leaving the wheel in the shop, I walked to the coffee house where Richard and I had arranged to meet.

'You must be Anna,' a tall, bearded man said as I wandered in, his smile broad and friendly.

'Yes!' I said, surprised, shaking his proffered hand, wondering if I looked that much of a cyclist even without my bike.

'Your photograph is on your blog,' he explained, eyes twinkling. 'I'm very much enjoying reading it. How do you find the time to write every evening?'

I smiled and sat down at the table. 'I often don't have the energy, in truth; I tend to catch up on my rest days.'

'Well, I certainly am enjoying it. I was shivering with you when I read your account of near-hypothermia in western Scotland. And hats off for that journey south from Oban – averaging fifteen miles per hour is hard enough with an unladen bike. With sixteen kilograms of luggage, headwind and hills, it's amazing!'

'Thank you!'

The blog, though sometimes a pain to keep up with, was proving to be a great idea. Through it I could keep family and friends updated with my progress, and I'd had many supportive messages from readers who'd stumbled upon it.

'Some say they wish they could do something like this too. That I'm living their dream! Which I think is lovely, but it's not as if I'm going round the world or anything,' I said.

'But that's one of the great things about this ride, Anna,' Richard replied. 'It's so accessible. It's *because* you're not going round the world that people have taken such an interest. This adventure means something – it's easy to relate to. You are undertaking an extraordinary journey in a place that is quite ordinary. People can read about this and think, "Maybe I could do that! Perhaps not all in one go, but even a small part of it."'

We whiled away the time, sharing cycling stories and discovering a common tendency to always be a bit late, never early. I'm always rushing to the next thing, squeezing too much in, panicking because I won't make it on time but not having left earlier because that was time well spent doing something else. It was hilarious to meet someone exactly the same.

'My partner Jennie is permanently frustrated with me. She'll amble down to the station if we're going somewhere, ready at least fifteen minutes before the train leaves, then I'll arrive just as the doors are closing and collapse panting into my seat! It must drive her to distraction!'

It was soon time for Richard to head home. 'I'll see you tomorrow,' he said. 'It looks to be a bit unsettled but quite warm. Let's hope we don't get a soaking!'

I bid him goodbye and set off to collect my wheel from the shop. I teased the owner that I'd be suing him if I had a puncture on this new tyre, then discovered that Richard had already picked up the bill. What terrific kindness.

The next morning, Richard was (typically) a couple of minutes late and I was (typically) not yet ready.

The day had started with a mugginess in the air, bright enough for sunglasses and warm enough for my thinnest cycling top. We cycled south from Lancaster alongside the marshes that line the River Lune, after 20 minutes or so almost unbearably hot, and we welcomed the light shower that came shortly afterwards. We made our way towards Knott End from where we would take a ferry across the River Wyre, the air calm, the sun bright, the landscape flat as far as the eye could see. The Lancashire plains were a marked contrast to the relentless lumpiness of western Scotland; I had almost forgotten what it was like for a vista to stretch unbroken into the distance.

At the ferry slipway I stopped to look across the sands of Morecambe Bay for the final time, the curved hook of Walney Island guarding its opposite entrance, the immense brown basin exposed by the low tide dotted with puddles of blue. Despite the sunshine, the clouds were closing in, the wind whipping up the water of the Wyre, making the short river crossing choppy. I gulped at the threatening downpour as we approached Fleetwood, hoping I wouldn't need a mac.

We disembarked, the sky now completely covered in clouds. Kite flyers stood on the vast beach, their toys dancing on the strong current, meaning only one thing. A great day for kite flying was not a good one for cyclists. And sure enough, as we turned the corner on the shoulder of the peninsula, the wind smacked in our faces, instantly slowing our progress.

Blackpool Tower stood tall in the distance ahead, growing no nearer even as we pushed hard towards it. The wind was blowing away the sunny mood of the morning with each gust. Every turn of the pedals became more frustrating, keeping up a conversation nigh on impossible, our eyes glued to the path, trying to avoid being blown off course, the views out to sea across the vast sand going unnoticed.

I grimaced. This was my least favourite type of weather. With rain you can wear waterproofs, with cold you can wrap up warm, with sunshine you can remove layers, but with wind, you can do nothing.

Without warning, it started pouring. Hard. Visibility went from good to zero in a matter of minutes and water started seeping into my socks. 'Ugh!' I squealed as Blackpool Tower became swallowed up, the long promenade disappearing behind sheets of rain. It was a brief squall and we laughed nervously as we reached the attractions, completely soaking wet. We rode along quiet pavements that should have been crowded, past outdoor seating that was unoccupied, passing Crystal Gazer palm readings and nightclubs, fish and chips and candyfloss shops, and places selling Blackpool Rock. An empty seafront train rolled past the flashing lights of an amusement arcade.

It wasn't long before another squall came through, drumming angry, beating rain on the promenade, the kind of rain that when you think it can't possibly rain any harder, it does. We dashed towards the Central Pier, joining several others who were already sheltering underneath.

'How about some chocolate to cheer us up while we wait?' Richard said. We devoured the chocolate. We waited. And waited. But there was no sign of a let-up, and the pier offered little shelter against the sheets of water that were blowing sideways along the seafront, so we emerged on to the sea wall, gritting our teeth.

A few people were out for the day despite the weather, determinedly screaming on the Big One and licking their ice creams under their umbrellas. Richard remarked about their stoicism and I harrumphed; I was in a poor mood, unwilling to chat, just wanting to get my head down and get on with it.

'You don't think so?' he asked.

'No, it's just bloody raining!' I retorted.

I felt bad for snapping, but the rain had drained me of all humour and my temper was short. The sunshine of the morning felt like an age ago as we wrestled onwards, the squall coming straight at us. That seafront cycle track was 13 miles long. It felt like a hundred.

Eventually we reached the mouth of the River Ribble at Lytham St Anne's and the track turned east, taking us out of the headwind. And once more, the day transformed: the rain stopped, the wind eased and a rainbow shone bright above Preston. We brought our bikes to a halt in order to gaze, our heads no longer bowed by the rain, our eyes no longer screwed up against the wind. It was as if we'd emerged from a dream, shaking our heads, realising that it was all OK. A couple strolled hand in hand along the shores of the river in the sunshine that peeped through the rapidly scattering clouds. Across the river lay Southport, Liverpool and, beyond, the hills of Wales. We stood still for several minutes, our earlier frenzy replaced by a deep calm. I regretted my outburst. It all felt trivial now.

We followed the gradually narrowing river towards Preston, along new waterside developments, over the lock gates and towards the marina, away from the city traffic. The sky was blue, the air warm. Had we really fought so hard to get here? Sheltering under that pier seemed like a distant memory.

'What a day!' Richard said as we reached the end of the cycle track and returned to the road. From here, he would head back to Lancaster by train, a mere 15 minutes away. 'Do you have much further to go?'

'About ten miles I think. I'm staying in Tarleton with a colleague; it's straight along the main road which will be quick.'

'Good. Thank you for asking me to accompany me today; it's been a privilege to share part of your journey.'

I suddenly felt embarrassed – Richard had been smiling all day, relentlessly cheerful and optimistic, patient with me even though I had let the weather affect me so deeply. 'I'm sorry you didn't see my best side.'

'Not at all,' he replied. 'I picked up on your frustration once or twice, but never felt it was directed at me. You've had quite a battle over the past few days, including with illness. I quite understand.'

I'd let the mask slip, allowed someone to see a side of which I wasn't proud. According to the outside world, I was having the adventure of a lifetime, the highs recounted on my blog and the lows glossed over in order to keep my audience entertained. But Richard was no longer just an observer; he now had an insider's view, had seen the ride for what it was, warts and all.

DAY 42:
TARLETON TO WEST KIRBY

56 miles

For the fourth day in a row I was heading into the wind, and I was beginning to fear I'd be battling it all the way to Land's End. Groups of cyclists came zooming along in the opposite direction; I was jealous of their easy speed, wondering where they'd all suddenly come from – I didn't usually see so many. But then I realised it was a Sunday, when a nation of MAMILs (middle-aged men in Lycra) rises from bed, gives their wife a kiss and sets off into the wild. We exchanged cautious smiles.

The immense beach at Southport soon emerged and I turned inland towards the station; today, I'd be riding with my eldest sister Becca, her husband Lenny and their two children, Lara and Oliver. It was a tentative plan made months ago, before I'd set out, when none of this had seemed real; it had been impossible to imagine that I would reach this point on this date. But here I was, waiting on the platform as their train rolled in and my niece and nephew ran to greet me, arms outstretched.

The wind charged across the wide flat beach and we soldiered along the wide flat tarmac, our eyes screwed up and the collars of our coats flapping. The children quickly became cold in their child seats, staring mutely into their parents backs. It was no fun for any of us.

Becca called something over her shoulder.

'What?' I said, no chance of being able to hear her over the wind.

'I said, shall we stop for lunch? There's a nice part of the beach at Ainsdale that we could go to.'

We rode on to the sand and settled in among the dunes, hoping they would provide shelter. But the sand was flighty, quickly filling the lunch bag, so we hurried to finish our flapjacks before they became covered in grit. White foaming waves rushed to the shore and lifeguard's flags were almost torn from their poles. Even the seagulls had given up attempting to fly and sat static on the beach, unable to move.

We'd planned to continue to follow the Sefton cycle track through Formby and Crosby, following the wide sandy beaches that line the Lancashire coast, but the wind was proving too much, so we retreated inland in search of shelter, following the NCN 62 along a disused railway line. Beneath the leaves we could at last chatter without shouting, the children happier to be away from the chilling gusts. But returning to the blustery seafront was unavoidable if we wanted to see the Antony Gormley statues, the one hundred identical cast-iron men staring out to the horizon from the beach, silent and pondering. The figures stretched endlessly into Liverpool Bay, the water covering the heads of the most distant, others half-submerged, while the closest stood exposed on their plinths.

I was determined that I should have a photograph taken with one of them – I would join the figure in his endless gaze, he now the cyclist with my helmet on his head and my bike at his side. I wheeled Randy across the sand towards the nearest statue, dragging him through troughs of seawater as we approached; the installation had been in place for several years, the sand shifting over time so that great wells had gathered at the base of the plinths, which now protruded far above the beach. Randy's handlebars barely reached the man's iron kneecap, the rear wheel half-sunk in salty water. I jumped to place my helmet on the man's head, and it sat there, lopsided, as he maintained his sightless gaze. Becca took the photograph. It didn't look anything like I thought it would.

Leaving the seafront once more, we joined the Leeds–Liverpool canal, once transporting coal and textiles to and from cities across the Pennines, now largely forgotten about apart from by the city's youth, the water filled with plastic bottles and shopping trolleys. Mallard ducks sat on the edge of the path, diving warily into the water as we approached. The houses that backed on to the canal became more closely crowded, the graffiti more frequent as we approached the city centre.

Then there it was, the Liverpool skyline with its two cathedrals crowning the hill, the bronzed square tower of the Church of England at one end standing tall and majestic, the crown-like spikes of her Roman Catholic neighbour at the other. We made our way past the domed town hall, between the tall Georgian buildings that line the streets, the docks emerging as we descended towards the waterfront, arriving at the river where the Liver Building and the Cunard Building and the Port of Liverpool Building stood. We stopped at the water's edge, the paved Pier Head clean and spacious, a far cry from the smut of the industrial era that once made Liverpool among the busiest docks in the world.

'Can you take our picture?' we asked a passing man, laughing into the camera as the wind tugged at our hair.

'Thanks for coming today. I've had a really lovely time,' I said to Becca and Lenny as I hugged them both in turn.

'You're doing well,' Lenny replied. 'Good luck with the next few weeks.'

As Becca and her family turned for the station I stood looking across the Mersey, the river wide and grey, surging with the tide. The Mersey Ferry would depart from the jetty just a few metres away, but I had decided against taking it, the Sunday timetable making it a long and expensive journey. Instead, I turned to get the train, under the river, from James Street to Birkenhead.

As I sat on the train, travelling only one stop, I felt that crossing the river by boat would have been more appropriate. That was how I usually crossed rivers, on a vessel that would go no further. But on the railway line, all the destinations were laid out in front of me, including my final stopping point that day – I could be there in ten minutes if I just remained on the train. Or I could be in Wales by the evening. I felt as if I were cheating, conventional transport too 'normal' for my adventure, suddenly desperate to feel connected with my surroundings once more, relieved when I emerged above ground on the opposite shore. The Liverpool skyline stood across the water in an endless panorama of cranes and docks and cathedrals and skyscrapers and warehouses, the ground solid beneath my feet. And even though the remaining miles around the wind-lashed Wirral Peninsula would make me curse, the gusts tearing across my path, this is what I preferred, to feel the land beneath my wheels and follow the road as it unfolded ahead, inch by inch, mile by mile.

DAY 43:
WEST KIRBY TO BANGOR

76 miles

The mountains of North Wales had been drawing ever closer since I'd glimpsed them just south of Blackpool and today I would cross my third border, another new country waiting to be discovered. I knew even less about Wales than I had about Scotland, despite being part Welsh myself – my father's parents were from South Wales and both Welsh speakers. As a child I'd climbed Snowdon and spent family holidays in Anglesey, the photograph of the four sisters and my mother standing in front of the Llanfairpwllgwyngyllgogerychwyrndrobwllllanty-siliogogogoch railway station sign as faded as my recollection of it. These were now abstract events, old memories, ready to be replaced with new.

A river delineated what had once been the border between the two countries and I paused on the magnificent Flint Bridge as it flowed beneath, the third River Dee of the trip, the name taken from the Latin for 'goddess', which showed how important these waters had been to our ancestors. Another bridge took me over a dual carriageway and I found myself looking down on a huge dragon chalked on to the wide verge below, the national symbol of its neighbour, a lion, mirroring it on the opposite side. Another roundabout, then the long awaited 'Welcome to Wales' sign – *Croeso i Gymru* – with its bright red dragon. I pulled over to the central reservation, ignoring car horns, to take a photo of my bike resting in front of it. My Welsh aunt had told me that there used to be another sign here that said 'Land of 473 castles and 7 Starbucks'. What a splendid country.

Everything was instantly Welsh, bilingual road signs making this new country feel refreshingly foreign. Away from the rush of industry I rode, towards Flint and the first of those 473 castles. The ruined walls stood desolate on the edge of the marshland whose flooding waters would once have filled the moat, with the stones of the towers and keep crumbling on to the neatly groomed lawn. This was the first in an 'iron ring' of fortresses that King Edward I had built to quell the natives, forcing them into submission, his continued battles against the Welsh princes resulting in the building of eight gigantic castles and in him stealing the title 'Prince of Wales' for his own son. The sheer number of castles was testament to how much invading they'd suffered at the hands of their bullying neighbour.

From Prestatyn to Bangor I would follow NCN 5, the cycle path running traffic-free all along the coast. I'd looked at the map often enough, picturing myself hidden among the dunes or cruising along the wide path, sometimes separated from the waves by a wall, sometimes with nothing but a concrete slope leading to the sea. Now I was on those very tracks that I'd visualised, the route beautifully flat, the mountains inland the perfect backdrop, as close to the sea as I could possibly be. It was exactly as I had imagined. Except for the wind. The gale that I'd been grappling with for the past five days had increased in intensity; this was by far the windiest day since the trip had begun. But I felt that I'd made my peace with it, spent so long fighting it now that it seemed pointless to resist. No amount of pushing at the pedals would make me go any faster. I sent a text to my next hosts, Sally and Martyn, relatives of mine: 'Just arrived in Prestatyn. V windy. I'll be with you by 5 or 6 I hope.' This would give me six hours to ride the 45 miles to their house. No problem.

Five miles later I was exhausted. *Only 40 miles to go*, I told myself, regaining some strength as I ate my sandwich. The waves flew high into the air as they hit the sea wall.

'Windy day for a cycle ride, isn't it? Where are you off to, then?' a man asked as he walked past along the seafront.

'I'm going to Bangor,' I replied.

'You'd be better off going that way,' he said, pointing to the adjacent main road. 'The sand is blowing up over the path along here.'

'Thanks,' I said. 'I'm sure I'll be OK.'

'Well then, just be careful,' he said as he walked away.

It was more stubbornness than anything – I was accustomed to passers-by telling me I couldn't do it, so as usual I would go the way I'd planned.

But he was right. I turned the corner and instantly got a face full of sand, the grains being snatched from the beach and tossed into the air, and I had to breathe through my nose to avoid getting any in my mouth. I skidded through the patches that had collected on the path until the beach gave way to rocks and I could breathe easy again. What a struggle! I hoped there wouldn't be many more parts like that. Out at sea the spray leapt from the crests of waves, the sun shining nonchalantly above. Along the shore a line of Welsh flags flapped frantically.

Around the next headland stretched the Victorian resort of Llandudno where tall, gabled buildings fronted with big bay windows and ornate plasterwork stood shoulder to shoulder in long, elegant terraces, the sand-lined promenade extending at their feet. Stretching out over the water was the intricate iron pier, and I paused near to it to watch the waves, clouds racing across the sky above. It had taken three and a half hours of trudging to travel a mere 20 miles.

The bay was sheltered on one side by the rocky promontory of Little Orme, and on the other the immense Great Orme's Head, around which the coastal road spiralled. I started the climb. Halfway up, a passer-by warned me about the wind. 'Be careful when you get to the other side. It's like hitting a brick wall,' he said. This time, I was willing to believe it. The sea was far below but I could hear it crashing against the rocks, the spray being carried right up to where I was, the road engulfed in the haze.

As I turned the corner at the tip of the headland I was brought to an abrupt standstill. Randy's front wheel was blown to the side, then he pivoted right round on his back wheel and crashed to the ground, knocking the skin off my shin with a pedal as he fell. I took a sharp intake of breath as blood sprang to the surface, knowing that I'd have a deep bruise to account for my troubles. I stooped to pick him up, struggling against the weight of the bags and the wind in order to get him upright, but it wasn't long before he was on the floor again, this time taking me with him.

I sat there in the middle of the road wondering what to do as the wind tried to steal my helmet. A car stopped and the passenger wound down the window to ask if I was OK – at least I think that's what he said, as I couldn't hear a word over the howling wind. It took three of us to push the bike round a corner to where the wind was less strong so I could remount. I stood still, regaining my breath and gathering myself before attempting to ride once more. *This is impossible!* I thought. Using the shelter of the rock to gain some speed before the winding road became exposed once more to the gusts, I gritted my teeth and fought to reach the bottom, my knuckles white from gripping the bars, blinking back tears of frustration as I arrived there, exhausted by the psychological battle of having to pedal downhill.

The cycle route wove through the dunes along the edge of the estuary; it could have been a beautiful ride, but today it was bitter, great clouds of sand billowing around me, stinging my bleeding leg and flying into my eyes.

My cycle path ended abruptly, buried under a dune. The wind must have been shifting the sand for hours until it completely covered the route. Tyre tracks led the way, thick, sturdy mountain bike tyres. But mine were too thin for sand. I climbed from the bike and half pushed, half carried it, my feet sinking deep into the drifts, constantly stumbling in the gusts. I was on the verge of tears, desperate for the end of the path, half-frantic by the time the shoreline turned into the river mouth, where rocks replaced sand and my cycle path re-emerged.

I paused for a moment to steady my breath and look over to where Conwy stood on the other side of the river, the view dominated by the eight brooding towers of King Edward's castle. Ghost-like sounds floated across the water as the wind screamed through the rigging of the moored boats, ropes banging against masts like rattling chains. There were 18 miles remaining. Judging by the day's progress it would take a further three hours to reach Bangor. It was already 5 p.m., the time I'd suggested I might arrive. I texted Sally again: 'Taking much longer than hoped! Approaching Conwy now', then set off towards the bridge.

Conwy was a charming place, quiet and understated even with the massive presence of the castle, the tiny timber-framed buildings tucked into the town walls, one claiming to be the smallest house in Britain with just a single room upstairs and downstairs. I cycled in the shelter of the walls for a while, then returned to the cycle route.

Once more the route wound among the dunes, the wind now roaring through the grasses, hurling sand into the air to batter against my face. I no longer felt as magnanimous towards the wind as I had when starting out on this stretch over five hours before. My eyes stung, my leg was sore and I was rapidly losing energy. My strength ebbed with every turn of the pedals, the sand absorbing all my forward momentum, and I couldn't help crying as I kept going into what now felt like a full-blown sandstorm.

I fought my way through the drifts, freely sobbing, eventually finding a bridge over the railway that would take me back on to tarmac. But it led directly to the North Wales Expressway, the road roaring with trucks and HGVs, a low barrier all that kept me separated from the traffic. The wind gusted against me, pushing me again and again into the metal railings.

My nerves were in shreds as the traffic pounded by. At last the road disappeared into a tunnel, my cycle path heading around the outside of the cliff, but as I rounded the corner, I was stopped dead by the wind. My feet couldn't physically push into it as it beat against my bike and ripped at my clothes. It was all I could do to hold on to the railings. I tried to continue, refusing to give up, but each time I managed only a couple of pedals before I found myself clutching at the railings again. Randy was blown to the floor and I sat down a few yards away, tears of frustration and exhaustion soaking my cheeks.

I was torn: part of me wanted desperately to keep trying, to keep moving forwards on the bike, while the other part of me was reluctantly admitting that the wind was too strong, and

I would have to stop. I sat there, head in hands, as the wind howled round me.

Just then an enormous gust lifted Randy up and pushed him along the ground, striking my turned back. It was as if the wind were telling me to give up, using my own bike as a weapon. That settled it. I just couldn't keep going.

With no hope now of being able to get to my destination by bicycle, I composed myself and hauled Randy upright, turning back towards the centre of the town that I'd been fighting to leave for over an hour. The wind was now behind me, propelling me back along the narrow pavement at a terrifying 28 mph.

It took less than ten minutes to reach the town, its castle and tiny buildings utterly failing to impress me the second time round. All I wanted was to leave. But a 90-minute wait at the train station would have been too much; I called Sally, trying not to alarm her with my sobs, saying 'I'm OK,' as soon as she answered, but sounding anything but as I explained the situation.

'Oh, Anna!' she said. 'That sounds horrendous. Sit tight – Martyn will come and collect you right away. Go and get yourself a cup of tea.'

I found a corner shop with a tea machine, gratefully sipping the pale grey liquid. It was a pretty terrible cup but I didn't care, desperate for anything that might cheer me up as I waited outside the station for Martyn. I must have looked a complete mess – hair full of sand, tear-stained face, bloody leg. I was utterly deflated, desperately upset at having been beaten, but there was simply no way I could cycle against that wind.

Soon Martyn appeared and gave me a hug before picking up my bike and putting it in the boot of his car.

'What a day you've had!'

'Yes,' I replied, smiling wanly, hoping I didn't look as bad as I felt.

'Sally and I were amazed that you were even attempting to ride. But your texts kept coming in so we knew you were doing all right. It's impressive that you got this far!'

'It wasn't too bad up until Llandudno. It was after that that the wind really got the better of me.' I clambered into the front seat, apologising as the sand from my shoes coated the carpet in the footwell.

'Oh, don't worry about that. We can beat it out tomorrow.'

With the door shut, the sound of the wind was blocked out. It was the first absolute quiet I'd experienced all day. I absent-mindedly scratched my ear.

'I have sand inside my ears!' I exclaimed.

Martyn chuckled. 'It's not far to Bangor now. You'll be able to have a shower and get cleaned up. Sally has said you should stay for another night – the wind is forecast to be strong tomorrow as well.'

Even inside the car we could feel the gusting wind. In a matter of minutes we passed the point where I'd abandoned my journey and we finally left Conwy behind. Twenty minutes later we arrived in Bangor, the sky turning a deep red as we approached.

It was such a shame, but I couldn't have made those last miles on a bike. I had managed over 70 miles and I'd had one hell of a day. And I didn't mind at all that I was doing the last 15 miles in a car. There's hardy, then there's foolhardy; sometimes the elements get the better of you and they certainly had me.

DAY 45:
BANGOR TO CRICCIETH

78 miles

It took two days for the wind to drop sufficiently to continue. I'd never experienced such conditions! It wasn't until I had settled down with my laptop that I found out why: this was the tail end of Hurricane Katia, a tropical storm that had swept across the Atlantic from the USA. The winds that I'd been struggling against since Allonby had merely been a prelude to the storm that reached the UK on the very day I chose to head due west, straight into it. The top recorded wind speed had been 81 mph in Capel Curig, just 16 miles from where I had been riding. No wonder I had struggled. I later heard that the Tour of Britain riders had postponed their day stage because of the awful weather. Knowing that professional cyclists hadn't even attempted to ride made me feel better about having given up. It had taken over an hour to get the clogged-up sand out of poor Randy's chain, and almost as long to wash the beach from my hair. Riding for a full day in a sandstorm had been good for neither of us and I was picking grains from the bike for weeks afterwards.

From Bangor I headed west along a dismantled railway line, the island of Anglesey a stone's throw across the Menai Strait, emerging from the seclusion of the trees at the royal port of Caernarfon. Rows of yachts sat in the marina, the forest of masts standing straight and tall, jack stays and sail spreaders extending like bare branches. Behind the marina sat the magnificent castle, another of Edward I's, its walls extending to enclose the whole town, this bastide style of building typical of the king. Cobbled streets disappeared upwards from under small stone arches so, to save my wheels, I continued to follow the wide walkway around the outside of the walls, trying not to notice the '*Dim Beicio*' ('No cycling') signs. A high-pitched alarm began to wail and I jumped, worried that I'd been caught flouting the laws. But it was only the swing bridge opening to let through a leisure boat with its gaggle of tourists, and once the bridge had closed again I could cross it, turning back to get a full view of the castle. And what a castle, its angular towers strong and magnificent, turrets piled on top of one another, huge and impressive against the sky.

From there I left the cycle route to join the Llŷn Coastal Path, which followed the edge of the peninsula, the ancient pilgrims' route terminating at the turtle-like Bardsey Island. The roads were quiet, the mountains of Snowdonia rising steeply inland, the mudflats of the Menai estuary melting into the Irish Sea. A steep incline brought me suddenly into the hills, and from there I meandered along the top of the peninsula, past churchyards filled with Celtic crosses and fields of sheep, looking from a distance like the white scattering of petals on the hillside.

The deeper into the country I went, the more the Welsh language began to dominate; instead of saying 'Slow/*Araf*' (an 'f' in Welsh is pronounced as a 'v', so this would be 'arav') on the road, it would say '*Araf*/Slow'. The bilingual system had been in place since the early 1990s, giving the Welsh and English languages equal status for the first time since the language laws of the 1500s made it illegal to speak Welsh in the public courts. Children were even given a beating if heard speaking Welsh at school. But now, I was in the heart of a region of Welsh speakers, the chatter of Welsh in village bakeries making me feel delightfully out of place. It looked a confusing language – all those consonants plonked together in unfamiliar combinations. A billboard outside a farm advertising 'Tatws Newydd' made me laugh out loud. I could work that one out – pronounced 'tattus newith' – new potatoes.

I'd reached Aberdaron at the pointed tip of the peninsula, where Mynydd Mawr (pronounced 'munith mower' – 'big mountain') stood, blocking my view of the ocean. Its 155 metres made me stop for a minute, unconvinced that I wanted to climb it. I was close enough to the end of the peninsula to turn around and head back along its southern side, surely? After pondering for a while, I saw a cyclist emerge from the top, which was the incentive I needed. I fairly sprinted to the top, the gradient nothing for my hill-climber legs. What a view! The Irish Sea stretched for miles, Anglesey on the horizon one way, Cardigan Bay on the other, Bardsey Island floating a few hundred metres away.

I stood still, waiting for my heavy breathing to abate, glad I'd made the climb, feeling on top of the world. The hurricane was over; now I could really start to enjoy being in Wales. I turned to look inland, the scattered villages minuscule from this height, the hills rich and green and blushed with heather, their tops tumbling with scree. My shadow stretched before me in the early evening sun, the peaks of Snowdonia scraping the sky in the distance. I started on the journey back towards the southern side of the peninsula and Criccieth.

But as I passed back through Aberdaron, things began to change. It was a longer ride than I had realised; already 6 p.m., I had over 20 miles remaining and the wind that I'd been riding against all day had mysteriously disappeared, just when I needed it to speed me towards my destination. As I pushed hard to summit a hill, I felt something ping in the back of my ankle and a jolt of pain shoot through the tendon.

This was not a good sign. I would have thought that by this point I'd be so accustomed to riding, I'd be beyond injury. I had been so careful to rest properly and not do too much too soon; I'd strained tendons before and I knew that this kind of injury could mean a premature end to my adventure.

I tried not to put too much pressure on it as I rode eastwards, letting the other leg do all the work, willing the hills to disappear so that I could take it easy. But the terrain wouldn't let up, each contour magnified by the pain. Six miles shy of Criccieth, I caught the eye of an old lady riding towards me.

'I'm Doreen,' she said, stopping in my path.

'Oh! Hello,' I replied, drawing to a halt. Doreen was my host for the evening.

'I knew you'd be coming along here so I was sure I'd see you. How are you getting on?'

'My heel has really started to hurt,' I replied. 'Do you mind if we cycle slowly?'

'Not at all,' she said. 'It's an easy ride back to my house.'

We followed the cycle path alongside the main road, mercifully flat and wide enough to ride two abreast, chatting as we rode, the conversation distracting me from my growing discomfort.

'We ride along here with the club sometimes,' she said. 'We call it the coffee and cake club – most of the people who join us are of the older generation, you know? They want an easy ride to a tea shop and to get out a bit on their bikes. It's not hard but it's great fun. I do a bit of long-distance riding too, to keep my hand in. Not bad given that I'm seventy-five!'

Soon we were approaching Criccieth, the sign '*Traeth*/Beach' pointing down a side road. 'Would you like to see the castle?' Doreen asked. 'It's a bit of a detour.'

'Yes, please,' I replied; despite the heel pain I wanted to add this to my castle collection. We looped round towards the seafront along Heol Castell (Castle Street), where the ruins of the Edwardian fortress lay at the top of the rock, the two-towered gatehouse still standing strong. It was then a near vertical ascent to Doreen's house, and I followed carefully behind, wishing I could get off and push, but not able to admit this to a lady who was more than twice my age.

Later, from my bedroom window, I looked down upon the floodlit castle ruins, the long curving line of Cardigan Bay stretching out beyond. Clusters of lights punctuated the coastline, each of the towns that I would be passing through over the next few days sparkling in the midst of a vast blackness. I was looking forward to reaching them and hoped that a good night's sleep would be rest enough for my aching heel.

DAY 46:
CRICCIETH TO ABERDYFI

47 miles

I awoke stiff as a board. Struggling to get out of bed, I began to worry seriously about my heel. The Achilles tendon felt swollen and tender; even climbing the stairs hurt and if it continued to worsen I'd never make it up the Cornish hills in a couple of weeks' time. As with any other type of strain, the only way I'd get better was to rest.

But I was reluctant to add days to my itinerary, hoping that if I cycled gently and tried not to push too hard with that leg, it would mend – not the easiest thing to do in the Welsh hills.

I tried to put it out of my mind as I rode away from Criccieth, stopping in a bakery in Porthmadog to buy myself some Welsh cakes. Clutching the packet in my hand I wheeled my bike up the street, pausing to eat them on the bridge over the river. Mountains rose inland and a polished red steam engine puffed and whistled as it waited to depart along the Welsh Highland Railway. I could hardly contain myself as I ripped open the cellophane – Welsh cakes in Wales! What a treat. I bit into the soft fruity scone. It wasn't a patch on my Welsh grandmother's.

Disappointed, I continued, becoming more and more despondent. Was this really the result of a bad packet of Welsh cakes? I suddenly had no interest in anything, not the castle at Harlech, not the outline of the Llŷn Peninsula that sat like a crested monster ever shrinking into the sea behind, not the hilltop views over sand dunes, not the endless sea. The things that I loved about my coastal trip were in abundance, but they were no longer working their magic.

Riding had suddenly become a physical struggle. How could it be that I had summited the Bealach na Bà, broken a century twice, and was only now suffering? My heel hurt more with each hill, my wrist had developed a strain from constantly shifting through the gears, and a large red welt had appeared at the very top of my inside thigh. After 2,600 miles and 46 days, my body was starting to complain. Vaseline and plasters were small relief.

Despite my earlier optimism about the hurricane being over, the tail end of it lingered, a constant headwind sapping my energy and my motivation. 'Go away, wind! Haven't I dealt with you enough already?' I shouted more than once. I wished I could allow myself to cast aside my carefully laid plans and take a few days off. But I'd had the guts to start this thing in the first place, I'd cycled through illness and near-hypothermia and hurricanes, everyone I'd met had applauded my adventurousness, my gumption and my determination, and I didn't want to give up my planned route and accommodation. Stubbornness and foolishness prevented me from admitting that I should stop and rest. No one would mind if I did, but onwards I struggled.

Then, coming down a short but steep cycle path, I felt my front wheel start to lose control and, leaning forward, I heard the faint but unmistakeable sound of air hissing from the tyre. A puncture! I plucked out the offending thorn and stopped by the seafront to fix it. This could have been the thing to make my black mood blacker – a small part of me had started to believe that I might make it all the way home without getting a flat. But I was also a little relieved: the longer I'd been puncture-free, the more pressure there had been to keep it that way. At least now I could stop worrying about it. *There are worse places to patch a tube*, I thought as the waves continued their endless roll in to the shore.

Off I went, the long rickety footbridge at Barmouth carrying me over the Mawddach Estuary, the wooden slats rumbling beneath my wheels like an approaching train. I took a deep breath of the fresh Welsh air to try to lift myself out of this mood, my ears straining to hear the far-off whistle of the steam engine. But it was no good; my eyes were closed to the scenery – I was just cycling to get there.

I arrived in Aberdyfi where I was staying with a colleague's parents, reluctant to knock on their door. I didn't want to be in anyone's company that evening, couldn't face answering the same questions about my bike ride. It was the first time I had just wanted to be alone, to sit in solitude by the beach and watch the sun fade over the horizon. I sighed and tried to pull myself together, fixing my face with a half-convincing smile as Helen opened the door.

'Hello,' she said, her smile changing to concern instantly. 'Oh gosh, you look exhausted. Let me help you with these bags and I'll put the kettle on. Would you like some cake? And a bath?'

'Thank you,' I replied, almost bursting into tears.

After dinner I wandered down to the beach, the light fading, the windows illuminated in the long line of houses and hotels that sat back from the sandy river mouth, the horizon tinged with a faint line of pink beneath the clouds. Lobster pots were stacked high on the jetty, fishermen's hooks lined up neatly on the railings. I looked across the estuary to where I'd be cycling tomorrow. I wasn't looking forward to it; my senses were numbed. This was my journey, my adventure, which had given me such joy and excitement. But I'd had enough. I just wanted to go home.

DAY 47:
ABERDYFI TO LLANGRANNOG

63 miles

Setting off in the morning, none of it felt better. It was the hills, the never-ending wind, the monotony of following the same damn road for three days straight. It was the long detour round the Dyfi Estuary; with no ferry it was a 20 mile ride just to reach the mouth of the river again, the houses of the town I'd left over an hour and a half before clearly visible over the water. I didn't pause to enjoy the spectacular scenery as I cycled, and nothing inspired me about the towns. I was bored with cycling; I didn't want to do it anymore.

Each rain shower further diluted my mood. There was something about the Welsh rain: when it rained, it really rained. Roads went from tarmac to torrent in a matter of minutes. Then it would blow over and I would find myself picking my way through gutters that surged with roadside debris.

The hills became battles, and I bemoaned the constant ups and downs. No sooner had I conquered one than I'd plummet to the bottom, greeted there by another climb. The long drags were slow and draining, my legs working hard to reach the summit. I kept checking my rear tyre, convinced another puncture was slowing me down, but it was merely the combination of heavy bags, long inclines and relentless wind. There was no longer any joy in reaching the top, with the subsequent freewheeling robbing me of the altitude I'd taken so long to acquire. And the steep hills were really tough; as I was climbing out of the town of Borth, a lady shouted, 'Good luck – it gets worse!' I would try to remain seated for as long as possible to take the strain off my heel, but I'd eventually have to give in and stand up, creaking my way agonisingly to the top. I'd then worry about the effect the constantly applied brakes would have on the wheel rims and brake blocks as I descended.

Each time I approached a town starting with Aber (which was a lot), I groaned; *aber* is Welsh for river mouth, which meant going all the way down to sea level, undoubtedly followed by a huge climb. Through Aberystwyth, Aberarth, Aberaeron, on and on. I cut a few corners, trying to make it easier on myself; Aberporth would have to wait for another trip. It could have been so lovely, I thought, as I crossed the bridge at Aberteifi (Cardigan) before making my way once more into the clouds. Pity I so massively failed to appreciate it.

I'd arrived in the country excited to get to know Wales, but Wales did not seem to be reciprocating. I frequently thought, *Why am I doing this?* Couldn't I just get a train back to London and hide there for a few weeks, arriving at Tower Bridge on my return date? No one would ever know. The only things that kept me going were the fact I had a place to aim for each night and the thought that I would never have to do it again.

I approached the tiny settlement of Llangrannog, tucked into its dimple in the hills, houses with grey slate roofs placed wherever there was enough level ground on which to build. The descent was brutal, but this time I'd have a break before climbing out again. I sat facing the tiny bay, the coastline a serrated edge of rocks, the waves swirling in huge pounding eddies at my feet. The roar was almost deafening, the sea like a creature thrashing against its shackles. I sat, brooding and sullen, staring through glazed eyes at the incredible power of the water, hugging my knees to my chest as the spray flew around me.

DAY 48:
LLANGRANNOG TO TREFIN

43 miles

Llangrannog disappeared beneath the cliffs as I climbed, pounding mechanically at the pedals; the raw elemental power of the sea that I'd experienced the previous night had given me a steely determination and an almost robotic rhythm to my cycling. I had a job to do, and I would do it; it didn't require me to think or feel, just pedal.

Yet a few miles down the road I was in tears: I'd become hopelessly lost coming out of Fishguard, and was running late to meet my next host. I'd set off early that morning, estimating optimistically that I'd be in Trefin by lunchtime, but the headwind and hills were adding to my journey time and frustration. I'd pushed my bike up a short but steep slope to get on to the cycle path, but when the heavy bags made it topple over, I'd started to sob with self-pity. I was utterly exhausted by the constant struggle. Standing invincible on the top of Mynydd Mawr was a distant memory.

'I can't do it!'

It was a Welsh dragon that made me stop crying. It was just one of the hundreds that I'd seen, adorning door frames, decorating letter boxes and hanging from lamp posts. This one was a bright-red stuffed toy, sitting on the grass verge flanked by a pair of wellington boots, each with a Welsh flag sticking from its top, and it looked so comical that I burst out laughing. What an odd thing! I wondered who had put it there, and why. Whatever the reason, it had temporarily snapped me out of my despair, and, accepting that there was nothing I could do about the wind and the hills and the time, I climbed back on my bike. Even though I was feeling desperately sorry for myself and hopelessly incapable, I knew I could do it, really. I took a deep breath, texted Gary to let him know I'd be late, and kept going.

'Where are you?' came Gary's reply.

'On the road out of Fishguard,' I wrote back. There were three roads out of Fishguard.

Despite my unhelpful reply, a short while later, a car pulled over and a stocky man with a shaven head climbed out.

'Hello. You must be Anna,' he said, his Welsh voice gentle and relaxed, deep dimples transforming his entire face.

I shook his hand, then stood there for a moment, too exhausted to even attempt small talk. 'How far to go?'

'Trefin is about five miles down this road. Would you like to put your bike in the boot? I can bring you back to this spot tomorrow.'

'No, I'd rather get this over with now,' I said. 'Do I have time?' Gary had arranged for us to go coasteering that afternoon. He looked at his watch.

'We have an hour before we need to be at the coasteering centre. You get riding, I'll go and check in at the hostel and find out where you can leave your bike. I'll meet you there in a bit.'

I watched him pull away in his car. Perhaps I'd been foolish to refuse a lift and I hoped I hadn't come across as rude. He'd only been trying to help. But he'd gone, and I would rather ride now than tomorrow, so I set off in his wake.

An hour behind schedule, I pulled up at the Old School Hostel in Trefin. I didn't know much about Gary; he was a fellow Green Party member who I'd found by emailing the South Wales Green Party and asking if anyone could host me. He would also be staying at the hostel that evening and the following evening we'd be staying at his home in Tenby. He had initially offered to accompany me for the final few miles to Tenby, but as our email plans had evolved it had turned into a day and a half's trip together. As I pulled up I thought what a gamble I was taking. I knew nothing about this man and now I had to spend the next 36 hours with him!

'What do I need?' I asked Gary.

'Just your togs, spare trainers and a towel I should think.'

I grabbed my things and jumped into Gary's car. We zoomed off in the direction of St David's.

'Sorry I'm so late,' I said – the first apology I'd offered. 'I hope we get there in time.'

'Don't worry,' Gary replied, his lilting voice calm and reassuring. 'If we make it we make it, if we don't we don't.'

We sat there quietly as the hedgerows flashed by, the things that usually caused such fascination to my daily journeys gone in seconds. I rested my head against the back of the seat, content to let it all zip by. Having an easy ride was a welcome change.

'So, what exactly is coasteering?' I asked a few minutes later.

Gary chuckled. 'I knew you were a bit unsure,' he said, 'when you kept saying that kayaking would be fun!'

I laughed. Gary had emailed offering to book us an outdoor activity and I had pointedly ignored his offer of coasteering given that I'd never heard of it.

'It's just kids' stuff really – scrambling over rocks in and out of the sea,' he explained. 'But with a hard hat and buoyancy aid.

I've not done it before but I know someone at the centre so I've wangled us a couple of places.'

I munched on an apple as we chatted, suddenly realising how hungry I was. Soon I was left holding just the core, but there wasn't anywhere in the car to put it and I didn't want to throw it out of the window. I looked at it for a minute, then ate the whole thing. Then I smiled. Jon would have been proud of me.

We pulled up at the adventure centre just as the group was assembling outside, so pulled on our wetsuits as quickly as we could, the rubber sticking to my legs as I hauled it up over my knees. I didn't have a second to worry about what I was letting myself in for before the group set off across the town, past the site of St David's birth, towards the cliff edge.

'Has anyone been coasteering before?' asked our group leader as we stood looking down on the whirling sea far below. A couple of hands were gingerly raised. 'We'll be making our way from here to another point further down the coast, doing a mixture of climbing over the rocks and swimming. The waves look a bit daunting, but we can use the swell to our advantage. It's more difficult if you resist it. As the waves bring you towards the rocks, use your feet, not your hands, and let them carry you up. Help each other – if someone is struggling to get out, hold on to their forearm, and they should hold yours. Don't hold hands as you're more likely to lose the grip. I have ropes and extra buoyancy aids, so I can help if you get into real difficulty. But don't worry, as long as we respect the sea and don't do anything stupid, this will be fun!'

He led the way down the steep coastal path to where the sea swirled and foamed, caressing the top of each rock then draining away with its steady rhythmic swshhhhh. 'Be careful to step where I step – once you've been in, your shoes will be slippery. And if you can, open your eyes under the water!'

Gary and I glanced at each other.

'Nervous?' he said.

'Nah!' I replied. And, after the first jump, when the initial cold shock had been overcome, I absolutely loved it. Submerging myself in the frothing sea was a fantastic antidote to the past few days' riding, feeling the power of the water, letting the swell lift me effortlessly, being at the base of the cliffs instead of riding along the top. I laughed and shrieked and squealed as we followed each other through sea caves and between boulders and across jutting walkways, the sea carrying us along in its watery grip. I'd forgotten my hunger and the pain in my ankle. I looked into the distance, at the Pembrokeshire coastline extending for miles to the east and wondered if I could just do this all the way to Tenby.

'OK, great stuff!' said the group leader as we gathered on a rock an hour later, grinning and breathless. 'Now for the final challenge. See that ledge up there? We're going to jump from that into the pool below. It's seven metres high. You don't have to do it if you don't want to. Who's in?' Ten hands shot into the air. 'OK! Follow me!'

Don't look down. I repeated the leader's advice as I took up my place, slowly plucking up the courage to hurl myself into the water far below. *Hands folded across chest, take one large step forward, keep your head up...* My involuntary shriek became a comical grunt as the descent knocked the air from my lungs and I plunged into the water. I rose to the surface, giggling uncontrollably, desperate to do it again.

It was a jubilant group that made its way back to the activity centre, dripping salt water through the streets of St David's.

Back in the car, warm and dry and glowing from the exertion and adventure we'd just had, I thanked Gary sincerely for arranging it.

'I don't even like kayaking,' I said.

He laughed. 'Lucky they were booked up then!'

We drove towards Trefin, completely relaxed in each other's company despite only having met a few hours ago. Gary had already seen me grumpy, hungry, flustered and in a wetsuit. My late arrival meant it had been a frantic introduction, with no time for all those questions about my bike ride. But it hadn't mattered in the least – in fact, it made a nice change.

'I've been feeling very melancholy the past few days,' I said as I leant back in the seat. 'I hope you don't mind. I'm not usually like this.'

'That's OK. You seem pretty normal to me. To be honest, I was a bit worried about what you might be like. You never know with these Green Party types.'

I laughed. 'I had worried the same about you!'

We pulled in to the tiny harbour of Porthgain, passing the rows of workers' cottages which now housed art galleries and retired couples, the waterfront overcrowded with sheds and boat trailers and warehouse-style buildings, the sea almost obscured by jetties and docked boats. Reaching up from either side of the harbour were steep grassy slopes, and built into the slopes, an incredible array of bricks arranged in gigantic hollow cubes, which glowed pink in the dying light.

'Wow!' I said, climbing out of the car. 'What are all these bricks?'

'This area was big on slate mining so they could have been part of that. They look a bit like hoppers, you know, like you find in a mill to separate the grain. Perhaps they were used to separate the slate that was quarried.'

In the centre of the harbour was The Shed, an old machine house that now housed a fish and chips bistro. 'Shall we?' We walked into its cosy interior, past the fresh fish counter, sitting down at a wooden table laid with a gingham cloth and candle.

'They catch a lot of the fish here themselves,' Gary said, 'so if you're after local and sustainable, this is it!'

Was it just because I was so hungry that it seemed by far the best fish and chips of the trip? My plate arrived with not one but two pieces of beer-battered hake resting on a pile of hand-cut Pembrokeshire chips.

'The first piece looked a bit small so we gave you an extra one,' the waiter said, placing it in front of me. My eyes almost popped out of my head, but I ate it all, every bit.

DAY 49:
TREFIN TO TENBY

53 miles

The approach to St David's along NCN 4 is possibly one of the most dramatic parts of the entire cycle network. Quiet, narrow roads wind their way through the countryside, the tall hedges that line the route increasing your sense of isolation. Glimpses of grand stone houses in the middle of large country estates flash by behind the waxy leaves of rhododendrons. Light peeps through the trees that line the way, dappling the road beneath. The medieval ruins of the Bishop's Palace emerge at the end of a narrow street, the cathedral beside it hidden until the last minute when, rounding the final corner, you see the grand stonework of that ancient place of worship dominating the view, its square tower stretching endlessly into the sky.

Unfortunately, we missed the turning for the NCN so we didn't see any of that.

Instead we reached the UK's smallest city on the main road, thankfully quiet on that Sunday morning, and approached the cathedral from the opposite angle, looking down from the elevated roads on the crucifix-shaped building, the walls adorned with arch windows and delicately pointed turrets. We zoomed from the hilltop into the grounds.

'Oh no! Look, this is where the route comes out.' We both looked up the country track. 'That would have been an amazing approach!'

Actually we had seen the turn-off, but had ignored it. 'I'm sure we won't miss anything,' I'd said.

'We're following the NCN religiously from here on in!' Gary said. 'You never know what you might miss.'

Gary's idea of cycling was nice and slow, with frequent tea stops, and I was happy to indulge him as we picked our way steadily along the Pembrokeshire coast.

'I'm about ready for my second breakfast,' he said after only 12 miles, and we descended into the pretty port of Solva, finding a tea shop that overlooked the yachts moored on the river mouth.

'You probably cycle much faster than this usually,' he said as he sipped his coffee.

'Yes, I do, but I don't mind going slowly at all,' I said. 'It's a good idea that I slow down a bit; I need to let my Achilles recover.'

'We can put some ice packs on that when we get to mine this evening. Perhaps do some yoga as well.' How very Green Party.

We traced the coast past wide pebbled beaches and through open farmland, and after ten steady miles we stopped again. 'I put a note in the local paper for people to join us here,' Gary said. 'I told them you'd buy them a pint if they came...' We waited for our companions to arrive. But no one did, and as we sat there watching the gusting wind knock our bikes from their resting place I didn't blame them.

For the first time in a long time, however, I welcomed the wind. St David's had been the most westerly point of my journey through Wales, and the route had turned a corner, meaning that most of the time we had a glorious tailwind pushing us up the hills. And we certainly needed it. Pembrokeshire was just as hilly as the long slog around Cardigan Bay had been.

'If only the pleasure of the down lasted as long as the pain of the up!' Gary would shout as we zoomed to the bottom of yet another.

NCN 4 is the Celtic Trail that stretches from Fishguard on the west coast of Wales all the way to London. It took us towards Haverfordwest along an old railway line, and from Johnston to Neyland a gentle downwards gradient pulled us back towards the coast with hardly any need to pedal. Another tea stop, then we crossed the Cleddau Bridge high above Pembroke Docks, with views of the oil refineries and power stations that line the river mouth. Then into Pembroke where the huge castle sat in the middle of the river, the NCN following a long curve round the edge of a park. I took a short cut straight through the middle, then looked back to see Gary racing along the NCN around the edge, panting and grinning. 'I don't want to miss anything!' he said.

Soon we were once more among farmland, a chorus of bleating rising from each field as sheep scattered from our bikes. 'This is the farm your dinner has come from,' said Gary.

'Really?' I said, unable to tell if he were teasing.

'Of course. I thought you would appreciate some local Welsh lamb. I know the farmer.'

We arrived in Tenby, where a row of pastel buildings teetered on the brink of the ruined town walls, their colours such a feature of the coast. London seemed so grey in comparison.

'Here we are, then,' Gary said as we passed a deli. 'Would you like a coffee? I know the barista.' He walked behind the counter and helped himself to an espresso. Then as we reached his flat, he put his hand to his forehead. 'You'll be wanting a shower, won't you – and I forgot to wash the towels. Hang on a tick,' and he disappeared out of the door again, returning a short while later with a pile of white fluffy towels that he'd collected from the nearby hotel. 'I know the guy who owns the place.'

I laughed in bemusement; it seemed Gary knew everyone in Pembrokeshire.

DAY 50:
TENBY TO LLANELLI

66 miles

As Gary had promised, the day began with yoga on the beach. 'All three of Tenby's beaches have a Blue Flag for cleanliness,' he told me. I removed my flip-flops to feel the award-winning sand beneath my feet. Gary began, instructing me in his gentle way, this the second time I'd ever done yoga, the first being on the clifftop in Humberside with Jon over a month ago. 'Relax!' he said after I fell over for the fifth time.

'I'll ride with you as far as St Clears,' Gary said, as we climbed the cliff path back to his house.

'Don't you have to go to work?' I said.

'Nothing that can't wait,' he replied. 'I need to collect my car from Trefin anyway, so I might as well come with you then get on the train. And this stretch is easy; we'll be following the old coal tunnels through the cliffs at Saundersfoot so we can avoid the worst of the hills.'

'If only they had these all the way round the coast!' I said as we pedalled through the huge rectangular holes carved in the limestone, linking concrete walkways that had once clattered with coal trucks. We had our final cake stop at Laugharne (pronounced 'Larn') where Dylan Thomas had written much of his poetry in his boathouse, then set off for St Clears.

236

'This is where we part ways, then,' he said, as we reached the station.

We stood facing one another for a moment.

'Thank you for such an enjoyable weekend. I appreciate all the organising you've done. You've really cheered me up.' I wasn't sure what else to say. I was accustomed to bidding farewell to my hosts, but I'd never yet felt a loss at saying goodbye. I wanted him to know what these last couple of days had meant, that he'd come along at just the right time, that his brief role in my adventure had changed it for the better. But I think he knew.

'Take care, Anna,' he said as he kissed my cheek. 'Perhaps our paths will cross again.'

I took a deep breath then cycled away, quietly pensive as I rode. I'd had a wonderful couple of days. The mixture of good company, easy pace of cycling and tailwind had begun to bring me out of my melancholy, and my heel had started to recover, helped no doubt by the submersion in the freezing cold sea and Gary's icepacks. Things were looking up.

From a hilltop I could see the River Tywi snaking inland, my destination that day lying just out of sight beyond its opposite banks. I followed the water into Carmarthen, reportedly the oldest town in Wales, once drawing folks from far and wide for its cattle market. But I couldn't get a sense of its history in the least as I cycled down the busy high street, any architectural gems hidden beneath the blaring signs of national chains and coffee shops, the first time I'd genuinely thought I could be anywhere.

Soon I was back on the river banks, and mist was fast descending. The bed of a railway track traced the water past the old station at Ferryside and through a waterlogged plain on whose far side sat Kidwelly Castle, then entered Pembrey forest where the grey evening haze settled on the concrete remnants of a disused airfield.

'Evening,' a man out walking his dog greeted me. 'Where are you off to with all those bags?'

'Just Llanelli,' I replied.

'Oh yes. Enjoy your ride then. Pity about the weather. This place is lovely. On a sunny day you can almost imagine you're in Spain!'

I looked around the deserted landscape in the evening light. It didn't feel like Spain. It felt like the set of a horror movie.

I was soon swallowed up in the thickset forest, the evergreens oppressive in the gloom, the fading daylight blocked by their spindly branches, their narrow trunks eerie and ghostlike. I was glad to emerge on the Millennium Coastal Path where a way-marker pointing towards Llanelli brought me back to reality. The cycle path was wide, with Gower across the water, and soon I passed the town sign, 'Croeso i Llanelli'.

I'd finally reached the place my grandfather was born, where I was to meet my father who would ride with me to Cardiff.

DAY 52:
LLANELLI TO SWANSEA

56 miles

The mudflats of the Loughor Estuary glistened in the low tide of the morning, the ridges of the Gower Peninsula rising up like the scaly crest of a dragon.

'That's where we're going, Dad,' I said.

'Looks awfully hilly,' he replied.

'At least it's flat to start off with.'

'Yes,' he agreed. 'A bit windy though. I'm not sure I ordered that.'

Dad had told me that he would only come and join me on the ride if it was flat with no wind. 'I don't think that's possible on a coastal cycle, Dad,' I'd said.

'Are we nearly there yet? I'm exhausted already!'

'Well, you didn't tell me that Maureen lived in Hendy when I planned the mileage!'

We'd stayed the night before with Maureen, one of dad's cousins, six miles outside Llanelli. Those were six miles that I hadn't counted on, especially as the distance that day would already be further than the 35 miles I'd promised. I glanced at my dad pedalling his heavy mountain bike, frowning in concentration. He was an active 65 year old, always getting about on his bicycle, but never this far. We'd trained together for the ride, doing a 40 mile trip from my house in London to his house in Hertfordshire. Then I'd bought him some cycling gloves and shorts. I hoped that was preparation enough.

We pedalled away from Llanelli along the riverside cycleway, past the head of the old docks. Dad had spent holidays here, visiting his grandparents when he was a child. 'I remember these being full of redundant warships, waiting to be broken up,' he said. 'Rows of old trolley buses too. You see that hill beside the play area? We used to call it "The Bal", because it's actually created from the ballast that the ships used to dump when entering the docks. I wonder if it's still called that? This area has changed an awful lot. There used to be railway lines running behind the houses, carrying the wagons between the docks. I remember playing outside one day, when a shunting engine stopped and the driver asked if I'd like a ride. I knew I shouldn't without telling my parents, and he could obviously see my indecision because he said: "It's OK – I'm your dad's cousin." So I climbed up and had a ride to the other end of the block.'

We'd reached the point where the NCN headed for Swansea in one direction, but where we would turn off for Gower instead. We looked at the signpost: 'Swansea: nine miles'.

'How about you ride the peninsula and I'll just see you there?'

'Ha ha, Dad. Come on.'

Along the wide plains of the Llanrhidian marshland we rode, fighting the wind. Horses stood stock-still in the fields while their manes danced in the gusts.

'Are we nearly there yet?'

'Ha ha,' I said again. But quietly I worried – we were only 16 miles in, and that had been the easy bit.

A short, sharp hill brought us from the Llanrhidian plains to the main road west through the peninsula.

'Only ten miles until we turn around!' I said. But ten miles sounded long, too long for his untrained legs, and he grunted in reply. The preparation ride now seemed pathetic in comparison, those four hours spent in the rolling hills of Hertfordshire incomparable to this windswept and rocky foot of West Glamorgan.

It took an hour and a half to reach Rhossili Bay at the end of the peninsula. Dad couldn't dismount quickly enough, propping himself against the fence as we quietly gazed upon the sand and the protruding ribs of wrecked boats. The three-mile sweep curved into the distance, the Atlantic rollers breaking with calming regularity on to the beach. We had travelled 30 miles, just under the mileage I'd promised as our daily maximum. I swallowed guiltily. For me, an extra few miles or an extra 20 didn't make much of a difference. But for my dad, I now realised, it would be too much. He was already nearing his limit. There was no option, however – we were at our furthest point from Swansea. At least now we'd be heading in the right direction. I hoped the tailwind would help.

'You can see why it's an Area of Outstanding Natural Beauty, can't you?' I said, trying to justify our journey. 'That's Worm's Head,' I added, pointing to the rocky promontory jutting into the sea, the mid-afternoon sun sending sparkles flashing around it like refractions from a shattered piece of glass.

'Lovely,' he replied, his voice weary.

'There's a cafe here,' I said a few minutes later. 'Shall we have a cup of tea?'

'No, thank you. I'd never get going again.'

The southern Gower coast was just as stunning as the guidebooks had suggested, tiny rocky coves hidden within rich green woodland, turrets of castles peeping from hillsides, the three cliffs towering like the Pyramids over Three Cliffs Bay. But the further we went the harder it became, the terrain merciless, the tailwind providing little relief. Dad had become subdued, obediently following me up each hill, too exhausted even for his, 'Are we nearly there yet?'

The sky turned to flame as we reached the final hill into Mumbles. I stopped at the top to take a photograph of the colours, my father making steady progress up the hill far below.

'Last hill, Dad!' I called. But it was too much for him, and he grew slower and slower, until eventually he slowed to a halt and simply keeled over on the grass verge.

'Oh, Dad!' I cried.

'I'm OK,' came his faint reply.

After a minute he picked himself up and walked up the hill, his heavy bicycle by his side. We'd been on the road for eight hours.

The expanse of Swansea Bay appeared and we followed it for five gloriously flat miles until we reached the city and could finally stop riding. Dad told me later that he felt embarrassed for having struggled so much, felt guilty about complaining at a day that was substantially lower in mileage than my daily average. I felt terrible for having dragged him all the way round Gower on his first day, almost twice the distance I had promised, and much hillier than I had hoped. I had the benefit of seven weeks' training for this. I hoped I hadn't ruined it for him.

DAY 53:
SWANSEA TO LLANTWIT MAJOR
45 miles

Swansea Docks spread immaculately before us; no trace of the grime of industry or the tangle of railway tracks remained, the defunct pump house and warehouses now home to museums, cafes, and the obligatory bars and restaurants. Smart new apartment blocks stood dockside, neat lines of trees springing up from clean pavements, the water full of yachts instead of cargo ships.

'How about we visit a museum?' Dad said as we rode by the water. I think that mostly he was trying to avoid going cycling again. We tied our bikes up outside the National Waterfront Museum and stepped inside, the exhibition telling of Swansea's glorious maritime and industrial past. The huge copper smelting industry that boomed here in the eighteenth century had given the area the name 'Copperopolis'. A two-seater recumbent bicycle with huge wheels was part of one display.

'Handsome. It might have been easier to use that,' Dad said.

'Come on, we've been here long enough. It's much flatter today, and we'll be heading east, so the wind will be behind us.'

'Oh, yeah,' he said. 'I've met you before.'

We rode away from the sprawl of the city, the Brecon Beacons rising sharply inland like huge forested boulders, punctuated by steep valleys raked out by the rivers that flowed to the sea. Once the luxury of the docks had been left behind, our cycle route succumbed to the overwhelming industry of Port Talbot, sandwiched between a steelworks and the motorway, surrounded by piles of rubble and concrete. Meandering down alleyways at the back of people's houses, we had to pick our way through broken glass amid abandoned shopping trolleys and graffiti. The wild beauty of Gower, still visible in the distance behind, was tainted by a smoky haze that hung in the air, the vapour that rose from power station chimneys scudding across the sky like little lost clouds. Back on the seafront we rode along a wide concrete pathway, the deserted beach bereft of colour, framed by grey skies, a grey sea, white foaming waves and the dark silhouettes of cranes.

In Porthcawl I insisted we stop for tea and cake – I could see Dad was flagging, even though he protested that he would rather just keep riding.

'No, Dad, we must rest. You'll feel better.'

We sat on the elegant Victorian esplanade with its embellished lamp posts and balconied buildings, drinking our tea. As I gazed across the water I caught a glimpse of something, a grey outline so faint that I wasn't sure what I had seen. But the more I looked, the more certain I became that it was land.

'Look, Dad, it's England!'

'No, it can't be. We're not that close, surely?'

'I'm sure it is! What else could it be?'

I felt the same excitement that I'd felt when standing at the Isle of Whithorn, of seeing my home country again, of wanting to return to its shores. But it was tinged with something else. After crossing back to England this time, that would be it: the final stretch home. Despite the hardship of the past couple of weeks, I was suddenly reluctant to continue. England meant the end of my adventure, the final chapter of this life that I had chosen. I squinted into the distance, trying to make out any detail of the land on the other side. For there was another reason for my hesitation – those hills looked monstrous, even from this distance.

We arrived in Llantwit Major as the sun was turning the surrounding hills to gold, riding down to the beach where we jumped over the rivulets carved into the sand by the Afon Colhuw as it completed its journey to the sea. The late sun glistened on the seaweed-covered rocks. To either side of the bay a vast wall of cliffs extended, complex layers of limestone and shale and sandstone harbouring the fossils of Jurassic sea creatures, which drew people from far and wide to hunt for their remains. Across the water, on the North Somerset coast, similar cliffs stood and we could just make out their faces, imagining a time when we could have walked across, before the glaciers melted and the channel filled to create the coastline we now know.

'It wasn't too difficult today, was it, Dad?' I asked. He made a face. It had been an easier day, but still, he was exhausted.

We returned to the town, finding Annie's house. 'If you get there before I do, please, make yourselves at home,' she'd said. 'The key is under the mat.' We crept in, not sure where to put ourselves, not wanting to touch anything. She arrived on her bicycle soon after, sitting us down with a hot drink each, insisting we rest while she cooked some food.

'Oh, you have a piano,' Dad said after we'd finished eating. 'May I?'

'Yes, please do,' she replied. 'It's nice to hear it played properly.'

Dad took his place on the stool, coaxing music from the stiff keys, his exhaustion forgotten. Soon my eyelids were drooping and I made my excuses, the tiredness that comes after cycling all day sudden and all consuming. The music drifted up the stairs to my room, reminding me of my childhood, when I'd often fallen asleep to Dad playing the piano. I heard him quietly talking with Annie, playing tune after tune after tune, continuing long after I'd succumbed to sleep.

DAY 54:
LLANTWIT MAJOR TO CARDIFF
31 miles

As we made our way east along the gradually narrowing Bristol Channel, the hills of England remained on the horizon, drawing ever closer, sometimes clear, sometimes hazy, always dauntingly high.

'This is more like it,' Dad said as we rode through the quiet rolling farmland in the Vale of Glamorgan, through villages where wisteria-clad houses sat behind low brick walls and ponds rippled in the wake of ducks. At Rhoose, the runway lights of Cardiff Airport shone brightly over our cycle path. From there we turned down an unlikely looking track, unsure of whether it would lead to where we wanted. But Annie had said it was this way, telling us, 'It looks like nothing – like an overgrown path. But it will take you to Porthkerry Country Park and you'll get a lovely view of the viaduct.' We fought our way through the undergrowth, worried that our laden bikes would sink into the mud and wondering whether it might have been a better idea to follow the main road. But the track soon emerged into the shadow of the viaduct, the huge brickwork arches marching across the field ahead.

From there it was a quick descent into Barry and the docks; these had once been the busiest in the world for coal exports, overtaking Cardiff just 20 years after they were built. It was yet another seaside village whose face had changed beyond recognition because of industry, the population booming, terraces springing up to house the workers and extending far into the surrounding hills, a network of rail lines clattering across the landscape to bring the black gold down from the mines. The long sandy beach at Barry Island would have been crowded with the Victorian working classes at weekends, and Billy Butlin himself had built a resort here, one of his grandest. But Barry had changed once more with the closure of the mines: the railways running up the valleys were now hidden beneath undergrowth, the pits themselves lying vacant, the network of industry which had brought such wealth to South Wales now silenced. It was a forlorn picture of boom and bust, the Butlin's hotel derelict, the beach near-deserted as I paddled alone in the gently foaming waves.

The roads became busier as we made our way up the final hill into Penarth.

'Nearly there, Dad!' I said as we reached its crest, the city of Cardiff emerging beneath us, the buildings appearing as matchboxes from this height, sprawling along the network of buzzing roads.

The docks glinted in the midst of it all, two of the original four still used for shipping, one now surrounded with housing, and the other filled in to create the long, straight avenue that connects the waterfront with the city. There was the Millennium Stadium, nestled in the centre like a spider on its web, and there was the vast bay, the Cardiff Bay Barrage having transformed the tidal and muddy estuary into a massive freshwater lake, where hundreds of leisure boats enjoyed their new playground.

We plunged down to sea level, the old Custom House at Penarth sitting tucked away at the bottom of the hill, all but forgotten about. We made our way towards the heavily engineered barrage, not quite believing in the cycle signs that allowed us to be there – the gates looked so forbidding, the girders so industrial, the power of the water that poured through the sluices beneath us making my heart pound. Once we'd cleared the barrier, the water became calmer, and we curved around the pebbled shores of the lake, drawing closer to the Millennium Centre, home to the Welsh National Opera, and the Senedd, the seat of the Welsh government, on the way passing the tiny Norwegian Church, an indication of a community that had once existed on the busy dockside.

'It was good today, wasn't it?' I said, anxious that my dad should have enjoyed at least part of the ride.

'I feel a lot older than I did a few days ago,' he said.

I wished there was something I could do to make it up to him. Because, for me, it had been perfect. Simply having him there had distracted me from the last of my melancholy, and the low mileage had been all that my heel and my wrist and the saddle-sore had needed to fully recover. The relief I felt was immense. Standing on that beach in Aberdyfi, I'd been frustrated and tearful and desperate for it all to be over, convinced I would be defeated by the challenge I'd set myself. All the things that had followed the crossing of the border, 13 days and 500 miles previously, almost exactly due north of the spot in which I now stood, had combined to make this physically and mentally the hardest part of the trip. Perhaps it had been the seven-week itch: well over halfway but not quite there yet, I'd grown bored with the monotony of my adventure. I felt as if I'd been sleepwalking through the past two weeks, and was only now waking up. Finally, I was able once more to look forward to the next stage.

As we pedalled northwards along the Taff Trail that evening my speedometer ticked over to 3,000 miles. I was three-quarters of the way round Britain.

PART 5:
SOUTHERN ENGLAND

Days pedalled = 46
Days spent resting = 9
Days to go = 17
Miles travelled = 3,034
Miles to go = 996
Counties pedalled through = 39
Countries pedalled through = 3
Punctures = 1
Ferries taken = 13
Days been rained on = 15
Sea swims = still only 3

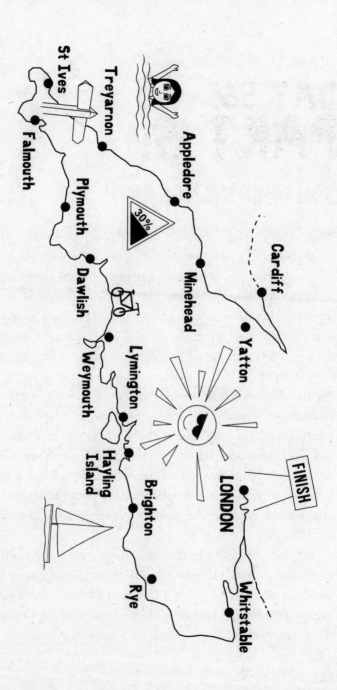

DAY 56:
CARDIFF TO YATTON

73 miles

What does it mean to be on a cycle tour? You wake. Dress. Pack everything in its place. Eat. Check the weather. Check the route. It takes a while to get going in the morning, the mind slowly clearing of sleep, the muscles slowly waking, but soon the rhythm returns and you remember how wonderful it is to ride, how simple it all is. The freedom of knowing that, whatever else may be going on in your life, the most important thing is this journey. Sometimes the road is your enemy, the miles passing slowly, sometimes the road runs effortlessly beneath the wheels. Stop to eat every couple of hours. Check the map. Think about where you were this time last week, and imagine where you might be next week. Why do we do it? To discover, to escape, to challenge ourselves, to feel free, to experience simplicity. Each pedal brings the end of the day closer. Arrive, shower, dinner, bed. A new day. It begins again.

This was the routine; this had always been the routine – nothing had changed. But it felt good again. I had remembered what the ride was all about. I smiled as I rode; I could put the hardship of the past two weeks behind me and look forward to what remained.

'Can you ride faster?' Pete asked. Pete was the policy director for Sustrans and a founder of the Transition Network, an organisation that promotes low-carbon living. He was a vegan and a serious cyclist, riding 100-plus miles for fun on a Sunday, having already cycled to Cardiff from Bristol that morning.

'Don't let him bully you!' said Ryan. Ryan was a Bike It officer in Bristol and we had worked together during my time at Sustrans. He had arrived in Cardiff by train along with Ed, who also lived in Bristol and worked for the Transition Network.

'Yes, I can go faster,' I replied, grinning at my fellow riders as I pushed harder and harder.

'Go Lara Croft!' Ed said, and I laughed. The name had been given to me that morning by the hostel owner, impressed by my adventuring. Or perhaps he had been referring to my huge bike rack.

We were on the Newport Road, flying east from Cardiff, our speed aided by the tailwind as we made our way towards the Severn Bridge that would take us back to England. I led the team through the winding lanes, unable to stop smiling, all trace of the strain in my heel and wrist gone, my saddle-sore cured. It was as if I had been under a spell, cloaked in the misery of pain and boredom, which had now been lifted.

'Wow, what is that?' Ryan said as a pylon-esque structure emerged ahead.

'It's the Newport Transporter Bridge,' Ed replied. 'You can see it from the railway line. It's impressive, isn't it?'

I paused to look, nervous as I recalled my experience with its little brother in Middlesbrough, but somehow it seemed less imposing, the huge metal struts that held the gondola magnificent rather than monstrous, its legs curved at a softer angle, the gun-metal paint less startling than the electric blue. We were the only passengers, and took our seats after leaning our bikes against the ornate railings, the gondola swinging smoothly and quickly across the water.

'What a remarkable invention!' Pete said. We grouped together for a photograph as the bridge made its passage. 'How long has it been here?' he asked the operator.

'It's only just re-opened after restoration. It was built at the turn of the twentieth century to replace the ferry that used to run here; the tidal range is so large that running the ferry became impractical. This was the solution, and there was a spate of transporter bridge building around the world at that time. They soon went out of fashion, though; it's not an efficient way of carrying a large volume of motor traffic.'

The gondola arrived at the opposite bank and we disembarked, following the blue signs of the NCN.

'Your sense of direction must be incredible by now,' Ryan said.

'Yes,' I replied, barely glancing at the map.

'Er, Anna, I think we're going the wrong way,' Pete said as we approached a sign for Cardiff.

'Oops!' I laughed as they tutted.

The Bristol Channel gradually narrowed as we rode our final Welsh miles, the hills of Somerset clearly visible across the water, all signs of being in Wales disappearing as we closed in on the border. A gap in the trees revealed the struts of one of the Severn Bridges, stretching across the river like a hump-backed dinosaur. The older bridge sat further upstream, the gentle arc of the suspension cables soon coming into view. I could barely contain my glee as we approached. This was the last of the big bridges that I would cross, the English border now only a few minutes away.

I let the others ride ahead as we joined the cycle path on to the bridge, wanting to slow down for a minute. They were simply crossing the Severn. For me, this was a moment I had anticipated for days, since the darkest misery the previous week had made me weep and want to go home.

The wide cycle track ascended as it crossed the water, and soon the others had disappeared, leaving me to pass slowly beneath the first of the suspension towers and upwards to where the bridge levelled off, the blue lamp posts mirroring the sky, the stark white cables matching the clouds. I paused at the top of the rise and looked upriver to where the Severn flowed from Gloucester, then turned to see the Second Severn Crossing silhouetted against the shimmering sunlight. I wanted to stand there forever, halfway between Wales and England, the waters flowing endlessly beneath my feet. After a minute or so I pushed on, passing under the second suspension tower and gathering speed as I descended towards England where the red rose, my national emblem, would welcome me back. The others were waiting next to the sign and cheered as I approached, laughing with me as I beamed wider and wider, unable to contain my excitement. This was it. Back to England for the final time, with less than 1,000 miles to go. I climbed from my bike and jumped for joy.

After the bridge, NCN 4 would continue eastwards, through Bristol and towards London; if I continued to follow it I could be home in two days. It would be a tailwind all the way. The claw of Devon and Cornwall was one more of those peninsulas that turned me away from my ultimate destination. Ryan joked that he would have to ride on my left hand side to prevent me from making a dash for it. But there was no danger of that – I was fully signed up to the adventure once more and nothing would stop me from riding these final 1,000 miles.

With already 85 miles under his wheels it was time for Pete to head home. 'Good luck with the rest of it!' he said and turned for Bristol, waving over his shoulder as he disappeared round the corner. Ed, Ryan and I turned in the opposite direction, riding southwards along the banks of the Severn through the clank of industry at Avonmouth and to Portishead. The land rose ahead, the climb up Dry Hill steep and long, but I was ready – I'd been anticipating this since my first glimpse of England in Porthcawl. I reached the top easily; it was the first hill I'd enjoyed climbing since the Mynydd Mawr. I turned to share my joy with my companions, but they were nowhere to be seen. A few minutes later they arrived at the top, panting and sweating, Ed grimacing. 'Can we find a shop? I'm desperate for a Mars bar or something.' It was a long time ago that we'd been zooming along that road out of Cardiff.

We freewheeled along the top of the ridge, gazing out over the Bristol Channel and forgetting our tiredness. 'This view is incredible,' Ed said. The early evening sun picked out the white sails of the yachts that bobbed on the vast waters, the Welsh coastline sitting on its far reaches. The magnificent bridges sat one behind the other in the distance, reaching their arms across the gap from England to Wales.

It would soon be time for Ed and Ryan to turn back and catch a train to Bristol to resume their respective lives. They'd glimpsed just a fraction of mine, perhaps not realising how much their brief inclusion in my adventure had meant to me, how their very presence had made my spirits soar, the significance of crossing a border for the final time increased simply because they'd been there to witness the moment. I'd had a fantastic ride, and the photograph of the four of us grinning on the Newport Transporter Bridge was a lasting reminder of the utter joy I'd felt that day.

DAY 57:
YATTON TO MINEHEAD

64 miles

Before the Severn bridges and tunnel were built, crossing the Bristol Channel by paddle steamer was the quickest way to travel between North Somerset and South Wales. Piers sprang up along both shores in order to launch the boats, and soon there was a constant stream of holidaying Victorians travelling between Penarth on the northern side and Clevedon and Birnbeck on the southern. We had passed the pier at Clevedon the previous day, the structure having been lovingly restored, slender wrought iron legs holding up the boardwalk, a pagoda sitting at its far end – it was the most strikingly pretty pier I'd seen.

I now looked down from the cliffs on to the delicate structure of Birnbeck Pier. Built as a landing stage for the steamers, the pier had soon been developed beyond the functional: refreshment rooms, reading rooms and a concert hall were added in order to entertain boat passengers, and it grew in size and stature as the attractions became grander and more extravagant, with a skating rink, an alpine railway and the famous flying machine. There had even been a water chute that plunged visitors straight into the sea. It had become so extensive that there was no need for people to even step on the shore – the pier was entertainment enough. Now all that remained was the metalwork that spanned the distance between Birnbeck Island and the shore; the arms that had once extended seaward had been damaged by fire and fallen victim to the hungry sea. A lifeboat station sat on the rock, its slipway gently sloping towards the waves.

Around the corner was Weston-super-Mare, its pier built to rival that at Birnbeck; it had once been a place for promenading, to see and be seen, a place to satisfy the Victorian fascination with walking on water. The frontages of grand hotels along the shore were elaborate, not just for their own sake, but for the view from out at sea. This pier too had been destroyed by fire, its modern replacement a far cry from that which had once entertained the Victorians. It sat as a huge white blob in the water, at odds with the gilded lamp posts that lined the seafront.

The channel of the River Parrett led me inland to Bridgwater and out again to the floodplains, the steep muddy banks shining silver with the remnants of the tide. Across the Bristol Channel I could still see the Welsh shoreline, a yellowing haze in the sky above Port Talbot. The ancient coaching route of the A39 wove its way through the hills and I felt as if I had been transported back in time, wrought iron signposts directing me from Kilve to West Quantoxhead along twisting roads where motor vehicles didn't seem to belong. Churches stood tall by the verge and the turrets of castles peeped from woodland. At Doniford I crossed the Great Western Railway, a heritage line that cut its tracks through the fields towards Watchet and Blue Anchor, passing platforms covered with advertising boards for products long gone and station buildings adorned with elegantly pointed roofs and delicate iron awnings. A sign was there to warn trespassers:

*Great Western Railway. NOTICE. All persons are
warned not to trespass upon the railways or stations
of the company. And notice is hereby given that
pursuant to the provisions of the company's Acts
every person who trespasses upon any such railway
or station in such manner as to expose himself to
danger or risk of danger renders himself liable to a
penalty of forty shillings, and in default of payment
to one month's imprisonment for every such offence.
By order.*

Much more elegant than our 'Do not trespass on the Railway.
Penalty £1,000.'

The line's terminus was Minehead, where the beach stretched
golden in the late afternoon sun. I sat beneath the bulge of
North Hill, watching the waves moving steadily towards the
sand, their tops curling as they reached the shore, over and over.
I removed my shoes, intending only to paddle, but after seeing
someone else in the water I stripped down to my bikini and
followed them in. The water was bitingly cold but I soon grew
accustomed to it, kicking towards the horizon with legs made
strong by eight weeks of cycling.

My hosts' house was nearly at the top of North Hill, the road
disappearing into the trees as I climbed, sweat accumulating on
my sea-salty skin. I went out for a walk after dinner, darkness
swallowing the path. My torchlight bobbed along the wooded
trail and I zigzagged up the hill, high above the street lights of
the town, hearing the soft rush of the waves far below. I found
a gap in the black canopy of leaves and extinguished my light,
my face upturned towards the stars. All this time and I hadn't
seen them – by the time it was dark I'd usually be settling down

for the evening, digesting my dinner, ready to climb into bed. The white pinpricks of light shone brightly, more stars than I had ever seen, the black cloth of the sky dotted with tiny holes. I stood still, staring, until my neck became tired, then I turned around and made my way back down the path.

DAY 58:
MINEHEAD TO APPLEDORE

65 miles

Minehead marks one end of the South West Coast Path, a hiking route that traces the coastline all the way around Cornwall and Devon to Poole. It winds its way around each headland and along each beach, rising and falling with the hills, up cliff-side steps and along river valleys. Most of it is not traversable by bicycle, so its 630 miles would be reduced to 500 as I followed the straighter coastal roads and cycleways. I'd tried to ride a part of the path on a previous trip, my stubborn determination to be next to the sea long ingrained, but I'd quickly discovered that it's not meant for bikes, greeted by an impossible incline that I could barely push up let alone ride up, then later by steps and stiles on narrow bumpy paths.

A huge sculpture of a pair of hands holding a map on the Minehead seafront marked the start of the route. My host Paul had ridden down with me that morning, along with his cycle club friend Andy, and we stood looking at the structure, the coming week's ride marked on the metal. It looked so straightforward, the protruding line giving away nothing of the contours. But I knew it would be far from easy. Ahead lay 500 miles of hills.

We headed away from Minehead, almost instantly caught up in the climbs. My co-riders were familiar with the route and they rode gracefully, knowing the point at which each hill would bite and where the road would carry them swirling towards the bottom. I tried to hide my laboured breathing as I followed. We soon arrived in Porlock, a collection of tiny thatched buildings standing nonchalantly at the foot of what appeared to be a vertical slab of hill.

'It's impressive, isn't it?' Andy said, as we paused in the middle of the street to crane our necks upwards.

'Don't worry, Anna,' said Paul, laughing as he caught sight of my face. 'We're not climbing Porlock Hill. There's a toll road that goes up the side; I think it's a mile longer, but the gradient is only ten per cent, so it's much less steep.'

We emerged from the village, passing a red warning sign: 'PORLOCK HILL. Gradient 1 in 4 UPHILL' and branched off to the right, towards the 'Scenic Woodland Toll Road – the pleasant alternative'.

'Have you ever cycled up Porlock hill?' I asked Paul as we began the climb.

'Yes. It's a tough climb. The steepest part is at the bottom, so by the time it flattens out you're completely done in. Drivers don't take too kindly to you being on the road. But it's do-able, as long as you don't end up following a coach or something. The hairpins are very sharp and sometimes long vehicles get stuck. Although it would be very tricky with luggage; you'd have trouble keeping your front wheel on the ground.'

'The Tour of Britain comes through Exmoor sometimes,' Andy said, 'although they take this toll road rather than the main road. They can get to the top in nine minutes or something ridiculous.'

'My record is twenty minutes,' Paul said. 'It's a popular challenge for cycle clubs.'

We made our way upwards, the woodland estate providing some shelter from the sun as we tackled the incline, gaining height gradually along the switchbacks. We had the road to ourselves, the toll booths unmanned, and emerged from the trees 45 minutes later on to the heather-strewn moorland.

'Well done, Anna!' Paul said. 'That was quite impressive.'

I laughed, sweat running down my face. The climb had been intense, but not nearly as bad as I had anticipated. How funny that I had been dreading that hill for weeks, but here I was, at the top. It had been the same as I'd made my way up the east coast, worrying about the hills of Scotland. I wondered when I would stop being nervous about the next part. Probably when I returned to Tower Bridge and could stop riding.

We rejoined the A39 on the edge of Exmoor, where a group of tourists were climbing from their coach to explore the National Park. The undulating road brushed the moor, steep valleys falling away across the land, ponies grazing at their flanks, the gorse and heather scrub colouring the slopes in hues of purple and yellow.

Andy and Paul turned back as the road began to fall at Countisbury, not wanting to make the descent only to have to climb back up again. I felt the road drop beneath me; my pace increased steadily as I flew round the gentle curves, passing old coaching inns and picnic sites, riding comfortably in the middle of the carriageway as I descended from 1,000 ft to sea level in just a few minutes.

Signs warning motorists of the gradient flashed by – '25 per cent – Low gear now!' – but for me this was fun. No longer was I desperately clutching at the brakes, keeping my speed in check because of the constant twisting and turning that had characterised the roads back in Scotland. The speed of the descent forced droplets from my eyes, my legs redundant, my weight thrown backwards in the saddle. I went as fast as I dared, knowing I might have to pull up short – a road often gives a kick at the bottom of a hill to cross the river or wind its way through a village, meaning that I might not be able to use my momentum to carry me up the other side. On this occasion, it was neither of those things that halted my progress, but a queue of traffic inching its way down the hill on the final turn to Lynmouth. I hoped the smell of burning rubber was not my own brakes as I tried not to breathe in the clouds of exhaust fumes that were being spat on to the hot tarmac.

I stopped on the bridge in the village, suddenly not minding at all that the slow-moving traffic had prevented me from zooming straight out again: Lynmouth was fascinating, nestled at the foot of a large gorge, and I watched the river dance over the rocks as it streamed down to the sea, the steep sides of the valley criss-crossing each other into the distance. The Lynmouth Flood Memorial Hall caught my eye so I stepped inside, a scale model of the village and countless newspaper cuttings recounting the drama and destruction of the floods in 1952:

> *Rivers became raging torrents; trees were uprooted and carried away; bridges blocked and then burst asunder, and boulders weighing up to 30 and 40 tons were torn from the river beds and banks, to become instruments of destruction. Ninety-three buildings were either swept away or damaged; 132 vehicles were missing, presumed swept out to sea; every boat was washed away from the harbour and smashed to*

pieces; the harbour arm, surmounted by the Rhenish
Tower was carried away, leaving only a shattered
remnant.

Unusually heavy rain that summer caused immense run-off from the barren plateau of Exmoor. The East and West Lyn rivers rampaged down the steep valley sides, converging in Lynmouth, and the harbour didn't stand a chance. Given the speed at which I'd plummeted towards the bottom, it was easy to imagine.

As I left the village, the now familiar sign for a 25 per cent incline greeted me, and I took a deep breath as I powered upwards, determined to keep the pedals moving. My pace slowed almost instantly and I found myself in bottom gear after only a few metres. Tree roots grew vertically from the cliff edges, each curve of the road hiding the next hideous section. Eventually I ground to a halt and dismounted, but pushing wasn't much easier, the metal cleats in my shoes slippery on the moss-covered tarmac. This was no solution. I stood still, catching my breath, wiping the hair from my moist brow, and then remounted, standing on the pedals to gain some momentum before the gradient could force me off again. Progress was agonising, my leg muscles burning with the strain, but at least I was going somewhere. At last I reached the turning that would take me off this hill, though all it did was replace it with another one. I continued, walkers in the village of Lynton watching my crawling progress.

Finally I reached the top, the tough hills at Porlock and Lynmouth now behind me, but the day's trials were far from over; this section of the ride would prove to be the most punishing stretch yet, tougher even than the Drumbeg road back in western Scotland. It wasn't that these hills were steep, or constant, or long, but that they were steep *and* constant *and* long. After the plateau at Lynton came the Valley of the Rocks, jagged boulders crowning the clifftops in glorious formation, and I plunged between them to ford the Lea, slowly climbing around Woody Bay, the panorama before me giving no clue as to when it would end. I mustered all my strength to overcome the steep stretch to Martinhoe, my eyes glued to the road in concentration as I was swallowed up by woodland then blasted by the sun on the exposed edges of the moor. The road then tumbled sharply downhill to the river Heddon, and up once more to Trentishoe. A sign's ominous words 'Unsuitable for motors' made me pause for a second, wondering if I should take the main road. As I attempted to climb an impossibly steep drag, I decided that this road should simply have been marked 'Unsuitable'. No amount of heaving at the pedals would make the wheels turn. This time, pushing was the only option.

Once back on the dizzying heights of the moor I paused to regain my breath and survey the scene. Hills were tough, but boy did they give spectacular views. Heavily wooded valleys dipped towards the sea, revealing tiny coves with sands rippled by the buffeting waves. The gentle curves of the hills rose and fell into the distance, their endless slopes adorned with greens and rusty browns. I could see, this time, why this was an Area of Outstanding Natural Beauty.

After another steep descent to Combe Martin and a slow climb out, I arrived in the bustling town of Ilfracombe and made my way towards the bay, where great slabs of slate shelved lopsidedly into the sand. It was hot for the time of year – though late September, the summer I had sought had finally arrived. The heat of the day induced a calmness among the people that wandered past, the distant sounds of the seaside filtering towards where I sat on the wall: the shrieks from children bathing, the laughter that accompanied a game of beach cricket, the bark of a dog toying with the waves. I bought myself a bag of Devon clotted-cream fudge and slowly ate the whole thing. It had only been a 35-mile ride since leaving Minehead but I was finished. I flopped back against the wall, silently pleading for the end of the hills.

I'd been following the National Cycle Network for much of the morning and soon resumed my journey, following the signs through the streets towards the edge of the town. But a flight of steps loomed ahead. I stopped, confused, and almost turned back, wondering why the NCN had told me to come this way. But, looking closer, I saw a wheel rut to one side. It was almost impossible to drag my bike to the top of the leaf-filled gutter, but I persevered, emerging next to a sign with the miraculous words 'Ilfracombe to Barnstaple railway line'. A railway trail! No more hills!

The line turned out to be not exactly flat, the unforgiving camber of this stretch meaning that it rose at a 1 in 36 incline – this had once been the steepest railway line in the country, giving me no chance to freewheel – but it was nothing compared with the terrain I had fought that day. I soared above the cliffs, smiling all the way, trying to convince myself that I should continue to follow it all the way to Barnstaple. But that would take me inland; my conscience wouldn't allow it, so I left the bed of the railway line at Mortehoe and returned to the coast.

From the railway path it was a quick descent to Morte Bay, a bridleway that followed its three-mile sweep gradually ascending then descending towards Saunton, the air that streamed past my ears almost deafening as I gathered speed. Below I glimpsed a remarkable beach; it stretched far into the distance, the late afternoon sun causing the sand to glow, a tiny collection of beach huts huddled in one corner. Hundreds of surfers peppered the water, waiting to catch one of the Atlantic rollers that slowly tumbled to the shore, breaking as if in slow motion, the huge waves mere ripples from this height, the surf steadily dissolving as it hit the sand. Behind the beach rose the great mounds of Braunton Burrows, an impressive collection of dunes stretching for what seemed like miles. I stopped and stood for several minutes, just staring, wanting to tell each driver that passed what they were missing. My destination lay beyond the end of the sands, across the estuary, and I could just make out the settlement of Appledore in the distance, boats crawling in and out of the harbour like bugs on the water's surface. This was where I was to meet Sarah; she and her boyfriend James were driving to meet me, as his parents had a guest house there.

I picked up the phone to give her a ring.

'Hi!' she answered. 'Are you there yet?'

'No, but I can see Appledore. I'll be another hour I think. Where are you?'

'We're just coming over the bridge at Bideford. The view is incredible! Are you coming this way?'

'I don't think so; there's a ferry that crosses the river mouth from Instow.'

'OK. See you soon!'

At Braunton I once more joined the disused railway line, this time completely flat as it followed the River Taw through quiet woodland and along narrow plains with views across the estuary. I crossed the river at Barnstaple and followed the opposite bank to Instow, the Tarka Trail tracing the journey of the otter from which it took its name. The River Taw flowed into the Torridge and I headed towards the estuary, a concrete slipway extending into the water. I sank into my seat as the tiny ferry set off, an old fishing boat that bounced on the waves as the sea breeze blew upriver towards the bridge that Sarah had crossed an hour previously. I'd missed the view that she had so enjoyed, but this journey more than made up for it, weaving between the fishing boats tethered to their mooring buoys, the land unfolding as we approached. Soon I could make out Sarah waving from the sea wall.

'That's my twin sister!' I told the crew. 'I haven't seen her for eight weeks!' It had been a long 3,000 miles since that rainy day in Cromer. I jumped ashore as soon as the bow touched the jetty and ran up the slipway to greet her, leaving my bike to be unloaded by the crew. 'Sorry,' I said, coming back to fetch it.

We walked arm in arm along the quay, chattering about the ride, the boats, the view, not finishing one conversation before we started another. The narrow streets curved round the headland, and we wandered along rows of old fishermen's cottages, each of them adorned with nautical door knockers and model ships in the windows. Though I had grown to love being by myself, nothing would ever be better than having the company of my twin sister. We had sent messages back and forth online and spoken often on the phone, but being able to recount tales in person, being able to look upon the same view while standing side by side, meant more.

The three of us, James, Sarah and I, went to the pub for dinner, ordering fresh fish and local English wine; I allowed myself a rare glass, it being Devonian. We talked long into the evening, reminiscing on Sarah's time spent on the ride, and those miles ridden with Jon. We walked back along the fishing jetty once it had grown dark, passing the ship yards and the blackened outline of moored boats, the street lamps at Instow glittering clearly over the water.

DAY 59:
APPLEDORE TO TREYARNON

69 miles

Sarah and I sat on the Appledore seafront watching the fishing boats head out for a day on the waves. Not a cloud sullied the sky and I rolled my shorts up as high as they would go, looking forward to another scorching day. The sky had a freshness about it, the sea breeze bringing with it a faint suggestion of salt, the sun blinking from the water's surface.

'Do you have enough water? Do you have enough sun cream? Do you know where you're going?!' Sarah said as she hugged me goodbye.

'Stop worrying,' I laughed. I mounted my bicycle and set off along the seafront, trying not to overbalance as I turned to wave as often as I could.

I rode westward to Westward Ho! past the beach where I'd once learnt to surf, the penny arcades and chip shops quiet in the morning. A steep hill took me up and away from the town, glimpses of the huge dunes back at Braunton Burrows visible through the thick foliage that lined the road, and soon after I rejoined the A39, which would take me into Cornwall.

The road was wide and busy, thick with fumes, the traffic passing fast and close, a far cry from the ancient highway through Exmoor and Somerset. Each junction signposted me to a different coastal town – Clovelly, Hartland, Hardisworthy,

Morwenstow – but I ignored them all. I'd had enough of hills; after yesterday's ride I was keen to keep my distance from the coast, nervous of the double chevrons that littered the map so casually as the roads dipped in and out to the villages. I laughed out loud at the irony; for the entire trip I'd wished I could have been closer to the sea, frustrated when the roads took me away from my coastline. And now, my resolve had utterly disappeared. The 'A' road carved a smooth pass through the hills, from which I could see the ocean, and that was good enough.

The heat clung to the road, causing the tarmac to shimmer in the distance as I pedalled towards the westernmost county in England, and soon I approached the sign for Cornwall, the words 'Kernow a'gas dynergh' welcoming me to the place that would be my final turning point, the county squashed into the toe of Britain. I'd visited only a handful of times, my family's loyalties lying with Devon, the land of my maternal grandparents. It wasn't that Cornwall had been forbidden exactly, but there was always a reason not to go. And it wasn't as if we hadn't asked:

'Mum, can we go to Cornwall?'

'Oh, well, there are so many tourists there,' or, 'No, darling, it's a bit too far,' or, 'It's nothing special, love, let's stay here in Devon.'

'Have *you* ever been to Cornwall, Mum?' we asked once and she'd smiled and said, yes, she had been. So she'd driven us there, at the end of a day when we'd been visiting friends of Grandma, taking a detour to cross the border just so we could see it. My ten-year-old eyes had looked around at the trees, the river, the undergrowth, feeling disappointed – it was exactly the same as Devon.

But here I was in that far-off land, exotic, secret, the neighbour that I'd never been allowed to get to know. Each time I'd passed into a new county I'd savoured the moment: one more region ticked off the list, one new place to become familiar with, one step closer to home. But reaching Cornwall was more than that. I couldn't wait to explore.

I struck off the main road on the approach to Bude, instantly hidden among hedgerows as I traversed the narrow roads. The streets were bustling as I arrived in the town, finding a bench in the central gardens to sit and eat my sandwich. I felt nervous – would they be able to tell I was Devonian? I was now just one of those many tourists Mum had mentioned. I looked around, but there was no sign of the reputed gruffness of the locals. Perhaps everyone else was a tourist too.

The couple sitting on the adjacent bench commented on my bike, the man keen to know if I found the roads here dangerous. 'What's the traffic like?' he asked.

'It's nothing compared to London!' I replied.

But later, coming down a steep, twisting hill, sitting in the middle of the road with no chance of being able to see if anything was coming round the corner, I wondered if this was what he'd meant. It wasn't the volume of traffic, it was that it came unexpectedly, and there was precious little room for it to pass. Occasionally I had to hurl myself into the hedgerow to avoid a vehicle, and almost wished I was back on the 'A' road where at least people could see me and keep their distance. A woman beeped as I crawled up a hill, leaning out of her window once I'd pulled over to shout at me for being in her way. A second car followed shortly afterwards and I turned sharply as the driver wound down the window, defensive and ready to retort.

'Did you just cycle up that hill?' he asked.

The admiration in his voice caught me off guard. 'Yes!' I replied.

'That's amazing,' he said as he drove off, and I breathlessly followed in his wake.

But soon I came up behind the most fearsome vehicle of all: the hedge-trimming tractor, its greedy blades swiping at the hedgerows, scattering thorns and twigs in my path, as if laying tacks to halt my chase. I cautiously followed, eyes glued to the road, swerving to avoid another puncture.

From Boscastle and Tintagel to Trevalga and Trethevey, Treknow and Trebarwith, I pedalled through the Tres feeling cheated – why had I never been encouraged to visit Cornwall before? This was some of the most startlingly beautiful scenery that I'd come across. A rich patchwork blanket draped itself across the hills, the distant knolls hazy with the late summer, the berries in the hedgerows bright with the early signs of autumn. Each beach sat golden in the crook of the cliffs, each village as picturesque as a postcard, the grey slate buildings gathered tightly around trickling streams. And the sea! Crystal clear and unspoilt by industry, the water shone with an infinite variety of turquoises, blues and greens. Never before had I seen such colours.

Once again, the day's ride would finish with a ferry trip, and I arrived at Rock, from where the boat would depart for Padstow from a tiny slipway on the beach. I cycled over to the sign that showed the departure times, clicking my right cleat loose as I slowed to a halt. But my weight went the other way, where my shoe was still firmly attached to the pedal. The bike pitched over, and with no chance of being able to free my foot I grabbed at the sign with my hand, letting out an involuntary shriek and slowly sliding down the pole as my bike toppled over beneath me. My yells ensured that the folk waiting in the queue couldn't fail to see what had happened. I boarded the ferry blushing.

The approach to Padstow was wonderful, the bow of the boat cutting through rich green water so clear we could almost see the bottom. Cliffs guarded the mouth of the estuary, the wide stretch of water dotted with fishing boats and sailing boats and lobster pots. I settled myself in a waterfront tea room, ordering a Cornish cream tea, buttering my scone, emptying the jam pot on top, then finishing it off with a huge dollop of cream. I almost felt guilty about it, this being the exact opposite of how they do it in Devon.

It was a short ride to Treyarnon, my hostel shored up next to the beach. The day was fading fast but I was determined to enjoy some al fresco dining as I watched the sun beat its rapid retreat over the sea. One by one the windows of the houses lining the bay were illuminated, the light of the sun replaced by the glow of hundreds of bulbs as families went about their business. I sat looking out to sea long after the last of my chips had gone cold and the last of the evening strollers had disappeared, watching the moonlight sparkle on the water in the velvety darkness, listening to the waves break on the rocks as the tide retreated from the shore.

DAY 60:
TREYARNON TO ST IVES

47 miles

The sun rose at 7.30 on that warm morning in late September, the pale-blue sky edged with the purple remnants of daybreak, the tips of the hills tinged with pink. Colour crept across the scattered clouds, painting the edge of each one with delicate brush strokes that grew bolder as the sun slowly released its rays. Pinks were joined by orange, the deepening shades rippling across the sky as the sunlight spread its fingers. Soon the sky was ablaze with hues, the blue growing more intense with every passing second until the tip of a squashed golden sphere burst from the clutches of the hills, its arrival sudden and glorious. It grew rapidly, inching its way into the sky, the pinks suddenly quenched, replaced by infinite shades of orange and yellow. Then, wrenching itself from the horizon, the full orb appeared, freed by the dawn, its multicoloured prelude disappearing as the orange halo shrank into a small ball of hot yellow, its light pouring unrestrained across the sky, the clouds restored to their original white.

I walked on the beach amid the paw prints of dogs, the ebbing tide slowly revealing more and more of the sand. The surf was high: two surfers arrived on the beach as soon as the sun had made its spectacular entrance, perhaps grabbing a quick moment on the waves before heading to work. I watched the risers smash against the rocks, covering the cove in spray.

It would be a short ride that day, but I left early; once my hostel breakfast was finished there was no need to be lazy. I intended to spend some time in the popular holiday resort of Newquay, to see what all the fuss was about. I approached warily, anticipating hordes of tourists and a faint air of tackiness, but on this out-of-season Thursday the town was calm, the shops that spilt their wares on to the pavement uncrowded, and I wandered slowly through the streets with the time and space to notice the delicate detail of the Cornish buildings hidden among the surf shacks. For this is why people come to Newquay: to surf. Down on the beach, a group of ladies stood on static boards in a circle around their instructor, while bronzed men headed out to the waves in wetsuits. I sat in a cafe overlooking the beach, utterly intoxicated by the scene: the sunshine, the miles of sand, the cliffs that stood like wardens at the edge of the bay, the waves crashing towards the shore. The draw of the sea was strong. I left my bags tucked out of sight by a rock pool and ran down towards the water, its freshness making me gasp as it splashed over my knees, my thighs, my chest, my legs running hard against the resistance of the waves until the swell caught me in its grip, holding me suspended as the sand dropped deeper and deeper beneath my feet. The breakers that had so hypnotised me from the shore now crashed over my head, and I dived straight into them, ducking under the crest and emerging a few seconds later, breathless with exhilaration. Soon I had swum far enough that I was beyond the line of breakers, the swell lifting and dropping me again and again, and I bobbed with a few surfers, enjoying the blissful cool as I kicked my legs through the gentle current. I stayed for what felt like hours, reluctant to return to the shore, until the cold started to seep towards my core and I let the waves carry me back to dry land, exhausted and invigorated.

It was well into afternoon when I left the town, country lanes leading me slowly westwards, the Cornish peninsula gradually narrowing. Nearing St Ives I stopped to watch the sun set. The day retreated in much the same way as it had arrived, the golden sun growing orange as it sank lower in the sky, touching the line of the horizon and appearing to sit there, static, for a few moments before being sucked out of sight, leaving the sky scarred with flames. All around, the rose-coloured tint was reflected in the water, every part of the earth clinging to the dying light as pink became purple became grey. Colours lost their fervour, fields lost their distinction, towns lost their detail as the world was deprived of light. The twilight was rapid, the darkness that followed absolute. Another day was over.

DAY 61:
ST IVES TO FALMOUTH

75 miles

The streets of St Ives were near-deserted as I rode down to the seafront, the steep descent to the water's edge causing my brakes to squeal in the morning damp. Mist clung to the hilltops, the chapel overlooking the tiny harbour only just visible through the haze. I sat down at the end of the harbour arm, its high wall protecting the circle of moored boats from the Atlantic swell. The town had yet to awaken, the distant clank of trucks making their deliveries to the waterfront stores the only thing that disturbed the quiet, the rows of fishermen's huts that now housed art galleries and trinket shops quietly awaiting that day's visitors.

Today I would reach Land's End. The name had long been in my head, this my final turning point where the westward journey would end and the eastward journey begin. It was once again a destination for travellers, a corner of Britain steeped in significance, the most south-westerly point, a gradually narrowing strip of granite: the end of the land, where my road would simply run out.

I cycled away from St Ives, fighting the gradient out of the town, the mist becoming thicker. The road rose and fell, tucked between the barren moorland and the sea, which crashed against the rocks somewhere to the right, completely hidden by the eerie vapour that hugged the landscape. Farm buildings loomed from the mist, the long ribbon of road weaving among scattered settlements where whitewashed houses huddled behind grey stone walls. Cast iron signposts ticked off the miles to the villages, where wooden-beamed cottages sat among shops with squat frontages and the trade etched into the glass. It seemed to belong to another time. I recalled how, as I'd ridden towards John o'Groats, I'd felt as if I were cycling off the edge of the world. Now, with an eerie sense of familiarity, those thoughts returned.

Soon the road became straighter, the country lane replaced by the A30 as I pedalled the final few miles through Sennen, passing the First and Last Inn in England, then soon afterwards, the south-westernmost point of Britain. The excitement I'd felt all morning was instantly quenched. Ahead stood a gigantic billboard declaring my arrival at 'the legendary destination', beyond which lay an empty car park and the words 'Land's End' laid, Hollywood style, by the side of the road. Mock-Greek pillars held up the portico, the Cornish words 'Penn-an-Wlas', stencilled on to the frontage that looked like it could do with a good lick of paint. I wheeled my bike into the entrance, bombarded with posters advertising 4D cinematic experiences and movies featuring pre-historic monsters, past phone boxes, postboxes and the souvenir shops of this contrived village, the layout verging on theme park. What had all this to do with Land's End? I had no idea.

The resort was quiet; a hazy day in late September does not attract many tourists and at mid-morning any cycle tourers would already have left. At the cliff edge, away from the shops and amusement arcades, stood the famous signpost, its arms pointing the 874 miles back to John o'Groats, to the Isles of

Scilly 28 miles offshore, and, thousands of miles across the sea, to New York. I settled on the edge, the granite falling away towards stacks of rock piled precariously in the unforgiving sea. The Atlantic Ocean disappeared into the haze in every direction, haze that hid even the Longships lighthouse just a mile and a half off shore. Seagulls wheeled over the cliffs and somewhere below, the sea thrashed. This was what I had wanted: simple, dramatic, atmospheric, marking the end of a 2,000-mile, five-week journey along the west coast. For the final time I watched the waves beat against the rocks on the west coast of Britain, then I turned my back to the ocean, hopped on my bike, and pedalled back along the A30.

The villages sped by as I made my way east – Lamorna, Mousehole, Newlyn – and soon I reached the grand curve of Mount's Bay, Penzance nestled on its shoreline. On the far side of the broad sweep sat the hulk of Saint Michael's Mount, brooding and forbidding under the stubborn grey skies. I rode slowly along the sea wall, the fortress on its island becoming clearer the closer I drew. A trail of people walked across the causeway to the island, shuffling like pilgrims called to worship. Behind, the gigantic sails of a classic schooner could just about be seen. Pirates!

The gloom began to clear as I turned southwards for the Lizard; the mist had finally dissolved, leaving in its place a landscape alive with colour. Cliffs fell away to my right, hiding the tiny coves and caves that once served the legendary smugglers of the West Country so well. A road sign appeared: 'Lizard Village, 8 miles'. I automatically did the calculation: travelling at 12 mph as I now was, it would take 40 minutes to reach. At the next junction, there was another sign: 'Lizard Village, 10 miles'. What? It took a moment for me to stop trying to recalculate and forget about the mileage. Even at this stage, having ridden thousands of miles, I could still be governed by targets and distances and destinations. The mileage didn't matter – the distance to Lizard Village was the distance to Lizard Village, whatever the sign said, and it would take as long as it took, regardless of how accurately I did my sums.

So after eight miles, or perhaps ten, I arrived at Lizard Village and, passing the Lizard lighthouse, arrived at Lizard Point, the most southerly point on the British mainland. The rocks sat piled in the sea as they had at Land's End, these two extreme points so close in distance and geography, but the scene was wholly different – no pomp, no ceremony, just a plaque and a cafe, and the gentle sounds of chatter and the swell on the rocks far below.

I turned to head north along the eastern part of the peninsula, the landscape flat, green and lush, a stark contrast to the cliffs and coves of the jagged and windswept western shore. The road flowed beneath leafy tunnels where pheasants dashed into my path, their long thin necks extended in fear as they squawked and fled, trying to escape the danger of my bicycle wheels when staying in the hedgerow would have done just as well. Silly birds, I thought, laughing. The streets twisted and turned between thatched cottages towards the village of Helford, where a ferry would take me across the Helford River, an ancient passage across which horses used to swim while their carts were rowed. Between banks piled high with foliage, hundreds of boats sat moored on the sparkling water.

I paused in Maenporth to paddle before riding the rest of the way to Falmouth. The sun shone on my back; now I had turned eastwards I would no longer be chasing sunsets. The evening air was warm, the stubborn mist that had lingered for so long this morning seeming like a dream.

DAY 62:
FALMOUTH TO PLYMOUTH

68 miles

From Falmouth to Plymouth the coastline creeps steadily northwards, a rugged coastline indented by the searching fingers of rivers and estuaries. The shoreline alternates between crescent beaches and bouldered outcrops, the map crowded with the 'points' and 'heads' so typical of the Cornish coast. Roads tumble towards settlements where houses are built into the cliff, with perhaps a waterfall descending quickly between rocks, perhaps a river gushing to meet the sea, before they climb again to soar along ridges with unbroken views of the endless ocean.

Life here centres around the water, from the ancient fishing villages that still operate a working fleet, to the gigantic harbours where hundreds of boats swing on their moorings in a coordinated dance. I boarded the Queen of Falmouth in order to cross Falmouth harbour, the waters of the estuary almost as vast as the ocean itself, the black dots of boats appearing in silhouette against the morning sun. At the harbour mouth sat Falmouth Docks, the inert tankers monstrous even when stationary, their hulls towering over the yachts heading out to the open waters. It took a full half an hour for the ferry to reach St Mawes, the crossing followed straight away by a quick dash in an open-topped wooden boat to a place called Place, a secluded haven resting on the tip of the Roseland Peninsula.

I was heading to an old friend's house for lunch; I hadn't seen Becky since we'd both left our teaching jobs over three years previously. She didn't have any family ties here as far as I knew and I had intended to ask her why she'd moved away from Hertfordshire. But approaching the tiny village of Mevagissey from the hilltop path, I could see why. Below me lay a classic Cornish fishing resort, the tiny harbour filled with the usual jumble of yacht masts and fishing craft. The houses appeared to sit almost on top of each other on the hillside, and I descended to the water's edge through cobbled streets too narrow for motor traffic. It was an absolute delight, as far removed from the mean streets of Stevenage as one could wish.

We spent an hour and a half catching up on each other's respective lives, not feeling the three-year gap; she was now a mother, her lovely daughter inquisitive as we chatted. It was with reluctance that I left, promising to visit again soon. The long break had been wonderful, but I had two more ferries to catch to reach my destination that evening. The last would not wait and I was keen to avoid repeating my Oban–Arran experience.

The coastal road skirted Pentewan and Porthpean on its way to Charlestown. Two magnificent Tall Ships were docked in the harbour, which had, in the late 1800s, been a base for exporting the china clay mined at St Austell. The old dockside railways streamed along the coast to gather at Par, and I raced alongside them, catching a glimpse of the 'Alps' at St Austell, the heaps of slag left from the mining age.

The road from Par to Fowey (pronounced 'Foy') was familiar. I had cycled down it on the Penzance to Brighton bike ride that had sown the seeds of this trip. It had been our first day: a tough ride from Penzance to Looe, a distance of 80 miles, where we'd followed the NCN through Hayle, Camborne and Redruth before realising that we'd been cycling in a large circle just south of Truro. We'd decided we should ride the main A-road towards St Austell to save time, but had quickly discovered that dual carriageways do not make for a happy cyclist – busy, noisy and smelly, with rain seeming to attack us from all angles as great clouds of petrol-tainted spray were kicked up by vehicles hurtling east. We had reached Par and the road that I now found myself cycling down at the end of our stamina, tired, wet, cold and hungry, with 15 hilly miles remaining once we'd crossed the river. It had been a miserable group that had descended into Fowey, cycling simply to get there, not appreciating how charming a town it was, all narrow streets squeezed between squat shops selling fudge, nauticalia and Cornish cream teas. I remember it being dark but it can't have been – that must just have been our mood.

That trip had been much tougher than I had imagined; never having done a long-distance cycle ride before, I'd had no idea what to expect. Eighty miles had seemed a reasonable distance, but we were unsure of the route, fighting hills and weather, not really understanding just how much the dynamics of group riding can affect the pace. It was supposed to have been a 500-mile ride, but out of the five men that I rode with, none of us completed the whole thing. I suppose there was something in me that wanted to go back and do it right. Now, as I waited for the ferry in the sunshine, surrounded by the gentle buzz of the Cornish crowds and the chaotic jumble of buildings, I was glad that I had.

From the hard-fought heights of the road beyond Polruan I plunged to sea level at Looe, its guest houses clutching impossibly to the side of the cliff, then scaled the hills once more, descending to Seaton where the shingle beach disappeared under the haze of open barbecues, the heat of the day dissipating as the sun sank low in the sky.

After an endless climb through Mount Edgecombe Park I reached the banks at Cremyll to board the final ferry of the day. I turned to look back as the boat slipped from the jetty, a spectacular sunset reflected in the rippled wash of the boat. Somewhere in the middle of Plymouth harbour I crossed back into Devon. It had been just three and a half days that I'd spent in Cornwall, but I had absolutely fallen in love with it. It was the easy pace of life, the tiny settlements clustered around river mouths, the long beaches that shelved gently into the sea, the surf shacks and the pasty shops and the fish restaurants. It had felt almost tropical, from the turquoise of the ocean to the squat palm trees growing in front gardens. Everything centred around the sea: the surfing, the fishing, the sailing, the folklore. I had truly felt as if I were on holiday. The cycling had been challenging but had never felt arduous, or a means to an end. It had been an absolute pleasure.

DAY 63:
PLYMOUTH TO DAWLISH

67 miles

The Indian summer stretched into October without a sniff of autumn. A full week had passed since there had been any rain, and I cycled along in my bikini top (a ridiculous outfit finished off with cycling shorts and helmet), the sun glowing on my bronze skin. Each marina bustled, each beach almost hidden beneath a rainbow of half-naked bodies and windbreakers, bathers splashing in the cool waters. For the first time I wasn't remotely tempted to join them, happy instead to sweat up the hills and then feel the gloriously refreshing breeze on my damp skin as I coasted down.

I had paused on Plymouth Hoe overlooking the sound that morning, unable to drag my eyes from the panorama of the bay, the colours vivid yet the early morning haze blurring the detail as if it were a painting that the artist had smudged. Below, the tourist bustle went on, men offering boat trips to entice customers down from the crowded walkways. I rode quickly along the bunting-lined pavements past the relics of Plymouth's maritime past and towards the old dockyard warehouses until I was clear of the city's reaches, engulfed in tunnels created by steep rocky verges and overhanging tree branches, gliding over the sun-dappled tarmac as my wheels ate up the miles.

I soon passed a sign: 'Welcome to Modbury, Britain's first plastic-bag-free town'. On so many occasions as I'd progressed around the coast the view had been spoilt by discarded plastic bags, their flimsy handles snagged on tree branches, or their balloon-like bodies roaming on the breeze, or their remains washed up on the beach. My personal dislike for plastic bags had increased immeasurably on this trip, and I entered the town wanting to find out how plastic bag free worked and what it meant to the people who lived there.

Sunday trading meant that the only shop open was the Co-operative supermarket. Aha! I was eager to see how they were dealing with the bag ban, most supermarkets almost forcing bags into your hands as you pay. I leant my bike up outside and wandered in, horrified to see a plastic bag being handed over to a shopper at the till.

'I thought this was a plastic-bag-free town,' I said to the cashier when it was my turn.

'Oh, er, these aren't really plastic bags,' he replied, squirming under my gaze. 'I'll get the manager.'

A stocky lady appeared. 'We use bags made of corn starch. They're compostable, like potato peelings.'

'Oh. That sounds brilliant. Why don't all Co-operative branches use them?'

'You'd have to ask them that!' she replied. 'They probably cost more than regular bags to produce.'

'Are most people in the town happy about living plastic bag free?'

'Some people moan about it, but most people are happy, yes. It means something to the community here, that we are working together to help our environment. There are always going to be people who grumble, saying that it's an inconvenience, but it's a fantastic scheme in my opinion. It's easier than people might think – if the bags aren't there, shoppers quickly learn to bring their own.'

The Devon countryside rolled on, and across the patchwork fields I spied the vast waters of the Kingsbridge Estuary, its branch-like arms extending deep into the valley. This was not a river mouth at all but a ria, a drowned river valley, the streams that trickle towards the coast having been over-run by an influx of sea. A quick descent took me to Salcombe on the western shore. The town was heaving, popular among 'yachties' and fashionably dressed country types. I window-shopped for a while, gazing through the glass of Crew Clothing and Sea Salt, almost every store selling blue striped jumpers, wellington boots decorated with lobsters and coat hooks in the shape of anchors. I wondered what the town must be like in the winter, and if any of these houses were occupied year-round, or if they were simply second homes for city dwellers. What a different place it must be then. I bumped down the steps to the platform from where the ferry across the estuary would depart. The crowd soon piled into the open-topped wooden vessel that transported people to the sands of East Portlemouth, Salcombe's waterfront villas receding in the ferry's wake. NCN 28 disappeared into the trees, slowly gaining altitude until it emerged from the woodland to lead me high above the sea, following the gentle ups and downs of the ridge.

Soon the road began to dip towards sea level, so I crouched low over my saddle, readying my fingers at the brakes in preparation for the descent. The bike picked up speed and I glimpsed a flash of sparkling blue and what looked like a sandbar as I zoomed past a farm gate. The brakes squealed as I pulled up – this was a view not to be missed. I nearly fell over as I pushed the bike the few metres back up to the viewpoint, but the scene was worth it: a dramatic sand spit, Slapton Sands, curved away into the distance, separating a cornflower-blue sea on one side from a huge freshwater lagoon on the other, both shimmering, mirage-like, in the heat. A shingle causeway carrying the road seemed to float between the two sections of water. There was an information board by the gate telling of the history of the spit: its formation 3,000 years ago, its popularisation by the Victorians, storm after storm breaking the fragile sea defences, a proposal to fill in the lake and build a leisure resort, and the beach being used as a practice area for the D-Day landings. This had been a disastrous exercise in which over 900 American troops had died, a result of unreliable communication, the firing of live ammunition, poor training in the use of lifejackets and an ambush by a fleet of German U-boats. A Sherman tank sat at one end of the beach, one of those that had been lost during the operation, raised from the seabed after 40 years. It now stood as a memorial to the servicemen who had lost their lives, children clambering over it, perhaps unaware of its tragic story.

I joined the road at sea level and gazed along the length of the sand spit, the far end of the causeway hidden by the haze ahead. I set off across it, the heat continuing to burn, reaching the other side where I could climb once more into the shelter of the forest-clad hills. What a day! I plied my skin with sun cream, wondering if I should stop for a while to rest under the trees. But mad dogs and Englishmen go out in the midday sun.

Soon I rounded a headland and found myself looking down on the River Dart, another gigantic ria whose valley extends northwards towards Totnes, ten miles inland. Two forts guarded the river mouth, the Dartmouth Castle and the Kingswear Castle, built into the heavily wooded cliff face, the river they were built to defend crowded with yachts and motorboats and the three ferries that shuttle passengers back and forth across the water. I descended the steep valley sides, arriving on the bustling riverfront where the old station building stood, the ornate overhang unmistakably Victorian. But there had never been a railway on this side of the river. The steam trains from Paignton to Dartmouth terminated on the Kingswear side, and it was a ferry that transported passengers the final stretch to their destination. I rode along the quayside, the tiny harbour surrounded by huge buildings, the town behind it extending sharply up the hill to where the Royal Naval College overlooked the estuary. I arrived in the queue for the Higher Ferry, the 'floating bridge' that carries the main road across the water.

The climb on the opposite shore was brutal, but I couldn't help grinning as the switchbacks carried me ever upwards. I was approaching the area in which my grandparents had lived, the place names now familiar – Brixham, Paignton, Torquay, the road leading me towards the endless stretch of Torbay and the English Riviera. The traffic became busier, fumes choking the tarmac, the seafront bursting with people. I rode past the funfairs and pier and Sunday crowds, and soon reached a small clifftop garden part way up the bay. I had stood in the same spot a few years back, watching the fireworks with Sarah and my parents on a cold New Year's Eve, where the jet-black water had shimmered under the row of lights on the promenade and bursts of colour had flooded the sky. Now I looked down on water that glowed a deep blue, the entire stretch between Hope's Nose in the north and Berry Head to the south filled with the swirling white foam of speed boats and jet skis and the flashing sails of yachts. The long stretch of Paignton beach faded into the distance to one side, Torquay Marina bustling away to the other, the hills above adorned with the white facades of huge hotels. From the shoreline rose the first of the famous sandstone rocks that line the coast as far as Dorset, the 'Red Rocks' as we had known them.

It was a hard climb to the top of Hope's Nose, the viewpoint at its tip a point from where we'd once spotted Portland Bill, 45 miles across the water to the east. But today there wasn't a chance of seeing that far, the late afternoon haze hiding the next section of coast, the detail of Torbay already fading behind. Zooming back down the other side, I joined the main road to Teignmouth, remembering how we'd cycled along it as a family to watch the solar eclipse in 1999. It seemed that the entire population of the UK had poured into the south west that day, keen to position themselves under the 'path of totality' that brushed the very bottom of the country. It had been cloudy so the view was disappointing, but I remember the moment of total eclipse: it had lasted barely a minute, but the world had become eerily calm as birds stopped singing, street lights powered up and a chill hung in the air. Then came the satisfaction of racing past queues of traffic on our bikes as the dispersing crowds quickly turned the roads to gridlock. The A379 round Babbacombe Bay was quiet this time, the road undulating among the folds of the hills, the first clouds I'd seen all day starting to catch the colour of the sun's setting rays.

I plunged down to Shaldon as the sky turned a deep orange, then stopped on Shaldon Bridge and watched the sun sink lower in the sky until it nearly touched the River Teign. The haze that had accompanied me all day sat on the horizon, the far end of the river lost in its rosy glow. Mackerel-skin clouds stretched over my head, spreading colour over the entire skyscape, and a flame-like reflection of the sun rippled on the water below.

The song that came on my iPod then could almost have been written for that moment: 'Soon as I Get Home,' from The Wiz. I sang along as loudly as I could while climbing the endless hill out of Teignmouth, 'Sooon as I get hooooame,' my legs determinedly pumping at the pedals and my lungs heaving as I tried to find breath for the words.

After weeks of staying in someone else's house or sleeping in a strange bed, it was with a sense of liberation that I reached the door of our family flat and put my own key in the lock. Maybe it was the beauty of the ride that day, or the perfection of the sunset, or the blessed familiarity of Dawlish, but as I stepped over the threshold I almost dissolved with tears. I was home.

DAY 65:
DAWLISH TO WEYMOUTH

64 miles

'Look at all those cyclists!' said one of my fellow passengers on the ferry from Starcross to Exmouth, as we rounded the spit of Dawlish Warren that extended into the Exe estuary like a gigantic claw. I looked up to see a crowd of high-vis waving from the pier.

'I think they're here for me,' I said. I had known that I would have company today, a gentleman from the local cycling group having contacted me a week or so previously. But I hadn't anticipated there being so many people and I blushed as I disembarked to cheers from the group. No fewer than 15 riders had turned up, including Alistair Cope, another round-Britain cyclist.

'Hello, Anna!' he said as he stepped forward to take my hand, his face bursting with smiles. 'Now, everyone gather round, Anna in the middle, and we can take some photos.' He set up his camera, running forwards so he could be in the picture before running back to set up the next.

'Excuse me,' said the ferryman, pushing through the crowd that blocked the ramp. 'I need to load my next passengers.'

'Won't be a tick!' said Alistair, returning to the camera. 'One more! Smile!'

'I feel like a celebrity,' I said as we cycled away. 'I hope I don't fall off!'

'How's the journey been?' Alistair asked as we rode along the Exmouth seafront.

'Brilliant,' I replied; having done the same trip, Alistair knew what I meant without me having to say more.

'The UK coastline is absolutely stunning, isn't it?'

Alistair's circumnavigation had been with the Great Tour, a group ride in stages around the coast of Britain that had had its inaugural outing the year before I'd set out. But 'inaugural' had turned into 'only', the logistics of such a massive trip making the promised annual ride difficult. Alistair had been one of the few who had ridden the whole thing and I'd picked his brains frequently during my own preparation.

'The landscape in Scotland is staggering, isn't it? Part of me wanted to turn round and ride all the way back again!'

'What about the road at Porlock!'

'That hill into Lynton was immense – I had to zigzag up it just to stop my bike sliding back down!'

It could have been either of us that had said it – our experiences were interchangeable.

But as I'd recounted the tale of near hypothermia in western Scotland, Alistair's eyes had grown wide. His experience there had been the complete opposite, riding across the moor on a beautifully sunny day. 'I remember saying to my fellow riders how hard the cycling would be if we'd had to ride those hills into wind with rain blasting in our faces.'

We began the descent to Budleigh Salterton, arriving on the seafront with its multi-coloured beach huts.

'Did you manage to secure accommodation all the way round the coast?' Alistair asked.

'Mostly. People have been so generous, though I sometimes worry I'm taking too much. Why should I receive all this for free when others have to pay?'

'I can understand that. But if it were the other way round and you were doing the hosting, wouldn't you want to give that person as much as you possibly could? These people want to help. You worked hard to organise your accommodation and other travellers could do the same, if they so chose. You thought to ask for it. I think the key is to accept, not expect.'

The hills rose and fell and rose and fell as the day went on, the pack spreading and regrouping with each one, the cafes on the route a convenient way to collect everyone back together. I quickly forgot everyone's name, flitting between riders as we tackled the terrain, becoming disorientated as I answered the same questions over and over, unable to distinguish one Lycra-clad roadie from the next.

'Where are you heading to now?' they asked as we settled for our final tea stop in Seaton, the seventh Seaton of the trip, unsurprising given that the name means 'town on the sea'.

'Weymouth. I'll have to ride a short section of the A35.'

'Oh, gosh, you don't want to go along that road! Far too busy. The NCN goes inland from there – it's a much nicer ride.'

But the winding country lanes were hilly, and the A35 was the coastal road, so after the immense descent and climb from Lyme Regis I joined the dual carriageway, pounding in the wake of exhaust fumes, not caring about the noise: it was smooth, it was flat, it was quick. I had crossed into Dorset. The counties were flying by now, just four to go until I reached the mouth of the Thames once more.

As soon as I could I ducked away from the road, a farm track leading me towards the water, where I emerged on to Chesil

Beach. I stopped my bike and tiptoed on to the shingle; I'd long been fascinated by Chesil Beach, had seen pictures, had read books, it being one of the world's collection of spits, those miraculous formations caused by the shifting power of the ocean. But I had never before stood here. There had been other spits that I'd passed: Slapton Sands, Dawlish Warren, Spurn Head on the Humber, but none so impressive as this. The 18-mile stretch was flanked by the gentle sea on one side and the brackish Fleet Lagoon on the other, the waves breaking in a neat white line on the seaward side. The long causeway curved southwards as if rolling away from the land, a perfectly formed brushstroke of pebbles, at its tip the outcrop of Portland, poised like a giant teardrop about to drip into the English Channel. 'There are so many gems right here on our doorstep, just waiting to be discovered,' Jan, my host in Humberside, had said. This was one that I had especially looked forward to and I stood for a while, watching the waves foam against the shingle as the sun's rays spread in a perfect fan over the sea.

DAY 66:
WEYMOUTH TO LYMINGTON

73 miles

'South West Coast Path' read the finger post, pointing back in the direction I had come. This was the end of the 630-mile route, a wooden arrow all that marked the terminus of England's longest path. My shoes sank into the sand, the dunes stretching back towards Swanage and the hills that had characterised this stretch. And in the other direction, across the entrance to Poole Harbour, lay the gloriously flat sweep of Bournemouth seafront, its wide arch extending as far as I could see. At last, I'd reached the end of the hills.

I stood watching the ferry make its passage. Pleasure craft zoomed in and out to Poole Quay, some nipping through just in front of the ferry, their daring making me catch my breath. Beyond them the water was lined with hotels and villas and private yacht moorings, the Sandbanks stretch of real estate the wealthiest in the country.

On the opposite side I made my way past the homes of the rich to join the endless seafront, the cycle path drawing me steadily past the towering wall of cliffs and chines (the south-coast word for valleys leading down to the seafront): Canford Cliffs, Branksome Chine, Alum Chine, Middle Chine, Durley Chine, West Cliff, East Cliff, then onwards past Bournemouth Pier and Boscombe Pier, and towards Mudeford Quay and

Christchurch. The roads became engulfed by the trees of the New Forest and soon I found myself in Lymington. It was early; despite the long ride, there had been a tailwind all the way. I found the marina and sat on the wall, waiting. And then, striding towards me from across the quay, was Nick.

Nick and I had been in sporadic contact since I'd broken it off with him all those weeks ago and the gut-wrenching feeling that had initially accompanied thoughts of him had begun to fade. It had always been the idea to meet when I reached the south coast; he had a boat in Chichester harbour so I had planned an overnight stop there and maybe even a day's sailing. As I'd drawn ever closer we had decided to go ahead with the plan. I was on the home straight and keeping up an enforced separation just seemed silly. He'd meant to sail to Lymington to meet me with the boat, but sailing wasn't going to happen – wind and tides had made it impossible to get the boat out of the harbour, so he'd driven instead.

I jumped up as he approached, smiling nervously, holding his cheeks in my hands as I kissed him, just to get it out of the way. Then a nine-week hug.

'Hi. Sorry about the boat. I've booked us a hotel.'

We walked back to our hotel hand in hand, but I couldn't relax. I'd lived another life for the past 60 days, one that he'd been utterly separate from. I worried what it was like for him, to suddenly be here with me, now a part of the adventure from which I'd forcefully excluded him. I wanted him to know that I hadn't hurt him on purpose, hadn't taken that decision lightly, that I felt guilty for having made that choice. I found myself overcome with nerves, unsure of what to say, or how to carry myself – things I'd never had to consider with him before. His familiar face was no longer familiar. There were 3,500 miles between us.

DAY 67:
LYMINGTON TO HAYLING ISLAND
55 miles

Nick set off to drive back to the boat at Chichester harbour; I was to meet him there after I'd ridden round the Isle of Wight. Going there was breaking my 'no islands' rule. I could have taken the short route through the New Forest and across Southampton Water, hopping across to Portsmouth on the Gosport ferry. But I was worried that I wouldn't hit my projected distance of 4,000 miles. I couldn't return without having reached that milestone. The loop round the Isle of Wight would add the necessary 20 miles, so as Nick was driving away, I boarded the ferry to Yarmouth.

Five hours later I found myself sitting on the return ferry from Ryde, watching a rainbow emerge from the deluge that drowned Portsmouth. I vaguely remembered standing at the Needles viewpoint, gazing down on those famous shards of chalk, the lighthouse seeming toy-like from the clifftop. The main road had passed in a blur of hills and more chines, as 'Zig-Zag Road' and 'Steep Hill Road' zigzagged up steep hills. I'd sat at St Catherine's point at the southern tip of the island to eat my lunch and then passed through the yacht-filled eastern towns of Shanklin, Sandown and Bembridge, the marinas sitting pretty in the shallows. I had thought of Nick the whole way, wishing I'd taken the shorter ride, wishing he'd brought his bike so we could ride together, worrying about what might happen between us, wanting to be there already, the 43-mile circuit of the Isle of Wight an inconvenience to get around. I knew then that I'd made the right decision to break off contact. This was exactly what I hadn't wanted. To have felt like this throughout the entire journey, wishing he was there, riding to get it over with, wanting to go home each time we'd spoken, would have been awful.

The ferry pulled up to Portsmouth Quay and I disembarked, riding quickly along the seafront towards Southsea, the light fading as I waited for the ferry to Hayling Island, the last ferry I would take in my circumnavigation, the 13th of the river-strewn south coast and the 28th of the trip.

Nick was astonished by my appetite as we sat snugly below deck on the still water of the marina, eating fish and chips straight out of their paper. I'd polished off my fish and a cheese fry, as well as all my chips and half of his, then sat there, rendered immobile by my full stomach. I tried to stay awake, knowing that the next day we would have to say goodbye once more, but the gentle rocking of the water hastened sleep, the creaks and sighs of the boat an irresistible lullaby.

DAY 68:
HAYLING ISLAND TO BRIGHTON
49 miles

I pedalled hard, pounding the tarmac, completely oblivious to the traffic that roared past on the A whatever-it-was, in my own cyclist's world. The days spent with Nick had confused me – it had been wonderful to see him, but it had been more complicated than I had anticipated. I wasn't sure what to feel. Would we be able to pick up where we left off? Well, in a few short days I would be home and there I could worry about what would happen between us.

Home. I no longer wanted to reach home. Because this was what I did now. Each day I would pack my bags and ride to the next place. Each day I would look at the water and think, this is where I live, on the road, by the coast. I had jumped off the treadmill, that expected path that society pushes us along: school, university, job, mortgage. I was simply a cyclist – my bike was all I had. We were inseparable, dependent on each other. This was starting to be true in a physical sense, too: I was much more comfortable hunched over the handlebars spinning the pedals than I was upright with both feet on the ground.

The tailwind was strong, the road flat as I looped down from Chichester to Felpham and pelted along the seafront. I was to meet my colleague Ben in Littlehampton, and I stopped by the side of the road when I saw him, by coincidence beside a road sign pointing towards London. I had assumed that when I first saw that word I would want to follow it straight home.

'London,' said Ben. 'You want to take a shortcut?'

'No way!'

Ben was also a Bike It officer, the local cycling celebrity, 'Bike It Ben', most likely to be found riding along the seafront with several kids in tow. I'd definitely found my kindred spirits working for Sustrans. Gone were the days when colleagues would look at me strangely for cycling absolutely everywhere, offering me a lift so I could have a rest, not understanding that, no, I want to ride! At Sustrans we were an eclectic group, some who came to cycling for environmental reasons, some for health, some for the sheer enjoyment. There were the 'serious' cyclists, the racers, the mountain bikers, the BMXers who would spend their coffee break talking about the new bottom bracket they'd just bought. But whatever their motivation, the utter joy that each took from cycling was tangible. And what a network: 17 of the nights I'd spent on the road I'd stayed with people found through my job.

Ben and I dipped down to the seafront cycleway at Goring-by-Sea, once again on the familiar route of my Penzance–Brighton bike ride. I remembered the exhaustion and relief I'd felt when pedalling this route previously, the finale to a ride that had literally crippled me (I had been unable to walk for a week afterwards), from the power station chimneys at Shoreham, across the industrial-sized locks towards Portslade, able to see the faint suggestion of Brighton seafront in the distance and following the long, slow curve of the coast to reach it. Each district blended into the next until we passed the huge lawns at Hove that sloped down towards the promenade, enclosed by the pristine bricks of Regency homes, and finally reached the buzz of Brighton itself, the culmination of 350 miles of riding. I had half-fallen from my bike and lain there looking at the sky, certain I never wanted to do anything like it again. But here I was, back on that seafront, this time whizzing past the pier among the other cyclists who crowded the cycle track, no fanfare, no significance, pushing onwards to Ben's house and tea.

There was something special about Brighton, reminiscent of its heyday as 'London-on-sea', all the usual seaside fare presented with Victorian elegance and a certain amount of extravagance. There had been not one but three piers that had stretched into the English Channel, the innovative Chain Pier joined by the West Pier in the mid 1800s and eventually replaced by the Palace Pier, the only one still in operation today. King George IV commissioned the oriental Royal Pavilion, a spectacular and flamboyant pleasure palace. There had even been a railway line that had run underneath the water to Rottingdean, part of Volk's Electric Railway, the 'Daddy Long Legs' carriage carrying passengers high above the waves. It was a quirky, colourful place where the individual spirit is encouraged. I was to stay an extra day in Brighton; at this stage I didn't need a rest day, but I wanted to eke out the adventure for as long as I could. There was no need to rush. I would get home soon enough.

DAY 70:
BRIGHTON TO RYE

59 miles

The chalk cliffs stretched eastwards from Brighton, the cycle route at their base, the NCN following the bleached concrete from which the sun's light bounced. The pale clouds had no distinct edge, blending into a sky that glowed a bright white. Beyond the pebbles on the beach was a silver sea and a bright-orange lifeboat flashed across it, the whole scene like a monochrome photograph where just one colour has been picked out.

My friends Natalia and Katie were riding with me, having arrived from London by train. We shed layers as the sun grew stronger, fighting our way through a throng of motorbikes at the Brightona festival, passing the marina village with expensive flats and private moorings, and riding beneath the huge estate of the Roedean School. Katie and Natalia hadn't met before, but they both loved cycling and this had seemed the perfect opportunity for them to join me: an easy Sunday ride along the coastline of Sussex.

'So, I saw a girl on the train with a bike and I went up to her and said, are you Katie? She wasn't.'

I laughed. Natalia would have no qualms about approaching a strange girl on the train.

They entertained me with stories from back home, banal stories, but it was great to have a good gossip. I smiled as the two of them chattered in the background.

'How do you know where you are going?' they asked as I twisted and turned through the streets of Saltdean and Peacehaven; I'd been following signs for the National Cycle Network without even noticing.

'Is it flat, Anna?' Katie had asked a few days earlier.

'Yes,' I'd replied, assuming that the sweep of the bay would continue long past Brighton. And for a while it did, the cycle route tracing the foot of the cliffs, then following a woodland trail towards the river banks that dipped inland to Newhaven and back out to the sea at Seaford. We reached the beach, the spray high in the wind. Kite surfers span above the water and we removed our shoes and ran down the shingle, laughing as we tried to mimic their acrobatics.

But after Seaford the cycle route left the bed of the river and began to climb, higher and higher, the long road exposed to the sun, the cliff edge bare. I should have thought of this – that the climb to Beachy Head, Britain's highest chalk sea cliff, would be punishing. I looked back to see the dots of my friends on the road behind.

We flopped on to the grass at the summit, exhausted. There was no fence or railing to prevent us from going right to the edge and we leaned over in turn, gripping the grass beneath our fingers as we looked down at the sheer chalk face, the red-and-white-striped pillar of the lighthouse standing on the rocks in the low tide. Walkers made their way along the South Downs Way, the grass draped along the tops of the dazzling cliffs like a bright green tablecloth.

The road curved round the headland and then took us hurtling back towards sea level; it was almost as difficult riding down as it was up. We arrived in Eastbourne, a classic seaside resort occupied by the very old and the very young; retirement homes and mobility scooter shops were just as numerous as penny arcades and ice cream vans. Through the bay windows of Georgian hotels we could see groups of old ladies singing along with the local Michael Ball tribute act.

'This would be a good place to retire,' said Katie.

'You must have seen all the best places,' said Natalia.

'Yes, I have! That was a point of the trip – a recce of retirement venues,' I joked.

A land train hummed past as we sat by the pier drinking tea, children squashed into the armpits of their grandparents.

'I'm completely exhausted! I think I'll have to leave you here and go home,' Katie said. She had intended to come all the way to Rye, but the Sunday jaunt had been far harder than we'd anticipated.

'Sorry it wasn't as flat as I said…'

'I'll go back too,' said Natalia, jumping up to join her. 'I have a band rehearsal tonight.'

They turned for the station and I continued along the seafront, at the far end passing the impregnable Redoubt fortress and soon after two circular Martello towers squatting on the huge stone harbour arm. I'd not noticed such buildings elsewhere – they were undoubtedly more modern than the castles which had been built to protect other parts of the coast. Being an island, there was always something to defend against, any number of directions from which intruders could come. But this part of England was more comprehensively protected than most, a mere hop across the Channel from continental Europe, constantly threatened with invasion from the Normans to Napoleon to Hitler. Three further Martello towers followed in quick succession, the thick stone walls now housing families rather than cannons. Another emerged, blocking my way on to the shingle beach with a 'Private' sign that directed me towards the inland-bound road. The early evening sun bounced in a hundred colours from the pebbles, and I was reluctant to leave the beach. I stole through a gap in the fence, the shingle cascading in ruts where my wheels touched it, progress slow as I would occasionally have to get off and push, the pebbles not stable enough to hold my tyres. The beach was quiet, the occasional dog walkers not seeming to mind I was there, the breaking waves reaching up almost to where I trudged. I thought of all the beaches I had wanted to ride along, but hadn't, and now I could see why.

At Hastings, the burnt-out pier stretched into the sea in an uncertain existence between demolition and repair, the exposed beams of the amusement arcade warped from heat, the remains of the framework at the mercy of the sea. On the hill sat the ruins of the Norman castle, the first that William the Conqueror built once he had defeated Harold at Battle. I looked back towards the pier as I pedalled, flames appearing to leap from its tragic silhouette, the sky turning a deep crimson against the backdrop of the setting sun.

Through Cliff End and Winchlesea I rode, following Royal Military Road into Rye; another Martello tower loomed out of the rapidly falling darkness, the town's stone gateway imposing in the black. Beyond the streetlights of the town the unlit country lanes were a struggle; I was staying in a farmhouse a few miles away, the lanes just steep enough to make me anxious that I would hit a pothole or a hidden tree root while flying downhill. I'd rarely had to use my bicycle lights but now they were essential – autumn had snuck up almost without my noticing.

I looked through my photographs with my host that evening, all the way back to the beginning. Those pictures of me smiling on Tower Bridge, breakfasting in the sunshine with Sarah and making my way up the east coast with Jon seemed all wrong, as if they belonged to a different trip. At the time everything had been fresh and new, those initial days teaching me everything that I now took for granted, sowing the seeds of the cyclist I had become. Looking back, that seemed like another life, a time long gone.

DAY 71:
RYE TO WHITSTABLE

90 miles

It was to be a day of lasts. My last day riding alone, into Kent, my last county, past the last nuclear power station at Dungeness. I would cycle along the last eastward stretch where I would benefit from a tailwind for the last time, before passing the last corner of Great Britain.

I pedalled away from Rye, the plains lining the River Rother stretching for what felt like miles into the wide open countryside. I was alone on the road and felt as if I were the only person alive at that moment. It was a familiar feeling, but this would probably be the last time. The low sun flooded the fields, growing brighter as it rose, pouring unrestrained over the sea by the time I reached the coast. Hundreds of diamonds shimmered over the wet shingle, the gentle shhhhhh of pebbles being sucked from the shore resonating in the air as if the sea itself were breathing.

By late morning I had arrived in Folkestone, the town slowly waking, locals sitting outside cafes by the water and tangled fishing nets lining the harbour edge. From there I followed the Old Dover Road which perched high on the cliffs, the tarmac broken and pocked with weeds, a gentle breeze ruffling the tall grasses on the verge as the traffic on the A20 rushed far below along the valley floor.

Eventually the track led down towards sea level, and I joined the maze of dual carriageways and roundabouts in Dover, bombarded by signs pointing towards ferry terminals and the continent. Almost everyone else had only come here in order to leave. The surge of travellers through the town was disconcerting; it would be all too easy to become swept up in the exit current, so I pedalled hard until I'd passed the ferry terminals. I wanted to stay for a while, to go against the grain and make my experience of Dover count somehow. I could see the turrets of Dover Castle peeking over the hill, so I headed in that direction, toiling up the long drag to eventually arrive next to the castle walls that rose from their moat. The sign on the ticket office showed the entry price: sixteen pounds! All I really wanted to do was eat my sandwich in the grounds.

'I won't stay long... I'm on a bike ride to London...' I said to the man behind the window.

'Do you have an English Heritage membership card?'

'Well, I'm a member of the National Trust,' I said, not sure if this would help or hinder my quest. He looked at me for a moment then nodded, handing me my 'Member complimentary' ticket, turning his attention to the next customer before I had finished offering my profuse thanks. I crossed the moat and climbed the remainder of the hill to the grounds, signposts pointing towards the Barracks, the Keep, the Barbican, these exclusive places that I now had access to, trying not to look at any of them – that wasn't part of the deal.

The huge seaward-facing wall of the castle stretched for what felt like miles along the hilltop, its windows looking out to sea, as I now did. Below was the ferry terminal, long breakwaters sheltering the docking points, huge boats coming in and out with the frequency of buses. I watched the hustle and bustle, the queues of traffic, the lorries silently rumbling, the cars waiting, fabulously removed from it all.

Further up the hill I passed a National Trust property, the White Cliffs of Dover visitors' centre – feeling suddenly guilty that I'd begged my way in to the castle when this would have done just as well. The NCN led up behind it on a grassy track and there, on the horizon, was the shadow of France, grey and wide on the far side of the Channel. The haze was such that I wasn't sure if it was just my eyes playing tricks on me – until my phone beeped into life, a message welcoming me to France.

Standing tall by the side of the track was the familiar, distinctive NCN way-marker, just one of the hundreds that had regularly marked the miles around Britain. But this was different, the start of Route 1, the arrows pointing not just to the next town, but all the way to Inverness, 1,194 miles away. I wondered who had come here, to this spot, to follow the signs all that way. Inverness. It seemed so long ago that I'd been there, following this very route, having only been a quarter of the way through my trip at that point, the whole of western Britain yet to be discovered. And there were the other places on the way: Harwich where Sarah had joined me, Whitby where I'd said goodbye to Jon, windy and rainy Northumberland, Edinburgh, Aberdeen, Fraserburgh – I traced each of them in my head as the ferries continued their endless dance below.

Somewhere along that clifftop path I passed South Foreland, the south-easterly tip of Britain, unmarked and nondescript, the final corner of my journey passing without ceremony. How different it was to Cape Wrath, to Duncansby Head and to Land's End, each of these other corners having been a defined peninsula or point, each requiring the traveller to turn around once they'd reached it. Now, all there was to do was keep following the slow curve of the coast, gradually turning north, closer and closer towards home.

The cycle route traced the very edge of the land, alongside the great shingle beaches at Deal and Sandwich, then upwards on the wide tarmac of the Thanet Coastal Path to Ramsgate, where clifftop Regency hotels stood behind manicured lawns and wrought-iron gates. At the foot of the cliffs was the marina, the forest of masts bobbing in unison, the last time I'd see so many. A group of locals sat outside a fish and chip shop, people who lived here, who had always lived here and would continue living here after I'd gone. It suddenly struck me as odd that I was there too, in a town that I had no connection with, a place I would never have visited had it not been for this journey. Yet this had been the case in almost every place I'd been, each one with nothing more to link it than its proximity to the sea, a set of jigsaw pieces that made up the puzzle of the Great British coastline.

The final northward miles passed slowly, the cycle track leading me gradually through Broadstairs and Margate towards the mouth of the Thames. It was here that I would turn around for the last time. The cycle route sat hidden away at the foot of tall white cliffs, the entire scene drained of colour in the fading light of the day. The concrete blocks bumped beneath my wheels with a hypnotic kedunk kedunk kedunk. I would be meeting my old Sustrans colleagues David and Lucie for tea and cake at Herne Bay before riding the final few miles into the sunset to David's home. Tomorrow the whirlwind would begin, drawing me inescapably back to London, the Thames becoming narrower and narrower until once more I was in the confines of the city. I stopped for a moment to gaze out to the edgeless horizon, nothing but water as far as the eye could see, looking upon the wide open ocean and the wide open sky for the final time, completing my day of lasts. I breathed in the sea air, filling my lungs to the brim. This is what I had wanted, to look upon this each day, to experience every piece of Britain's edge, living here on the periphery.

DAY 72:
WHITSTABLE TO LONDON

78 miles

It was the final day, the culmination of the thousands of pedals that I'd spun over the past 71 days, and of the hours spent planning for the six months prior to that. I'd dreamt about this moment ever since leaving Tower Bridge two and a half months previously. Every single day I'd thought about getting home.

In the beginning, people would ask me which part I was looking forward to the most. I would say, 'Finishing,' not because I wanted it to be over, but because I knew that the feeling I would have when I arrived, the sense of achievement after having cycled round the entire coast of Britain, would be tremendous. I couldn't wait to trace the snaking Thames back into London as I had done in the opposite direction on the opposite bank all those weeks ago.

And, finally, it would happen. Today. I'd stuck to my schedule with amazing accuracy, despite the hurricane and the hills, the illness and the rain, and those long days when it felt as if the end would never come.

The previous night David had cooked a Herculean amount of food and we had sat round the table demolishing seconds: Lucie, David and I, David's girlfriend Fiona and their baby, the last in a long line of people who had unquestioningly welcomed me into the family home, giving me food, shelter and the open-hearted companionship with which I had been blessed so many times. Lucie and David would be riding the final leg with me, part of the peloton that would deliver me to the finishing line, and there was an excitement in the air, the buzz of anticipation, the significance of this occasion not having gone unnoticed by my friends. But for me, the excitement was just out of reach; this final stretch had been where it had all started to make sense, where the initial struggles and trials and tears had been left behind. And now it would all end. I had spent so long picturing the finishing line, but now it was within reach I didn't want it to materialise. So much had led up to this, it seemed impossible that it had actually arrived. I sat there quietly, almost numb, as time crept steadily forwards.

We set out early, cycling past the oyster sheds at the harbour, the morning air filled with the faint suggestion of the shellfish for which Whitstable is so well known. It was almost impossible to relax and enjoy the ride – I knew we had a time to keep – 6 p.m., Tower Bridge, where friends and family and two bottles of champagne would be waiting. I was nervous and excited and anxious to be there, all thoughts of the journey forgotten, the destination the only part on which I could focus. David asked me questions sometimes, but I was too distracted to answer them. He told me about the places we went through, and I nodded and smiled each time without taking it in. A couple of his cycling friends had come along for the ride, and I followed them, merely a witness to their conversation. The detail of the ride was a blur. A boatyard at Faversham, an industrial site at Sittingbourne, the chimney of Kingsnorth Power Station on the River Medway. We rode through acres of apple orchards, the wind strong when we came out of the shelter of the hedgerows, but I barely registered it.

Then suddenly there was a signpost for Rainham, Kent. I had been in Rainham, Essex, on the very first day and it was there that I had caught my final glimpse of London, there that the adventure had truly begun. It was there that I had passed under the Queen Elizabeth II Bridge, those perfectly symmetrical cables acting as the gateway from the city, the ring road of the M25 a concrete lasso reining in the urbanity of the capital. From there I had looked across to these very shores, something that I had gone on to do countless times as I'd traced the zigzag coastline around creeks and rivers, bays and firths, alternately looking towards the shore I was about to ride and back at that which I had just ridden. But this had been the longest time coming: ten weeks between here and the opposite side. No longer did I feel numb. The others had gone on ahead and I raced to catch them, my stomach contracting with excitement, devouring the long climb from Rochester where, from the top of the hill, I could see the silver path of the Thames and, striding across it, the cable stays of the long-awaited Dartford Bridge. I scanned the horizon – there! A winking light and the faint grey outline of skyscrapers. 'It's Canary Wharf!' I shouted, bursting into laughter as the hill descended, repeating over and over, 'I can see London, I can see London!'

The Thames Estuary had suddenly narrowed and we finally reached the river banks, Rainham Marshes now clearly visible across the water. Through Dartford, Erith and Thamesmead, we passed through industry and across salt marshes, once more following NCN 1, which had guided so much of my ride. Soon we reached Woolwich, the river revealing more of London with every turn: the Woolwich Ferry, the Beckton Alps, the Thames

Barrier, the sugar factory at Silvertown, the Yacht Club at Greenwich, all things that I had seen in reverse that very first day. It all seemed so long ago. Had I really just been cycling all this time?

An aeroplane roared from the runway at City Airport, the sound louder than any I'd heard for the past ten weeks. By now we were racing, with less than an hour to go before my party. I was desperate to be on time for once, running on pure adrenaline, David forced to keep up with me as we hurtled along, the others long gone, scattered as the speed of my quest defeated them.

The glass windows of London's skyscrapers began to glow orange as they caught the sun's setting light. I was going as fast as I could, but the cycle route was convoluted, the Thames Path often obstructed by private wharves, and cobbles blocked my way. I whacked my hip on a post as I took a corner too fast. Typical – over 4,000 miles under my wheels and it all starts to go wrong when the end is in sight. Then suddenly, we rounded the final corner in the river and there it was, Tower Bridge. This was it: my ultimate destination, my objective, my terminus. All around was the London I knew so well, the Gherkin, the Shard, the Tower of London, places that now seemed odd in their familiarity. How could they have been here as normal all this time, when I had discovered so much? The ride suddenly had the uncertainty of a dream, everywhere I'd been since last seeing these buildings strangely abstract, somehow removed from the here and now. *How was it?* – a question I was dreading, for how could I possibly answer?

Closer and closer to the bridge we drew, finally reaching Tower Bridge Road where I hopped on to the pavement to arrive at my finishing line – the foot of one of the two towers, where a crowd had gathered, with Dad and Sarah at the front holding a ribbon across the path. I started to grin as I approached, giggles spilling from my throat as I rode through the ribbon and came to a stop. Sarah handed me a glass of champagne and I climbed from my bike, about to lean it against the wall but someone had a camera out, insisting that I pose with Randy, the star of the show. I gulped at the glass in my hand, downing it almost straight away, Sarah quietly telling me to slow down – with no alcohol tolerance and very little body fat I would be in the river before I knew it.

Jon was there, and Mark, who I'd last seen in that tea shop in Oban and who had returned to his home in Oxford to continue to train for his world cycle. Cris and Jake, my wet-weather heroes, were there too; and Katie and Natalia; and Nick. He stepped forward to give me a hug, laughing into my ear, more proud of me than I was of myself.

Friends came and went throughout the evening, and I took a moment alone to stand in the middle of the bridge, looking down at the tar-black ribbon of the Thames as it flowed beneath my feet. Traffic pounded by, the lights of the city glaring on either shore, but there, in the water, all was dark. I imagined its path, running from here to reach the sea, then flooding round the island, passing everywhere I had been, connecting everyone I had met, touching every beach on which I had stood. The entire coastline appeared in my mind's eye, as if I were looking down from space, and round the island stretched a thin line, the tracks of my wheels.

My friends were waiting but I lingered on the bridge, piecing together the journey, trying to recall each stage, remembering what it had been like to ride those miles. I'd been given a hero's welcome but all I'd done was ride my bike. I alone knew what that had meant, what strength and courage it had taken, but also how simple it had really been.

What did they teach me, those long days on the road? To enjoy simplicity for simplicity's sake. To not worry about what's around the corner. I would miss the autonomy, those hours of solitude, that lonely contentment. What a wonderful thing to have done, to have lived on the road, my home not a fixed place but wherever I lay my head, and to have as my constants the sea, the wide open sky, and the ceaseless whirr of bicycle wheels.

Have you enjoyed this book?
If so, why not write a review on your favourite website?

If you're interested in finding out more about our books,
find us on Facebook at **Summersdale Publishers** and follow us
on Twitter at **@Summersdale**.

Thanks very much for buying this Summersdale book.

www.summersdale.com